I0154739

DISPATCHES TO GROVER
Unsolicited Letters to my Twin

Ludlow Smutt

To order this book
please visit:
www.ludlowsmutt.com
or
http://www.createspace.com/3497478

Ludlow Smutt

Dispatches To Grover

Unsolicited Letters to my Twin

Ludlow Smutt

To order this book
please visit:
www.ludlowsmutt.com
or
http://www.createspace.com/3497478

Ludlow Smutt

© 2010 by G and P Press
P.O. Box 3834
Mission Viejo, CA 92690
U.S.A.

Library of Congress Cataloging-in-Publication Data
Dispatches to Grover by Ludlow Smutt
ISBN-13   9780615417417
ISBN-10   0615417418

Cover design by Alixandra Mullins: http://alixandramullins.com

*To Jarvis Berp, who taught me
the joys of cooking and associated
self-immolation.*

Introduction

Ludlow and Grover Smutt are identical twin brothers who have always been close despite the significant difference in their ages. After a difficult childhood, made more difficult be their proximity to each other, they were rarely together. Ludlow lived for a long time outside the country while extradition procedures were being sorted out, and Grover's years in the "Home" also kept them apart. In addition, Grover had a history of unsuccessful therapy aimed at breaking him of his addiction to therapy sessions. "Dispatches to Grover" is a compilation of letters that Ludlow sent to his brother over a period of years, and it's unclear exactly when they were written—or why. The book will soon be released as a major motion picture starring the electrifying actor, Macon Sparks, in the role of "Gramps."

About the Author

Ludlow Smutt is an acclaimed author whose works include "The Shortstop in the Barley" and "Do-It-Yourself Interior Decorating for Aircraft Carriers." His books fill receptacles in libraries and book stores throughout the world and have been translated into twenty-three languages, none of which are currently in use.

Excerpts

In one of his letters to Grover, Ludlow includes the following excerpt from one of his newspaper columns:

"May 17. **Car Thefts on the Rise.** The city council announced at their meeting today that the incidence of car thefts in our city is on the rise. Last year one stolen car was reported, and this year the number has sky-rocketed to two, a percentage increase of ... er, let's see ... lots more. The number would have been three, but was reduced to two, because I had reported my car stolen and then realized that I just forgot where I parked the damn thing. In a future column I will deal with the lack of responsibility on the part of establishments where alcoholic beverages are allowed to be sold and consumed in large volumes. Police Chief Fawlty Flapp assured the council that his officers have undergone comprehensive additional training to instill in them the knowledge of just exactly what constitutes a stolen car. He reports that the majority of them have grasped the concept that it concerns automobiles. Our gendarmes, ever vigilant."

And Ludlow describes this particularly interesting science class:
"Bob set up a DNA experiment at the beginning of the class to show us how D reacts with N and A to form common table salt, and that's when the fun started. He had an elaborate arrangement mounted on the lab counter, composed of thistle tubes, Erlenmeyer flasks, titrating pipettes, a gumball machine and a trombone. Bob announced that he needed a volunteer to hold part of his equipment, and Tillie Terts rushed to the front of the room. Tillie's motor is always running a little hot and she's constantly looking for equipment to hold, so she never fails to attract attention. The lady is quite appealing, although a little on the chubby side (make that "kind of a lard-butt"). But not many muchachos would turn down the opportunity to grope around in her underwear. Or in anybody's underwear for that matter. It was therefore no surprise that as the experiment progressed, Bobby wound up inadvertently goosing the lady with what may have been unintentional vigor."

Ludlow Smutt

1

Hey Grover,

Since we moved to the West Coast and I can't tie your shoes for you anymore, I feel it's my duty to keep you informed about what's happening here in the land of the frequently abnormal. I know how much it means to you. California, what a great place to live! The land of beaches, palm trees, surfers, laid-back lifestyles, congested freeways, and the most dysfunctional legislature in the country. Only one other state requires a two-thirds vote instead of a simple majority to pass important legislation, such as the budget, and that's Rhode Island—with a population of 14, including household pets.

When we looked for a house, we found one that looked very nice. The realtor told us, "I want to be honest with you. The municipal dump is on the north side of the property, to the east there's a sewage treatment plant, there's a fish factory south of here, and the people who live to the west raise pigs." I said, "Is there anything positive about the place?" She said, "Well, you can always tell which direction the wind is coming from."

We finally bought a house, and we don't have to travel far to observe the changing landscape. Half the state erupts in forest fires every year and then when the rains come, they push the denuded soil down the mountains and the mudslide season begins. Gretchen (who, you remember, is a former "Miss Potato Harvest" from Bavaria) appreciates the sociable gestures of the neighbors when they wave to us as their houses slip past our property and plummet into the canyon below.

On my birthday, Gretchen wanted to surprise me with a car—but she missed. You may have a birthday soon yourself. We celebrated at the local gout factory with a bunch of (so-called) friends. The most prominent among them are two odd numbers we had met at another party, and since then it's been almost impossible to shake them. Madge and Earl have latched onto us like leeches. They invite us to their place all the time and seem to be around whenever we leave the house. I think they hide in the bushes and wait for us to come out. It's difficult to describe them without referring to a handbook on mental disorders.

Earl has a tremendous gut and is also hard of hearing. He's a tad slow, so it takes him a few days to get an idea across (in the unlikely event that he actually has one). He'd have trouble expressing the concept of falling if you shoved him off the Eiffel Tower. Earl is married to Madge, who is a far pudgier version of the Pillsbury Doughboy. Madge is a talker. She hasn't come to the end of a sentence since she participated in a moment of silence at a Fourth of July ceremony in 1952. She never gives Earl the opportunity to finish a sentence of his own, which is okay I guess, because he'd take the better part of a weekend if he were left to figure it out by himself.

The doctors are trying everything to bring Earl's fever down since he collapsed at the polka party last weekend. His injuries were the result of impaired judgement, in which he is eminently rich. They occurred when Earl got the impulse to do a polka with Ikon Gedditt. She's the biggest flirt in town, despite her age, which approaches triple figures. She stuck her pelvis in Earl's face and that got him up on the dance floor, which is a real accomplishment if you don't have a car jack. Once he was vertical, Earl stood in one place and tried to maintain his balance while Ikon danced around him, shaking her boobs and wiggling her ass. She didn't look bad. At the best of times, Earl is in no condition to interact with the laws of physics, his principal challenge being gravity. He took one step and did a Brody onto the parquet after striking the dinner buffet a serious blow. Bam! A first-class "keel-over." Fortunately, his head took the major portion of the impact. When Earl falls, it's like unloading a dump-truck full of boulders.

The team of physicians, who I believe specialize in burial prep with a minor in last rites, worked on lowering his temperature. They wisely ignored the possibility of pressure on the brain. The decision was to keep Earl in a meat locker overnight and then pepper him with snowballs in the morning, but a couple of them hit him square in the sack and created "oversize-testicle syndrome" on top of "ass creep." His feet smell too. Instead of a Placebo, they chose a Gazebo (in other words, they threw the clown out in the backyard). That helped a little, and they're now feeding him intravenously with embalming fluid.

The excitement at my party was similar to standing in line at the post office. Gretchen is always deliriously happy at birthdays and I try to join in the enthusiasm (meaning I don't really care). At this stage of my life, another birthday doesn't seem to be anything to get pukey-thrilled about. I did get a couple of nice presents, though, including a T-Shirt depicting the Kentucky Derby winner as seen by the horse that placed second, along with an Alex Rodriguez signature jockstrap. At one point in the festivities, even though we were supposed to be celebrating my birthday, several attendees wanted to know why I had been invited. People have forgotten the basics of simple etiquette.

You may have heard about our illustrious mayor, the first Latino to be elected *jefe numero uno* of our fair city. It was revealed that he has been doing the horizontal mambo for the past few months with a young Spanish-Language television reporter while still married to the pretty-good-looking Hispanic lady he is currently divorcing. The reporter (now referred to as *primer culo,* or "first piece of tail") was covering the mayoral beat, and he was covering her with a sweaty belly. She stuck her microphone in his face and he stuck a thing or two in her anatomy. Of course, the press and the voters were incensed at this disgusting behavior, right? Hell no! The public adores this kind of stuff. They love to hear about public officials and celebrities doing the bedspring boogie on the side. The news is full of governors, senators, congressmen, and athletes who are involved in sexual antics outside the elastic limits of holy matrimony. It seems to be the favorite indoor sport. If our fine role models didn't pull this crap, they'd be too boring for words.

The public wants the juicy details. Never mind what a politician, an entertainment figure or a professional athlete has to say. Their opinions are worthless. I wouldn't listen to any of them if the only alternative were a TV documentary on prostate removal with a band saw. Let's face it, we want our public officials, our multimillionaire sport figures and our film stars to screw around. How else would we know they're still alive? It's hard to detect a heartbeat with most of them. You sure can't tell by observing a politician in the act of public speaking or running an administration. When their extra-curricular nookey raids are exposed, we at least know that one part of them is able to function.

No one would blame our esteemed *politico fantastico de Sand City* for tucking his tortilla into the lovely Señorita. She is one hot *chica*. No guy in his right mind would kick her out of a *cama*. Now, you would think that our public servants want to avoid impropriety and scandal at all costs, but nowadays they appear to go out of the way to step on their own dongs. They always get caught. It's an epidemic, but it doesn't seem to affect their careers too often. Look at Billy ("Pipeline") Clinton. The Republicans tried to can him, but not for having his lever fondled. No, they wanted to ding him for lying about it, not for getting his baster caught in Monica's bridgework. They couldn't make it stick because the public's shocked and scandalized reaction was: "Who cares?   What's for dinner?"

I was personally mortified—for about two seconds. Let's face it, all the males in the world know how they would react to the same situation. Just imagine, you're President of the United States and a fairly good-looking bimbo offers to do the lollipop lunge on your Willie. So what if she only has six active brain cells? What would you do? What any red-blooded American male would do (and I brazenly include you in that category). Even if you were in the middle of your State of the Union address on world-wide TV, you would tell her to go to it—but try to stay under the podium.

What I love is that journalists then crawl all over each other in an effort to report every repugnant detail. They salivate at the prospect of bringing you the news and treat the guilty parties like royalty. And they glorify the woman. Let's not denounce immoral behavior. Let's interview her on every major television broadcast and then give her a show of her own. Our admirable TV executives, operating as moral ports in a sinful storm, try to develop a vehicle that stars the gal/dong-chaser, whose only qualification is the ability to lure a stiffy out of a high-profile personality's pants. It's what makes this country so rich in culture. There are so many of these cases you can't keep them straight without a scorecard. Who can forget the senator from an unnamed Northeastern state, the former late-night submarine captain, who showed us that you can get away with contributing to a young woman's death as long as you demonstrate that you've been bonking her every Thursday.

Our current crop of office-seekers should take a lesson from all this: Relax, folks! You can get away with anything! Even women should heed the trend. I've already contacted most of our female office-holders and candidates with the advice to show a little more chest meat during campaign appearances. In fact, in the interest of attracting the male vote, I tell them to take the bulges in their blouses out completely, but how far they go on a scale of one to HOLY SHIT! is entirely up to them.

Oh well, I remain philosophical about it all. In the words of Descartes, "I think, therefore I am. At least I think so."

Ludlow

2

Hey Grover,

This is a pre-written letter I ordered from Correspondence R Us. I just had to sign my name and pop it in the mail. It sure frees up a lot of my time. Now I can devote more energy to my inventions. I'm busy finishing up the prototype of my finest achievement yet—a motorcycle powered by a forty-gallon hot-water boiler. As a former mean biker, you're my first choice to test the vehicle, which sports a chrome-plated saddle and a holster for the coal shovel. Maybe you can find a good coal supplier in your neck of the woods. The bike is being delivered to your place so you can ride it out here and test it on the way. I'm relying on your expertise to tell me why the other fourteen prototypes blew up.

I want to put a myth to rest. It's amazing how the public accepts unsubstantiated statements as fact. For decades, people have believed that the angle of dangle is equal to the heat of the meat plus the mass of the ass. Using volunteers from Fifi's Parisian Clinic for Girls With (Lying) Down Syndrome, I have been able to show statistically that this statement is, in the parlance of the scientific community, so much horseshit. My mathematical research proves without a doubt that the source of the force is derived from the fever of the beaver multiplied by the expanse of the pants, particularly on a Saturday night where alcohol is involved. At all other times one must factor in the bump of the rump and the thrust of the bust divided by the hum of the bum, being careful to allow for the drool of the tool in case of willie fall-out. I feel better knowing that you are aware of the real story. The calculus theorems I applied in my research involve complexities that are far too profound to explain to you (like virtually everything else), but I can state with confidence that I always remembered to carry the 2.

Here in California we are located at the epicenter of refinement, and my respect for my fellow man is increased many-fold when I see the values of the Hollywood crowd—and observe my fellow citizens wearing shorts and shower clogs to the opera. The entertainment industry is the big thing out here, of course, so we're inundated daily with the latest news about surfing and Paris Hilton, which is where I used to stay when I traveled to France. We're secure in the knowledge that the media concentrates on the important issues. Yeah, right. The media fawns over Hollywood as though these people were actually involved in something important. They afflict us every day with stories about attractive celebrities like Chad and Boopsie, who are engaged in charitable activities such as cheating on each other and adopting six more kids before they divorce. And on any given day, the developing stories include entertainment types giving each other awards and where to find the best hamburgers in the area.

This is in addition to the daily list of well-known recreational pharmaceutical users posing as actors and movie-makers, who have successfully completed a drug rehabilitation program and are arrested the next day for assaulting their girlfriends or wives and then driving 200 miles an hour in a driveway while stimulated by a nose-full of synthetic pesticides. These show-biz types, who masquerade as actual mammals, stuff this goop in their nasal passages with garden spades. They spend most of their free time taking complex organic compounds in through their beaks, and the media reveres them for it.

Now that I'm warmed up, I want to say something about sporting events. I especially like to see a basketball player with the Los Angeles Fakers cross himself before he takes a foul shot. Come on, we all know God does not care about a one-and-one! He cares about the municipal water supply in Sioux Falls, South Dakota, and lunch-meat processing. I may be generalizing here, but as is so often the case, I don't give a muskrat's tailbone.

Gretchen and I have developed a wide social circle since we've been here, as I mentioned, which is to say that we can't avoid a lot of people. Our unshakable new acquaintances, Madge and Earl, are inseparable. Which means it usually takes four or five cops to pull them apart. I'll keep you advised about them. I want you to feel that you know them as well as we do, although it's not necessarily a great feeling. I'm sorry to report that Madge had to go to the emergency room just yesterday. She was brought in with a torn jug-muscle, because Earl likes to sleep with his arm around one of her breasts and he fell out of bed. The condition is known in medical circles as "saggy baggy." There isn't much they can do except soak it in brine.

A lot of our acquaintances seem to feel they should devote most of their time with us to sharing personal confidences regarding disgusting intestinal matters. We call it "the organ recital." Why is it that so many people are proud of their health problems? I keep asking if it ever occurs to them that I don't give a badger's butt pipe. But we hang around with them because we hope they will infect other people, and they sometimes leave money lying in convenient places.

You'll be interested to learn that I am now employed by our local paper, the "Daily Compost," as a reporter, columnist and washroom attendant. Here's a recent column I wrote. It gives you an idea of life in our exceptional community.

April 1. **Speed Trap Yields Lawbreakers.**
Responding to complaints of speeding, loud vehicle noise and gang-flatulence, our vaunted constabulary set up radar equipment on Santa Sadie Parkway a few days ago. Sergeant Bert Stingbladder and his squad manned the bushes around the clock and stopped a passel of vile motorists who were exceeding the posted regulations. In fact, in two days of vigilance the officers pulled over four hundred and thirty-two drivers, many of them in their own driveways. Most of the violators were teenagers, those delinquent scabs, so in addition to citations being issued, the cops administered violent maulings and worked their asses over good with lead-reinforced nightsticks. I had spoken at a city council meeting supporting the keister-kicking measure and it was approved by a vote of 9 to 1, the only dissenting vote cast by Junior Sturnprod, a sixteen-year-old member of the council and a kid we would personally like to hammer the shit out of.
The majority of the motorists were allowed pay their fines by mail or carrier pigeon, but the teenagers were required to appear in court, where Judge Seething Bungtrough not only levied high monetary punishment, but also used pointed and harsh language to curse the defendants and their parents, in addition to slapping a couple of them (forty-seven). He even came down off the bench to knee several kids in the groin. At one point, Mrs. Fowlrump, the slut, rose to defend her son and was promptly kicked in the ass by a

bailiff, setting off cheers in the gallery. I try to remain neutral, as my readers know, but I think they should de-nut some of these kids.

We hope that increased police vigilance and the stern application of justice by our peerless courts will reduce the incidence of speeding violations. It not, there is a back-up plan already rammed through by the city council (up yours, Junior!), in which random raids will be made at the homes of teenagers. Any young person within ten feet of a set of car keys will be flogged severely with a logging chain and have his rod stepped on (providing the subject is male). Teenage girls will be transported to the lock-up, where fingerprints will be applied to them in unseemly but exciting areas.

As for you, Grover, remember to abide by the rules of proper cattle-prod safety.

Until next time,

Ludlow

3

Hey Grover,

I am moved to share this professional break-through with you. I finally hit on a project that promises untold financial reward and I want to let you in on it. As you are certainly aware, we are bombarded with maddening regularity with ads for products that target males, like Viagra®, Pudd-Prop®, Torpedo-Tightener® and various other stiffeners guaranteed to put starch in your stroke. These medications are designed to cure Erectile Dysfunction (or "Slack-Sausage-Syndrome," as it's called in medical circles).

The ads for these pole-enhancing medications swear they will put real "hop" in your hammer, but they warn of possible side effects, such as fatal episodes, along with loose teeth and bowels. The ads advise you to contact your doctor if you have an erection lasting more than four hours. What a laugh! I can tell you I've had erections lasting more than four hours on numerous occasions and I didn't waste valuable time telling any friggin' doctor about it. I got on the phone and broadcast the fact to practically every female within a fourteen-mile radius, some of whom were still smiling when the coffin was lowered into the ground.

I was wand-loose and fancy-free at the time, and some of my lady acquaintances were almost too passionate to describe. For instance, there was Marie-Thérèse in France. Talk about a hot number! I was walking with her in the countryside one afternoon, discussing Plato's Republic and the overhead sewage system in Indo-China, and somehow my hand got caught in her underwear. It's an inadvertent movement that can happen to anyone. I said, "Let's slip over into that cornfield." She agreed and we climbed the fence into the agricultural environment, hidden by high rows of corn. I started to get undressed, and she said, "Better zat you keep zee clothes on, mon amour. We weel not be coming back down ziss row again!"

But we have to look at this situation seriously. As a person whose Johnson has gotten him in a load of trouble many times, I've come to the conclusion that a limp weenie is not the problem. No sir, the real problem is the exact opposite. Think about it. How often have you been involved in this scenario? You meet a hot number whose IQ is the same as her bra size and pretty soon you're chewing her face and whacking her on a regular basis—you know, doing the Dipstick Derby. The Plunger Polka, get it? Then after several months she starts asking embarrassing questions and trying to find out where you live, something that's none of her business.

What's the cause of this villainous problem? Hey, it ain't a case of putty-pecker. Careful scientific research has demonstrated that the swollen male apparatus (a.k.a. "Hardening of the Hog") is primarily responsible for AIDS, rape, incest, sodomy, single motherhood, orphanages and screaming children. It's true. You can look it up in any reliable periodical on sale at the supermarket. In addition, I can tell you from personal experience that the trouble with our schools is **not** under-funding or poor teachers. It's the fact that they contain all those damn kids.

We're living through a period of the vulgarization of traditional American standards. Our moral compass is threatened, and our culture is undermined. Common ethics have been subverted. Every book, every movie, every TV show is about sex. We're inundated with the promotion of sex. Ad agencies even use sex to sell farm tractors. It's disgusting. I thought about this issue one day while I was in the bathroom reading "The Layman's Guide to Unobtrusive Flatulence" (the chapter on surreptitious squeezers) and I decided right then and there to do something about it.

After long hours in my garage applying my vast knowledge of genital chemistry, I came up with the perfect solution. I combined the complex organic compound called di-hydroxyl-dong-bender-sulfate with cheap scotch and a powerful commercial drain cleaner, and behold!—a product that will de-fang the deadliest dork. It takes the "pow" right out of your pencil. It melts your meat quicker than you can describe a well-known defecatory substance.

Just a couple of drops on your Corn Flakes or in your coffee and you're good for twenty-four hours. Instead of the shameful condition known as a "Raging Crack-Buster," you obtain the more serene "Sagging Half-Master." And it frees up your hands for yard work. No more hormone-gorged harpoon that can get you in nothing but deep dog-poopy. I managed to locate the arousal center in the brain that responds to phrases like "nice ass!" and "look at those bazooms!" and found a way to convert those images, through subtle molecular manipulation, into gruesome pictures of your nuts caught in a trash compactor. Automatic turn-off.

My compound really gaffs your gadget. Isn't this great? Of course, there is one small drawback. The stuff tastes a lot like bat saliva, but I'm experimenting with peppermint to resolve that problem. In the meantime, my approach allows you to circulate in society without the embarrassing condition known as the "Non-Bendable-Boner." No more unpredictable rod-rigidity. The freedom engendered by a successful "flopper" is simply incalculable.

I have an extensive background in marketing, and therefore I've already developed a can't-miss commercial. How's this?

"Listen guys! Are you being held back by unwanted erections? Is your career or social life in jeopardy because of an untimely stiff one? DICK-WILT® is the amazing new product that deadens your dunker so you can avoid those awkward moments we all fear. You no longer have to go through life bent over like a hunchback to cover up the shameful zapper in your zipper.

"Don't be a slave to the puppy in your pantaloons. Use our revolutionary product and your dipper won't spring to life at inopportune moments (for example when you happen to gaze into the dress worn by your boss's big-breasted wife, thereby screwing up your chance for a promotion). Let's face it, a puffed-up prong, no matter how involuntary, makes you do things you shouldn't. For instance, we all know it's bad manners to try to spear the grieving widow before she even gets home from the funeral (although we've all done it, I admit).

"But now you can go anywhere, unfazed by the humiliating condition known as 'Protruding Penetrator.' You can take charge of your Willie, instead of having it dictate its disgusting needs to you and forcing you to respond to your copulatory urge in large crowds and on escalators. So tame your trowel with DICK-WILT®. Take the stiffness out of your splint and get your life back on track today."

Several large corporations are presently in early negotiating stages with me for manufacturing rights. The Hart-Donn Pharmaceutical and Air-Brake Company appears to be mighty interested. I'm poised on the threshold of unlimited wealth here, but I want to keep the business private and realize a vast fortune before I proceed to a public offering. In the meantime, because you are my brother (and also distantly related), you have the opportunity to get in on the ground floor. You could make millions on this deal. So if you're interested, send me a check for all the money you have and you'll receive a substantial amount of preferred stock in the company. You can trust me. It's completely safe.

Your most precious sibling,

Ludlow

4

Hey Grover,

Earl and Madge have been at it again. The local constabulary is called to their home quite often, for instance when the neighbors hear a steady stream of chilling screams and socially-unacceptable language emanating from their love nest. In the best of times, these two lovebirds have what I feel is an oddly confrontational approach to communicating with each other, but old Earl used poor judgement on this occasion when he told the Missus that he thought their sex life was shitty.

I have to say that I would consider any type of sex with Madge to be shitty, even by phone (and she paid for the call). You could take a survey of five hundred registered sex offenders and you wouldn't find one who would consent to crawl up on her frame, even for monetary incentives. No sane male would touch her chassis with a 3.28 meter pole.

Madge isn't what I would call remotely attractive (in the sense that she's uglier than a dragon's ass), although she's convinced that every man envisions her as eminently desirable. This gives you an idea of her level of intelligence. She's about five feet tall and has the figure of a Polish sausage. And she's a talker. I try to keep from dozing off when she's gabbing just to see if she'll ever come up for air. Hand signals are the only way to get a word in. Otherwise, you have to mail in your share of the conversation.

Madge figures any guy would love to do the tummy tussle with her, so she flirts shamelessly with them all. Earl is no prize, either, so I guess they belong together. He has this tremendous gut. I may have told you that before. His comment about his bride's physical deficiencies on this particular evening, though, was poorly chosen. The fur started to attain rocket velocity when he suggested they experiment with jumper cables as a marital aid. I think he should have stuck with the twelve-volt battery. But he didn't, and that's when the feces really collided with the ventilating system.

Madge demonstrated her distaste concerning his remarks by crowning him with a couple of choice pieces from her best set of crockery (from which the food had not yet been removed). Earl, feeling oddly slighted by this behavior, then rapped her resoundingly on the forehead with a wine bottle that was conveniently within reach. I'm happy to report that it was empty, so he didn't spill anything—which is normally the case. Madge responded by booting him in the nuts. Although it's hard to imagine, the level of animosity escalated from there to the point where Madge is sitting on Earl, who is flat on the floor with his big gut sticking up in the air, and she has her hands around his throat, trying to re-distribute the gristle that comprises his larynx. Earl is landing the occasional lucky punch, and they're both using unflattering linguistic phrasing at high volume to describe their mutual lack of admiration.

Now, Earl doesn't know the meaning of the word defeat (along with a lot of other words). He finally knocks Madge off him and tries to get out of the kitchen. Well, the guy doesn't move too fast, as you can well imagine from the size of his gut (which makes him look as if he's swallowed part of Rhode Island). And I'm not sure he knows how to get out of any room, once he's entered it. This means that Madge quickly catches up with him and conks him a resounding blow on the noggin with a giant skillet. It's one of her favorite close-combat accessories. This sends our hero flying along the tile floor on his face and out into the hall, where he is brought to a halt after fifteen feet or so by a large glass cabinet holding Madge's prize crystal. Not much of her collection survives the impact.

Ain't no verse in the Bible gonna hold Momma back at this point. Earl is a big guy, but he's no match for the little woman when she's in full-fury mode. Earl is not what you would call an accomplished bob-and-weaver anyway. The combination of his girth and the low level of voltage passing through his cerebellum makes him as light on his feet as Fred Astaire, who is currently dead (if you catch my drift). In fact, when Madge swings a roundhouse right at him, he tends to remain mesmerized and fixate on her approaching knuckles until she makes contact. Right on the beezer.

Anyway, Madge wades through the destruction, kicks some of the glass aside and picks up a poker from the fireplace. She is just about to put a new part in Earl's hair (right down to the brain) when a couple of neighbors, Hyphen Shingle and his wife Bessie-Mae, rush in and wrest it from her grasp. These folks have been through similar dramas many times before, and they really don't give a shit if the neighborhood pugilists murder each other. They're just trying to avoid another visit by the sheriff's stalwarts, who always screw up their flowerbeds.

Earl is lying on the floor like a paralyzed pachyderm, gasping for breath, with his big gut heaving. He has lacerations, contusions and welts all over his head and shoulders. He's covered with shards of glass from the cabinet, as well as minute fragments of what used to be an impressive arrangement of crystal tableware, much of which has been reduced to sub-atomic particles. He's also leaking a little hemoglobin. Upon realizing that their concerned neighbors have come calling, Madge (who is breathing hard and holding the poker over her head) ceases her rampage and turns on the charm. Her clothes are torn, a couple of teeth are loose, and she has one eye swollen shut and rapidly going deep-purple. Her hair is sticking straight out to the sides and she's sporting assorted cuts and gashes on her honker, where Earl has landed a few lucky ones.

"Oh ... hi," she says, smiling sweetly, "Earl and I were just re-arranging some household items." The Shingles are not fooled. They know full well that these two lunatics have been trying to re-arrange each other's topography. But the presence of the good Samaritans serves to calm the scene. Just another day in Loveland. I've advised Madge and Earl on several occasions that they should try to look for positive aspects in each other. Let's face it, there's a little bit of good in everyone, I tell them. Even Attila's wife called him "Hun."

Madge is a gourmet cook. She spends twelve hours a day watching cooking shows and the other twelve putting together elaborate culinary masterpieces that Earl wolfs down without the faintest idea what he's devouring, which is a blessing. She invites us over a lot to show off her prowess, and we've run out of excuses to turn them down. When they're not trying to kill each other, Earl is usually parked in front of the TV, viewing a re-run of the "Lawrence Welk Show" with his well-known intellectual intensity. He's hard of hearing, as I said before, so I don't know what he gets out of the program. The effects of blunt-force conjugal trauma have taken their toll on old Earl over the years. He's been exposed to a pretty steady diet of flying earthenware since he first said, "I do," and then, "No, don't!"

Sometime during the second hour of our visit, he registers the fact that we're present. He manages to hoist his lard up from the couch and mutters something that would resemble a greeting if he ever got it all out. Conversation with Earl is usually carried on at maximum volume in an attempt to penetrate his cranium, and even then I don't think we've ever come to any conclusion about what gets through. After trying to place us, he sinks back down like a dead horse falling from the mezzanine of the shopping mall and starts emitting sounds that resemble talking or something. His mutterings are interspersed with long intervals of silence while he tries to get a handle on whatever the hell his idea was when he started the sentence in the first place. His attempt to use a two-syllable word is genuinely ambitious. But Madge doesn't give him much of a chance. She interrupts him as usual and begins a totally unrelated soliloquy in a voice that's set on maximum *screech*.

"We've been so busy since the last time we saw you. And we had such a wonderful time at my high school reunion in Chattanooga. It was a thrill to see my old friends again, even though a lot of them look dreadful. Some of those people just never take care of themselves. Wilma Tuttle told me she had recently lost her husband, Herb. She said he had a heart attack in the bowling alley while he was trying to pick up a four-seven split. He hit the hardwood just as he let the ball loose and it wound up in the gutter two alleys over. The corpse, not the ball. Apparently, everyone watched in horror as the ball continued down the alley and only managed to knock down the seven. His team was pretty upset when they finished out of the money. But the whole town turned out for the funeral, except for Marge Diddle, of course, who always gets her nails done on Tuesdays and refused to change her appointment. Herb was buried in his favorite bowling shirt, just as he would have wanted. They laid him out face-down so everybody could read the ad on the back for Swenson's Bait Shop. Sadie Humper ran off for the third time with that no-account bum from Memphis. She never learns. He keeps promising to pay her way through manicurist's school, but he never comes through—although she does. I don't know how she could pass the entrance exam. She spells 'shit' with two t's."

And on and on. She's happier than a hillbilly with a car that starts once in a while. But her plan to nauseate her guests is succeeding nicely. While she's trumpeting about something completely trivial, my mind wanders to patterns in the carpeting, and Gretchen later told me that she was silently conjugating irregular French verbs.

Madge finally winds down and shouts, "Earl, go outside and put the steaks on the grill!" He gets up (an accomplishment in itself) and says, "I don't have time for that shit now. I'm going outside and put the steaks on the grill." He lumbers out to the patio with me in pursuit. Earl has what is considered an average California barbeque. It's about the size of a U-Haul truck, with more knobs and dials than the cockpit in an airliner. He gets it fired up, flames shooting out in all directions, and throws the meat on the grill. This exchange ensues:

Earl: I went to the ballgame last night.
Me.   Is that right?
Earl: What?
Me: You went to the ballgame last night.
Earl: Oh, did I tell you already?
Me: No. I thought you didn't like baseball.
Earl: Dave Klutterbeek had tickets. He wanted me to drive.
Me: Why didn't he drive?
Earl: What?
Me: Why didn't Dave drive?
Earl: He screwed up his leg. Slammed the car door on it. Silly ass thought he was all the way in. It's all black and blue now.
Me: Who was playing?
Earl: What?
Me: Who was playing?
Earl: It was probably the Cubs.
Me: Was it a good game?
Earl: Not worth a damn.
Me: Who won?
Earl: What?
Me: Who won the game?

Earl: I dunno. I fell asleep.

Me: Didn't Dave tell you who won?

Earl: Oh shit, I was supposed to drive him home!

Me: Good move.

Earl: I really like those Lennon Sisters.

Me: You like the Lennon Sisters?

Earl: No, the Lennon Sisters. And they look a lot alike.

Me: Maybe that's because they're sisters.

Earl: What?

Me: The Lennon sisters are sisters.

Earl: I don't know about that, but do you think they're sisters?

Me: It's a possibility.

We hear a voice from inside the house.

Madge: Earl, are those steaks done yet?

Earl: Never mind that shit now, the steaks are done!

Madge: What?

Me: He says the steaks are done!

Earl: That woman must be deaf.

We gather at the table, where Madge has dealt out loads of side dishes. I think she uses secret ingredients like basil and acetylene. She's made potatoes à la parisiénne, beans à la Bourdeaux, mushrooms à la Marseille, squash "oh, my god," and a shit-pot of other fancy grub. Most of it is unrecognizable. Earl spoons big heaps of this stuff on top of his steak, burying it under a huge mound of designer vittles. He applies a two-inch layer of ketchup to the food and the surrounding area of the table and starts forking it in like he's feeding a hay baler. Madge gives Earl a look that says she wants to kill him, which is probably what she'll attempt as soon as we leave.

Fortunately, the two of them gulp down wine by the bellyful, subtly tasting the unobtrusive bouquet and slightly cheeky personality of the two-dollar-a-gallon fermented paint remover from Earl's private stock. I figure they'll be so plastered by the time the evening is over that they'll just exchange a couple of half-hearted punches and go to bed. As we say our good-byes at the end of the evening, I slap Earl on the back. "The steaks were delicious," I say. He says, "What?" You can't put a price on this kind of entertainment.

That's pretty much the way things go around here. Too bad you have to miss it. Earl and Madge are painfully selective about the people they allow into their social circle, but I'm sure with a little coaching you could quality.

The One and Only,

Ludlow

5

Hey Grover,

I'm disappointed that you chose not to put some cash into my last venture, but I suppose you have your money tied up in safe, over-diversified mutual funds geared to pile up the profits through conservative management. It simply shows that you are an amateur in the financial area. You have to forget that stuff, because I'm giving you the opportunity to really hit it big.

Although you would never have suspected it, in all fairness I should mention that I have prevaricated on occasion, but this is definitely not the case here. I'm starting a combination Designer Language School and Travel Agency, geared to the discriminating wealthy tourist. I find that people need someone to arrange their voyage (French: *voyage*) and coach them in the use of proper communication tools. I will provide indispensable advice so my clients are guaranteed to achieve maximum fulfillment when tooling through some foreign landfill ...er, country. They learn, for example, that they will be going to countries that contain geography, among other things. I also warn them that the main problem they will encounter in another country is that it's filled with foreigners. This is often shocking news.

Here are a few general rules that every tourist should be aware of. I thought you might be interested too. First, you should never believe a brochure published by the locality you intend to visit. They use words like "charming," "historical" and "quaint," whereas most of the places they refer to are as charming as a public washroom in the Bronx. Visiting these foreign locations (toilets) is similar to having your scrotum slapped with a ping-pong paddle. If you actually visit the run-down piles of debris that they claim are quaint, you should have your head examined, along with a number of internal organs.

And who needs that ancient crap anyway? Other countries are so behind the times. It's mind-boggling (especially for those of us who have one). Most of their decrepit castles, cathedrals and other piles of junk need renovation, big time. They all saw better days years ago. Why don't they fix these eyesores up? But no, they just let the stuff go to ruin. Slap some paint on those damn things, for chrissakes!

The Parthenon in Athens drives me nuts. First they put it up on a hill where it's hard to reach and then they let it go to hell. All the windows were knocked out years ago, and those dummies never think of replacing the glass. Shitty management. And don't get me started on the Coliseum, the one in Rome or someplace like that. Hello!!? It's falling apart! I'll bet they can't hold a good motorcycle race there anymore. They should tear all those old trash heaps down and put up something attractive, like a strip mall or at least some condos. Maybe a whorehouse. They think they're so great just because everything is centuries old. We have old stuff in this country too, you know. Earl is a perfect example. And Disneyland is quaint.

Here's a subject that frosts my crotch. It's the concept of art. This is a real sore point with me. I know everyone thinks Michelangelo (or "Mike the Angel" as I call him) was a genius or something. Frankly, I don't see it. The guy was a free-loader, a first-class sponge. I guess nobody checked his expense reports. He must have spent thousands on paint and scaffolding. He worked for years on the Sistine Chapel when anybody with common sense knows it was a two-day job with a roller or a spray gun.

But realistically, a foreign country has a lot to offer if you're willing to look for it. Put on your grownup underwear and deal with it when you travel. Take a chance and explore the real thing on your own. Find the bar in an American hotel. You may meet some people from back home. When on the road, be aware that it's preferable to start your travel experiment in a country that has reasonable hygiene habits. In your case that might not be so important. There is a rule of thumb to use when packing for travel. The British always take seven pairs of underwear: for Monday, Tuesday, Wednesday, and so on. The French travel with twelve pairs: for January, February, March, etc. You can choose something that falls between these extremes. I don't know how far you want to trust the French, though. Those people actually eat snails! Ugh! Then they have the unmitigated gall (or Gaul) to speak French. Is that phony or what? And they suck half their vowels right up their noses. How inconsiderate can you get?

Before you leave home, work out the exchange rate for the currency you will encounter. It's not that difficult. You would be surprised how many ninnies travel with no idea of the relative value of their money. Financial arithmetic seems to baffle the average Yankee. Not only that, most people don't even know what the official currency is in the country they're visiting. Once I arrived at the Amsterdam airport to start a business trip. This was before the Euro was adopted by the European Union. Holland's currency at the time was the Guilder, also known as the Florin.

I went to the Currency Exchange to get some Marks or Pesetas, or some other silly damn money. A young woman with a Texas accent said to the girl at the counter, "I want to get some Amsterdam Francs." I am not making this up. The girl replied with a smile, "Madam, we have a lot of things in Holland, but we don't have Amsterdam Francs." Hello!!? It isn't that difficult. The exchange rate calculation is pretty simple. You just have to remember that the Euro-Dollar (or "Euro" as we pros call it) is worth 0.6537281 U.S. Dollars, but only on Thursdays if it's not raining. Otherwise divide by 17 and carry the 9. You have to keep in mind that the Brits didn't make the change to the Euro, and neither did the Scandinavian countries. I don't think it was because their economies were doing so well. They were just terrified to give up their currency because they knew they could never learn to calculate in another one.

The next point that frustrates Americans is the fact that most foreigners tend to be reserved. The Yankee tourist can't figure out why there is no red carpet spread out for him when he descends from the plane and nobody runs up with open arms and shouts, "Oh praise the Lord, you finally got here!" Yanks are on a crash program to expand their circle of friends, whereas people in other countries don't give a hairy damn about you—or each other, for that matter. They don't care one way or another, and neither do I. The American traveler then draws the conclusion that foreigners "don't like Americans."

Why wouldn't foreigners love us when we visit their country? We don't know where we are, we have no clue about their history or their culture, we can't say two words in their language, and we don't want to eat their food. The natives wonder why we leave the U.S. in the first place. In their opinion, if you want American stuff everywhere you travel, you should go to a VFW convention in Detroit.

And it comes as a major surprise that in many countries people actually prefer to speak in a different language. It's narrow-minded, but that's the way those friggin' wogs are. This means that they sometimes spit on you if you ask for directions, especially if they can't understand you. Can't they grasp what we need? If they come to our country they better by-god speak English. And if we go to their country they better by-god speak English. It's only fair. If you have trouble getting your point across you should try shouting. It assures an optimal level of social exchange. But try to avoid excessive slang. It's better to break the ice with expressions like, "*Excusez-moi*, you goddamn frog, where the hell is *le prochaine* crapper?" This is so much more diplomatic than coming right out with, "I gotta take a massive growl, man!" Try to put the accent on the final syllable.

Natives are always receptive to people who try to communicate even a little in their language, and the linguistic nuances embedded in the above sentence, once mastered by the traveler, guarantee several hours of rewarding offensive communication. Try to observe the rule that in any language, the plural takes two Umlauts and should be underlined.

Some handy phrases for travel situations:

Quanto cuesta eso?	If it's more than $1.99 you can stick it.
Entschuldigen Sie, bitte.	Who the hell do you think you're shoving?
Vous êtes très gentil.	How about a little service here, dickhead?
Dove posso trovare una donna?	Where can I get laid?
Wilt Uw met mij in het bed gaan?	Lie down, I think I love you.
Non voglio mangiare questo.	This stuff tastes like badger puke.
Ich bin ein sensibles Seelchen.	Don't give me that shit, buster!
Y tu mama tambien!	And your mother too!

Anyone using my services will certainly want me to arrange guided tours within the target countries. I use the word "target" because in some cases you will feel like blowing the place up before you leave. A guided tour can be the *pièce de résistance* (piece of resistance). This gives you the advantage of occupying a bus with some of the biggest idiots in creation, maybe fifty people who have the combined sense of a pebble. It has the added benefit of giving you the opportunity to make fun of the tour guide, the little lovely whose accent is incomprehensible, but who thankfully has an imposing chest. You may have trouble understanding the accents. Not everybody says "shit" the way we do—with the accent on the second syllable.

I guarantee that there will be a bunch of loud American females along for the ride who are over fifty, overweight, over-beveraged, and have never been out of their state before. At no time will they know where the hell they are. Fortunately, they also have big jugs. If you are on a boat, one of the women (many of them come from somewhere in your neighborhood) will at one point consider it necessary to jump in the water to cool off. It will take several strong men to pull her drunken ass back into the boat, and she will be soaking wet with her dress clinging to her body, at which time you will be grateful that she has really big jugs.

In addition, in every group you will be confronted with a passel of folks from the deep South who are built like Clydesdales, but not nearly so attractive. These rednecks will drawl the shit out of you, until you wonder why we didn't let the bastards secede from the Union when we had the chance. I guess it was more fun to try to shoot them. Also, several nuns will be on board. How do they pay for these trips? Do they have access to the collection plate?

A word about the food. Try not to eat. Outside this country you won't find a lot of food that's similar to what you eat in the States. Or edible, for that matter. It's tough to find a good burrito in Germany or decent spaghetti in Greenland. Just remember to order a coke with everything.

Avoid museums. They just have old stuff in those places, and although nerdy scholars consider this barf-material to be valuable, you wouldn't put it in an outdoor crapper situated on the farthest corner of your property—unless your property is in the Louisiana swamps. I don't know if anyone should go to Great Britain. On one hand, they're sort of civilized (so is everyone else compared to us), but I've always had the feeling that England is behind the times. Be prepared to wind your watch back to 1955. Besides that, the British approach to meal preparation lacks imagination. It's a bad sign when the stew and the pudding taste exactly the same. It's best to just watch them boil cabbage for an hour and then point yourself at the sweet trolley. Leave Africa off your travel schedule. I can't think of anything worth seeing there, unless you're partial to sand and charging rhinos. But the Sahara is nice in the fall when the leaves turn color.

Europeans always drink bottled water in a restaurant. In Latin America and Asia it's a good idea to avoid tap water unless you're intent on investigating symptoms associated with the government-issue shits. Mexico water is one of the top ass attackers. I don't know how they do it. Maybe they develop a tolerance over time to the black, hairy bugs swimming in the agua. Or maybe they don't mind shitting through the eye of a needle every day.

If you are anywhere in Asia, never order the duckbill marinated in napalm. Heartburn is guaranteed. Be warned that you won't find a large selection of ice cream in Antarctica. And airlines everywhere discourage passengers from riding in the overhead luggage compartments. With the right planning, travel can be a delightful experience. It all depends on your attitude, and that can be controlled with the proper medication.

I think I've covered the most significant points here. Once again, send me a large check for everything in your account and you'll get a bunch of preferred stock in my company. It can't miss. You may want to get a second mortgage. Earl asks about you frequently. I told him you died. You'll thank me for that some day.

Old "You Know,"

Ludlow

6

Hey Grover,

As I told you, we've developed a wide social circle here. Frankly, they're pitiful, but we don't have much to choose from. Most of our neighbors can't remember how many parents they have, but we hang around with them because they're entertaining in their dim-witted way, and we sucker them into paying when we go to a restaurant with them. They never catch on.

Every so often we rent a party boat for a picnic on the lake. It's a big, square thing with an electric motor and large comfortable couches. The boat, I mean, not the lake. It has a canopy and can easily hold over a dozen people. We did the sea-faring thing Sunday and invited the usual suspects. Gretchen made her popular sauerkraut sandwiches for lunch. There are some weird combinations among these people, not all of it the result of illegal immigration. We know a couple where one of them is from Ireland and the other from China. There's a gal from Argentina married to a Russian and a French guy whose wife is Egyptian. We also have various possible fugitives from justice, a Japanese girl hitched to a redneck, a guy from Albania with a Norwegian bride—and of course Madge and Earl.

Hugh Jass was there, along with his wife, Larr. Her can is not what I would call tiny. And she has the biggest jugs I ever saw. Those things are almost as big as her ass. If she ever took off her bra, it would pull all the wrinkles out of her face, but I don't want to be there when that explosion occurs. Hugh has been a flasher for so long he often forgets to wear his raincoat.

Inga Gundersen and her husband, Carlos Cajones, came with us. He just finished his degree in urinal maintenance. He's a mumbler. When he talks it sounds like somebody taking a dump. Carlos proudly showed me a picture of his family back in some cruddy village in Honduras. I thought it was a device to induce vomiting. You never saw such plug-uglies. Inga and Carlos brought some special food. I guess you could call it Scandinavian-Latino fusion cuisine. It consisted of a casserole that combined herring, reindeer nuts and refried beans, topped with Tabasco sauce and some kind of Chinese noodle dressing. Dousing it with urine would have improved it. Earl was the only one who ate any of it and spent most of the afternoon squeezing off several loud but artistically redeeming pants busters. His life has been a series of incidents that have often caused people to remark, "Is there a hit man in the house?"

We had a native from Dubai on board too. A pervert, but pleasant enough. His name is Jaleel-al-Hossein-al-Jesus-al-Michaels. Claims to come from a diverse religious culture and is a football fan. His wife is the lovely former Shaykya Noggers. She was born in Bolivia, grew up in the Philippines, moved to Zimbabwe after her Korean mother's divorce from her Hindu father, went to school in Switzerland, and worked for a couple of years in New Zealand as a Jungian psychologist, bus mechanic and part-time hooker. She met "Al" (as we call him) in Pocatello, Idaho, where he was managing a surfboard shop.

Our bantam-weight prizefighter buddy, Hector Borracho, sailed with us too. The "Mucho Macho Mexicano" (as we fondly refer to him) has been in the fight game all his young life and has a special vocation within the industry. You know that in each bout there has to be one loser. This is the role Hector has chosen for himself. Apparently, his job is to use his head to stop opposing punches from traveling too far. Between rounds of his last fight, his manager told him, "Don't worry, the other guy ain't hardly laid a glove on you." Hector said, "Then keep an eye on the referee, Gringo. Somebody's kickin' the shit out of me!" The only significant punch Hector ever connected with was when his opponent ducked and he shattered the ring-post, for which he was awarded three points. To say that his brains are scrambled requires the assumption that he had the necessary raw materials to start with. His whole head looks like a cauliflower ear.

Hector's wife is Carmen, a *muy* hot *chica*. Is she sexy? Does Earl fish around in his nose in public? Her subtle appeal can be traced to the fact that for a small woman she has a nice ass and really big milk cans. Carmen is a confirmed advocate of breast-feeding, but restricts her recipients to males eighteen and older. She has what you would call an outgoing personality. She gives it away to any guy who asks and a lot who don't. Her punchy hubby doesn't have a clue, though. Some guy could be pouring the meat to Carmen with Hector wedged between them and he still wouldn't catch on.

Carmen really knows how to almost dress. She was wearing one of those flimsy Hispanic blouses that hide everything but the boobs. Due to an unfortunate accident, she pulled up her skirt and sat down on my hand, which I had carelessly misplaced on the seat beneath her. But she didn't seem to mind when I proceeded to demonstrate my new bowling grip. And she asked more than once for details about picking up a spare.

Father Francis Waferchucker was also there. He's a priest who is primarily involved with administrative duties, meaning he runs a string of bingo parlors for the Archdiocese. Father Waferchucker got into a heated theological discussion with Strokka Pellvuss, who is a non-practicing, reformed, anti-orthodox, sectarian nun who doesn't believe in atheism or the Easter Bunny. They disputed the theological theory that communion wine is cheaper at Trader Joe's and other discount outlets than at the major supermarket chains. They also got into a rip-roaring dispute over which verse in the Bible requires church leaders to wear those silly robes and funny hats. Strokka may be somewhat confused about her spirituality. She left the mother church to become a Sixth-Day Adventist (obviously, she didn't complete the entire indoctrination course). But she has a good heart and a nice ass. She will soon leave to do missionary work in the Central African Republic—the poorest nation on the continent—where she intends to augment her religious salary by selling Avon products hut-to-hut.

Strokka has a brother, Wally, who couldn't make it to our picnic. It's just as well. They call him "Fingers" because he has his hand in his fly so often. This guy is what is known in cultured circles as a real ugly bastard. He has a face like a toothache. My guess is that he may have been the original reason for birth control. Wally was arrested once for tearing the labels off new mattresses, exposing himself to the Mormon Tabernacle Choir, and molesting farm animals, but they let him go with only a warning and a kick in the nuts. He had a terrible learning deficiency as a child. After sixteen years of schooling, the only word he ever learned was "no." He isn't terribly exciting in a social environment, but it qualifies him uniquely to be a claims representative for a large insurance company.

Buckminster Naykudd and his wife were also in our delightful bunch of sideshow candidates. Buck owns a successful business producing plastic tubular products such as rake handles and dildos, primarily the latter. He's managed to dominate the self-satisfaction market ever since he introduced the WOWIE! This is an improved insertional model with handles and brake lights. The WOWIE! comes in several colors and a full range of sizes, from the PETITE version for girls under ten to the CRACKERJACK, for more mature, full-bodied consumers. The WOWIE! offers a large selection of vibration settings. They start with the sedate "Oooh!" passing through the more rigorous "Gulp!" and finally culminating in the ultra-violent "Skull-Fracture!!!" The instruction manual shows how to use the 911 accessory with this last setting, along with insightful hints on how the neighbors can help extricate the user from ceiling fixtures.

Buck's wife, Wandarown, is a stately blond bombshell with a body that can best be described as "high-violation material." Every male eye was on her ass when she climbed into the boat and inadvertently allowed her duds to flutter upwards in the wind, revealing her lack of unmentionables. It was a major contribution to the afternoon's prong-thickening. Wandarown's charitable activities are mostly confined to fornication. Most women shake hands in a social situation. Wanda reaches for your crotch. Delivery men and other male well-wishers are lined up at Wanda's door all the time. You can tell how aroused they are by how far apart they stand. Although the rumor proved false, it was thought at one time that she also had a relationship with a large dog named Lowell. But Buck doesn't seem to mind. Maybe he's unconcerned because he devotes most of his spare time trying to harpoon the fair sex himself.

An Eskimo couple rounded out our group. We needed them to bring the ice. Nanook met Oona when she was hooking and teaching Sunday School in Nome. She has one of those flat Eskimo faces that looks like she was born while sitting on an intercontinental ballistic missile when it struck the target. Nannook runs a fish market and pimps on the side. He's trying to establish himself in the bordello business full time, but it's slow. His wife is his only employee right now and that keeps her busy, as you can imagine. She's a little on the chubby side. Okay, she's really pudgy. When she's naked, she looks like she's fully dressed.

You've heard me complain about the lack of culture and refinement in this part of the country. Well, on this day, when we expected to relax and enjoy ourselves while tooling around and trying to swamp the other boats, we saw one of the most vile, repugnant and disgusting demonstrations of tastelessness you can imagine. A guy was standing in his sailboat with his pants around his ankles and holding his wand up in plain view as we went past, with a big smile on his face. What's become of good manners? Is there no shred of common decency anymore? The cretin obviously has no respect for others and no grasp of appropriate public behavior. We mooned the bastard. Carmen held up a large card with a "1" on it.

The highlight of every picnic, naturally, is when Earl and Madge show up. It matches the thrill you get when you back into a paper shredder. You could tell they were pissed at each other right from the start, although Madge is usually the only one who remembers why. Earl plopped down on one of the couches like a sack of grain being tossed into a pick-up, which forced us to relocate everybody to the other side of the boat to avoid capsizing it. Earl has a big gut. He reached for a handful of beers and started sucking in the liquid refreshment like a newly-unstopped drain.

The big guy was already half-loaded when he arrived and still suffering from a head-banger from the night before. His few remaining cerebral molecules have convinced him that the best cure for a hangover is to drink some fur from the skunk that screwed you. It has never worked, but he is not about to give up on the research. Earl wouldn't blink if you hit him in the head with a two-by-four. I've tried it. The first time we witnessed anything resembling even mild comprehension on his part was when he figured out last summer that his pants were on fire from standing too close to the barbecue. Earl is involved in the new beautification project in our town. The first goal is to have him deported.

We had a CD player, so I put on my favorite, Julia Child singing obscene Armenian folk songs and Slavic goosing melodies. Everybody had a good time. Our picnics on the water are always pleasant when only one or two fistfights break out. We laughed and talked and shouted obscenities at passing watercraft. I was captaining the vessel, applying all of my remarkable maritime skills and perfecting my ramming technique, but I think I drank a little too much grape juice (read: firewater). At the end of our travesty, as I approached the slip, I kicked in the afterburners instead of reverse gear and took out half the dock. What the hell. Why do they put that thing so close to the water, anyway?

Earl fell on Wanda. She was delighted for a second, until she saw who it was. If it had been anybody else but Earl, it would have been planned. But Earl hasn't experienced the spark of a plan in years. He has to read directions to take a shit. Not more than forty or fifty casualties resulted from the pile-up, so I actually did a better job than the previous time. And I garnered extra style points for sinking two other boats and wearing my cap backwards. I also managed to keep my fly closed. That was a first, as well. Got a lot of compliments from the lake staff when they came back down from high ground.

This is how we amuse ourselves around here. Wish you could join us. Earl still asks about you a lot. If he ever shows up at your place, act like you're dead.

Your brother,
er .... .You can fill in the blank here.

7

Hey Grover,

I'm really excited! I'm in the process of developing several screen projects, and I presented one of them to a major film studio a few days ago. The concept is original and fascinating—a sure-fire winner, or as one film executive described it, "Worthless." But I remain confident, because I know that when film executives with real insight are confronted with overwhelming talent, they'll choose to develop my stuff because they don't know any better. The smartest one of the bunch pulled a hamstring in his brain a long time ago.

My submission goes like this: It's the inspirational story of José Canyusee, an ambitious young man from a popular barrio in San Culo, Colombia, who decides to leave his family in order to follow his dream of making it big in the complex and exciting world of professional plumbing. José is not the first of the siblings to be driven by burning ambition. One of his brothers has already published a manual to help quadriplegics put on their underwear, and his sister is studying for her advanced degree in prostitution. The family is engaged in casual fornication and intense narcotics trafficking, so José must give up a life that provides him with massive amounts of money, unimaginable luxury, unlimited sex and the possibility of having his ass shot off at any moment. But he's determined to make a name for himself in the vocation he cherishes—human waste delivery.

José steals the money for his tuition from his mother's underwear (she's wearing it at the time) and enters the United States in a UPS carton, where he enrolls in the Brooklyn Poly-Technical School of Toilet Studies and Plunger Dynamics. This is one of the most prestigious institutions of bathroom education in the country, right after the Vermont College of Sewage Diversion and Cesspool Storage.

At a Perverts-Anonymous meeting, José meets Shebang Zalott, a moderately attractive nocturnal affection distributor, and they realize that a mighty spark of mutual animosity has been ignited between them. Shebang is trying to reform and abandon her hooking activities, though somewhat half-heartedly. The intensity of their emotions, paired with their low-level of brain activity, quickly turns to disgust and after several bouts of vomiting, they decide to move in together. She decorates their cozy apartment in a tasteful military foxhole motif.

As José puts all his efforts into his studies, bribing his instructors and memorizing anal diagrams, Shebang lends him much needed financial assistance by turning tricks, copying Biblical manuscripts and giving banjo lessons to members of the New York Philharmonic Orchestra. The day he gets his coveted degree in Roto-Rooting, though, tragedy strikes. Shebang, whose pubic section is the only part of her body that functions adequately, runs off to Des Moines, Iowa, with a deaf, one-armed, insect-infested Albanian landscape-worker who does Elvis impersonations, and José loses a testicle in a freak hopscotch accident. But our hero overcomes one obstacle after another (including a low IQ and a small weenie) and moves steadily upward in his toilet-oriented career, from urinals to full-size porcelain blasters, proving that persistence lands you in the shit every time. There's a lesson in there somewhere, Grover.

My story targets rugby players and eleven-year-old special education students. The studio execs said it just needed a little "tightening up." They wanted to set the action in either Singapore or Kankakee, Illinois, and have the male lead (I'm thinking Matt Damon here) tortured, spit upon, castrated and kicked out of West Poopistan for deflowering a member of the royal family (female) and her mother. Twice. In church. They also want to change the name of the film from "Gardening Without Your Pants On" to "Gidget Misplaces Her Diaphragm." I'm willing to consider some modifications, but I'm going to hold out for Trixie Phoot in the title role, which involves about two on-screen hours of nude scenes with close-up penetration shots (four weeks in actual filming time).

My discussions with the Hollywood elite resulted in an invitation to a big party in Beverly Hills. A major studio player has a lean-to there that consists of thirty-seven rooms and over a dozen crappers. Gretchen could have gone with me, but she wanted to iron my socks, change the toilet paper in our bathrooms and read through some back copies of the Gestapo Gazette. Naturally, I was flattered with the invitation and decided to postpone bowel movements for a couple of days in order to attend. They sent a car for me (a 1943 jeep).

As each limousine drew up to the awning at the front door, a parking attendant rushed forward to assist the descending female film celebrity, pulling her out of the vehicle by her butt and trying to get a look up her skirt, sometimes scoring digitally. The paparazzi were on either side of the entrance, and their shouts could be heard in the darkness. When a particularly fetching group of large-breasted and only partially-covered starlets arrived, one of the lowlifes hollered, "Take out your jugs!" No, wait, that was me.

The festivities were going full-blast when I got inside. The house was a castle—expensive furnishings everywhere and paintings on the wall by Titian, Botticelli and Yogi Berra. The glitterati (people engaged in glittering) were drinking champagne and acetylene cocktails, eating those little finger things that look like little fingers, and bullshitting each other. A six-piece trio, Joe Banana and his Bunch ("Music with a Peel"), was playing excerpts from Puccini operas, interspersed with Sousa marches and amplified labor pains.

The host, a pot-bellied, old bald guy with his fly open, introduced me to his wife, Mitzi. His name was Durdee Shords, and his clothes must have been tailored by Waste Management, Inc. I wouldn't have worn his shoes to kick shit into a corner. The word "ugly" must have been invented just for him, but missed by a mile on the low side. Surprisingly, the little woman was a knockout, young and blond. Who would have guessed in a town full of trophy wives? Her upper torso preceded her by about ten minutes. The mother lode. I haven't seen mammaries like those since I went on a guided tour of Wisconsin dairy farms in 1980.

The old guy asked me if I liked cocktails, and when I answered in the affirmative, he told me one. I had heard it before. It was the one about the Jewish janitor in the convent who called the head nun Mother Shapiro. After subtly squeezing the wife's ass (and then her hubby's), I was led around the pool by a flunky wearing a sequined sweatshirt and open-toed football shoes. He pointed out some legends of the silver screen. I said, "Wow, there are a lot of people here." He sneered, "They're all here to advance their careers by sucking up to the boss." I looked at him quizzically (with considerable quiz). "Figuratively speaking," he quickly added. I asked him if he knew what "figuratively" meant. "Later in the evening?" he ventured. I supposed aloud that the guest list was probably très exclusive. He said, "Naw, any dumb ass can get in here."

Most of these people think they're infinitely important. They've had so much smoke blown up their tailpipes that the danger of anal cancer is appallingly real. Nevertheless (or never-the-more, whichever applies), it was a thrill to rub shoulders (and butts) with the stars. I shook hands with Poobda Liddel, a lovely young, plastic-augmented actress whose figure consisted of two enormous melons. At least I think so. In the ten minutes I spent in her company, I never managed to get a look at the rest of her. She had just finished a flick with Jamma Tinn about two college girls who start a banana-peeling business and wind up selling it (and their cans) at a huge profit to a group of Bosnian street vendors in Manhattan. Box-office returns were shitty, but the critics were lenient. Nobody said anything bad about the film, because nobody went to see it.

Lance and Missy, the current golden couple of Hollywood, stood at the side of the pool, watching people fall in. The glamour magazines have named them the pukey-cutest couple of the year, admired by fans everywhere for their good looks, their lack of acting talent and their determination to adopt more kids than anybody else. I'm pretty sure that wide-angle camera lenses were created to accommodate her frontal acreage.

The great Russian director, Lemmie Yankittov, was there with a dark-haired Slavic beauty. She was the sensational actress, Boobzer Shaykun. She had put on a little weight, but fortunately most of it had accumulated in her knockers. Her latest picture was big in Europe, a typical Slav sex-comedy entitled, "I'm Russian To Get Home." It's currently playing in the States, with sub-titles in Afrikaans. Yankittov said he was working on a three-part historical epic about the Soviet discovery of the female genital area and the molecular structure of DNA. Also the DNA itself, as well as a sack to carry it in. Lemmie planned to have a lot of sex.

Not in the picture, but while working on it.

"Call me Lemmie," he told me, putting one arm around my shoulder and a hand on Boobzer's ass (or was it the other way around?). "I gonna tell you what big success I am." This was a matter of staggering indifference to me. The only reason I didn't walk away is that Boobzer's jugs risked falling out of her dress at that moment and I wanted to keep my hands at the ready. But Yankittov wouldn't let up. "You want part in my next film? I picture you with lots make-up, bushy beard and maybe thick glasses. Anything for hide you face. You play part of shepherd with poor knowledge of personal hygiene. Can wear same clothes you got on now. Not much lines to learn but big chance to earn plenty rubles. Only have to do couple sex scenes with old peasant woman and spend few hours at low altitudes with animals who not mind how you smell. You always smell like this? What you say?"

I asked for a photo of the peasant woman and told him I'd get back to him. Actually, I like the idea. At that moment, Boobzer's chest fruit plunged from the front of her dress, as I had hoped, and I was in the right place at the right time. I didn't want them to hit the floor. She and I spent about twenty minutes stuffing them back in the flimsy garment she was wearing. She seemed extremely grateful, but not nearly as much as I was.

I really had to take a leak, so I went inside rather than doing it from three-meter board. There were free-loaders all over the place, power-people and fantastic-looking women, all feeding their faces and slurping down the root beer. I brushed my hands across a few really nice asses and then concentrated on the women. Next, I spent an interesting hour in the living room with a rectal thermometer taking people's temperature without their permission. Finally, I drained my bladder and went back outside. Next time I'll try to make it all the way to the bathroom.

These Hollywood types are really friendly. A handsome young couple invited me to sit down at their table. Her dress almost contained her frontal construction. She immediately made me feel welcome by putting her hand in my fly. She had to remove her husband's hand to do it. Later on, I accidentally got my hand caught under another woman's skirt and offered to do some obstetric work for her while I was at it. She declined, but agreed that my new bowling grip would definitely help me pick up more spares.

My scores are sure to improve, providing I ever make it to a bowling alley. I tried to repeat the accident with a girl who had a spiky haircut and purple nail polish (on her teeth), but some swine beat me to it. Courtesy is a dying concept.

I'd like to tell you how the evening turned out, but the indictment has been sealed. Maybe you can see it on the new TV series, "Life-Styles of the Rich and Voluntarily Abused."

Yer brudder,

Not that one, the other one.

Ludlow

8

Hey Grover,

I'm still waiting to hear back about my screenplay. Apparently, several studios are bidding for the incinerating rights. But that's not important now. I'm writing today to reveal a secret that I have never mentioned to a living soul (that description may include you). The truth is that I maintained a lie for many years and I need to tell someone about it. It's been weighing on my mind for a long time. Since you are my sibling (and also my brother), I know I can confide in you and count on your discretion. You must tell no one.

Back in the sixties, I was recruited by a government agency to perform covert operations of the utmost secrecy. One day a man suddenly appeared beside me as I was walking to the office. He had a face like a bagful of elbows and a bad limp in both legs that gave him a curious impression of proper balance. He gave me a card (the deuce of hearts) and asked me to have lunch with him the following day. Over a period of several weeks we met at famous Boston gourmet spots like "Hamburger Hamlet" and "The Skarf and Barf." We were deeply involved in the cold war at the time, as you may recall (I'm not sure whether your memory or your forgettery is more developed), and the gentleman assured me that my activities as a good-looking international businessman were a perfect cover for the type of work I would be requested to perform. In addition, my mastery of languages, including Cuban, Algerian, Obscene Serbo-Croatian, Mandolin Chinese and various scatological dialects, made me invaluable to federal authorities, including the Postal Service (Survivor Training Section).

I was sent for indoctrination and instruction to a place they call "The Farm," where I learned to raise chickens. No, wait, it was a place where I was coached in every aspect of furtive international politics, espionage and personal hygiene. I was also told to stay out of the washroom in the Minneapolis Airport. The world of covert stealth is an awesome place, not for the weak of heart or sphincter. I learned to deal with all the tools of the brutal clandestine trade, which included sophisticated weaponry, spying apparatus and pajamas with feet in them. I was also briefed extensively on how to resist torture by balling myself up into the fetal position, soiling my pants and whining at ear-splitting volume.

The head instructor (who spent a lot of time in the head) was Archibald "Gassy" Beans, formerly with the Royal Scottish Highland Cross-Dressing Regiment. A tough nut (maybe both of them were) if there ever was one. I considered volunteering for the project to describe his ugliness, but soon realized that the most appropriate adjectives were already being used to depict disgusting diseases of the dong. Gassy's face was an open book of undercover experience. He had Crow's Feet. Also Crow's Legs and Crow's Ass. He used to keep us up half the night recounting his adventures under deep cover, such as the time he attempted a nocturnal penetration operation, but the bimbo wouldn't uncross her legs. I wanted to kill the bastard.

Another of our training experts was Skabby Krodge. He was sort of like "Q" in the James Bond movies. As a weaponry expert, he taught us how to use ordinary objects as lethal devices. For example, Skabby showed us how to mount a dildo on a motorcycle for high-speed violation assignments. I was surprised to find that a common credit card was among the most interesting defensive tools. When confronted with a life-threatening situation, you buy a gun with it and shoot the bastard who's bothering you. And one normally doesn't think of scotch tape as particularly dangerous, but we learned that it could come in handy in threatening situations involving extreme flatulence. You use it to bind an opponent's rectum shut, thereby depriving him of much-needed anal oxygen and leading almost always to a quick and stench-less death.

I don't expect you to follow the complex workings of the deception trade. The average citizen has no idea of the danger, the elaborate undercover procedures and the advanced technology that were at my disposal. Therefore I will try to simplify these things for you, but it won't be easy. We had equipment that was unbelievably advanced. My compass could be converted into an ovary-extraction kit. And I was issued a fountain pen that was in reality a combination nine-millimeter machine-pistol, a sophisticated global positioning system, a land mine and an accordion.

The training was exhausting. Cleaning the latrine was also tiring. There was a lot of emphasis on hand-to-hand combat. We also learned foot-to-ass combat and knee-to-nuts combat. And that was just to get a place in the lunch line. I excelled in the maneuver called "Let's Find the Friggin' Door, Man!" One problem with the course was that I thought a "dead-drop" meant I was supposed to drop dead, and instead of one-time code paper I wanted to use Charmin. I learned things like the famous "Shanghai Switch," a clever means of communication developed by Howard Shanghai, who was a legendary spy and car wash employee. In a crowded venue, such as an embassy party, a public square or a whorehouse, it's sometimes necessary to pass vital information while remaining above suspicion. Since virtually everyone in a totalitarian state was constantly under surveillance in those days (often while perched on the can), the "Shanghai Switch" was an intricate procedure designed to fool even the most watchful eyes.

It goes like this: I approach the person to whom I want to pass a meatball sandwich, but more frequently a message. It's written on personalized, cream-colored, embossed stationery and naturally in code (usually a blind, double-digit, one-way, Chinese-character cipher with three carbons, and only readable by de-coding with the aid of a wrapper from a Hershey bar). I shake hands with my contact, greet him amiably, and sweep his feet out from under him with a vaulting pole (which I carry for the purpose). I pounce on his prostrate frame, choking him and simultaneously (at the same time, if possible) shoving my message into his mouth and down his throat. One healthy crap later, and voilà, the message is recovered. This almost always proved to be a detection-proof method of exchanging data. The only disadvantages are that serious constipation can occur or a healthy bowel movement may render even the best penmanship illegible. In such cases, the alternative procedure is used whereby the message is mailed to the recipient's home. Alas, poor Howard's career came to an ignoble end when his body was found a couple of years later washed up on a deserted beach in Idaho with a flagpole inserted two meters into his trap door.

As I said, the training schedule was grueling, with almost twenty minutes a day devoted to exhausting undercover (and over-cover) methods, including fetching sticks thrown by our instructors. We suffered severe deprivation and often had to wait five minutes or more to use the Jacuzzi.

When I had completed my intensive program, one of my instructors gave me a small, white pill. He told me it was very important to keep it with me at all times. I asked him if it was cyanide, arsenic or sodium iodide. He replied, "Actually, it's a breath mint. Whew!"

I was sent first to Paris, where within six months I was able to find a parking space, use the toilets by myself and call in massive air strikes on the French naval base at Toulon. I still hold the record for peacetime tonnage sunk. From my various bases in Europe (including first base on the softball team), I often went into East Germany, Greenland and other Eastern Bloc countries controlled by the Russians. I was successful in establishing business ties with those countries, because they needed our hard Western currency and we needed their inflatable plastic dolls. I can send you one. While engaging in legitimate business negotiations, I met with political officials in order to subvert them as agents in place. I would often use seductive females to accomplish my goal—like getting into their pants. Then I'd go back to work subverting officials. It was difficult and dangerous work, but I kept the CIA motto in mind: "We're going to throw Castro out if we have to exhume him to do it." I had to offer my target contacts attractive incentives. Sometimes a couple of bucks did the trick, but it was frequently necessary to provide season tickets to a local cathouse or a set of plastic dishes with little clowns painted on them. Occasionally, they held out for a change of underwear or a Millard Fillmore signature coffee mug. One difficult guy came around when I managed to procure him pictures of Charles de Gaulle exposing his stiffy while standing on the Arch of Triumph. I have a poster-size photo somewhere around here that I can mail you.

Those were heady times, hazardous but exhilarating. My colon was seized up around the clock. I never did find out who stuffed that clock in my colon. I was playing a risky game, usually a cut-throat session of jump-rope in an alley next to the toilet. When it was necessary to pass into East Berlin, I preferred going through Checkpoint Charlie, because I could get my parking ticket validated. It was a torturous process. The Volkspolizei searched my rented car with mirrors and a fine-tooth comb, often locating stray hair, as well as the AK-47's and rocket launchers I had lashed to the roof, while I shuffled through a long series of security buildings where my documents (and my anus) were examined. I managed to explain the weapons to the security people, assuring them that they were to be used to unblock East German toilet fixtures. They could identify with that. But still the thought of all those soldiers standing there with machine-guns and pinking shears was enough to freeze the waste in my intestines.

However the mission was foremost in my mind. Plus a cute little *Schatzie* who lived near Alexander-Platz. Her name was Irmgard Rottenbox, and she was the most beautiful person I had ever known up to that point, if you don't count Earnest Borgnine. We met at an industrial trade fair sponsored by the East Berlin Society for the Advancement of Colored People. Our eyes met and I felt a stab of pain pass through me. Some guy behind me at the buffet table had impaled my can on a salad fork. I still limp a little. She wore the standard Party reception fashion, a transparent gownless evening strap, long johns, high-heeled bunny slippers and a tattoo that read, "Ain't Nothin' Better Than This Commie Shit!"

I already knew she was a high-ranking officer in the First Directorate of the Second Division within the Third Department of the dreaded F.D.S.D.T.D. (First Directorate of the Second Division within the Third Department). She could be an invaluable source of information (and carnal recreation), and the story was that she was a whiz at removing your underwear without taking off your pants and could buff a shine on your car with her knockers. My contacts had told me Irmgard was dangerous, and of course they were right. She was swinging a fungo bat near the buffet table, taking cuts like a professional as she knocked out Brussels Sprouts to several tough-looking members of the secret police who were wearing outfield gloves. But I didn't care. I was drawn to her like a movie star to an adoption agency. After a few short moments of excruciatingly dull conversation (mainly my own), I managed to get her into an empty room, where I tore her clothes to shreds. Regrettably, she was not wearing them at the time. They were extras she had brought along for tearing. I took her in my arms and gave her my most seductive smile. My smile often causes women to quickly shed their vestments (most frequently when I'm driving a Goodwill truck). After several furtive meetings, she finally let me into her bed (while she went out for pizza with two other guys). But it was a start. My only complaint was that she always laughed during sex, no matter how difficult her crossword puzzle was. And she had another habit that was really kinky. She used to tie me up and then go out dancing with somebody else.

It was through Irmgard that I was able to meet the all-powerful Russian military commander in East Berlin, Colonel-Major-Captain-General Boris Borisoff. She worked in his office at military headquarters, translating Peruvian graffiti and securing hookers for office parties, often filling in at the last moment for no-shows. Irmgard was fluent in English, German, Russian, Old High Hindu and Hill-Billy. She was also the curator of the East Berlin Underwear Museum and kept the cars in the motor pool shiny.

General Borisoff was a typical Russian military man—mean, gruff, cruel, and by no means pretty. But he was important. If I played my cards right he could be my biggest coup (or as they say in French, "coup"). I spoke with my superiors and got some input from Irmgard (actually, it was output, and she was the one who put out). We came up with a plan to blackmail Borisoff, so I sent him mail that was completely black. At the same time, I developed a friendship with the General by buying him lots of professional female affection.

The next day some of my men were instructed to kidnap his wife, Stinka. She was no raging beauty, but she had a body that wouldn't quit, highlighted by two astonishing dairy containers. Four of my agents pulled up in a Mini-Cooper as she left her building and tried to get her into the car. They had chosen the wrong vehicle, the dip-shits! It was way too small. She was a big gal, and they couldn't squeeze her into the thing. There was only room for her balloons. They grunted and they shoved, but she wouldn't fit. General Borisoff saw what was happening and rushed out of the building. He saved the day. With one gigantic heave, he pushed Stinka into the car and my men took off like a teenager's orgasm. She pleaded with my men for mercy and promised to bang them all if they would let her go. Afterwards, she promised to bang them all again if they wouldn't let her go. She was spirited out of the country disguised as a living person. We had papers for her, but she continued to do her business on the rug. She currently lives in

Mobile, Alabama, in a *ménage à trois* (or four or five—the numbers change daily) and greets customers at a Wal-Mart, usually by opening her shirt and dangling her whoppers at the rednecks. Retail results have improved significantly at that location (a large percentage of the sales figures involve her butt).

Borisoff could now concentrate his energies on his lovely mistress, the sultry Ulrike Poon, whose father was credited with inventing the orange drink, Tang. This seductive temptress had an impressive display of milk vessels and a correspondingly poor display of common courtesy. The first time I met her, she refused to acknowledge my erection. And I had brought it just for her. General Borisoff intimated that he wanted tons of sex, so I procured six female sumo wrestlers for him, dressing them in lead loin cloths. That did the trick. Now he was ours. He eventually supplied me with information of the most important kind, including a subscription to Sovietsky Televisionskaya Guidesky, the batting order of the East Berlin baseball team, and a complete layout of the washroom facilities in Moscow Military Command. This intelligence was priceless in case we ever wanted to plant a device to interrupt the flow of Soviet excretion. I was already familiar with the physics involved in the movement of immense streams of excrement, having been required during my training to sit through a joint session of Congress.

But Ulrike Poon soon proved to be a surprising opponent. It turned out that she was a quadruple agent, working for East Germany, the Dubai ski-jumping team, the Vatican, and the Providence, Rhode Island, Institute of Bathroom-Stain Removal, often hiding tall pygmy operatives in her underwear (while wearing it). I had been too careless in trusting her with my lower anatomy when I wasn't using it. During an important meeting with the general, she surreptitiously (and also secretly) slipped a knockout pill into my shorts ... er, I mean my drink. As you are well aware, manure sometimes occurreth. I hit the floor like a quadriplegic sky diver and blacked out, without the remotest opportunity to look around for small change. When I awoke, my hands were tied behind another guy's back and my mouth tasted like the bottom of a bird-cage, which may have resulted from the fact that I was imprisoned in a large bird-cage. The East German officer who interrogated me was relentless. A nasty number if there ever was one. It may have been eleven. His name was Jürgen Noff and he had a scar that ran from the top of his bald head down one shoulder, across his stomach and around to the crack of his ass (he showed me). It seems he got it in a potato-sack race at a secret police picnic. His partner was trying to peel the potatoes in the sack while they were competing. His demeanor sent shivers up and down my spine, as did the air conditioning, which was set way too high. He told me that unless I admitted everything, there would be no more ice cream. I laughed in his face and didn't flinch when he threatened to do impersonations of Jimmy Carter, but then he got tough. With a cruel smile he brought out the apparatus I had feared most. It was a long handle with a cluster of feathers at the end. Ignoring my screams, he forced me to dust all the furniture in the room. But even that didn't break me. It wasn't until he threatened to slit my sack with a power drill that I screamed and cried and soiled myself and agreed to tell him what he wanted to know, which was primarily where to get laid in Milwaukee.

It would be difficult to describe the terror of those days, the constant fear of betrayal, the dark alleys and lack of adequate street lighting. It's not easy to perform at your best when you devote all your energy to sphincter control, but I saw the job through. I could tell you of courage, heroism, personal sacrifice and lots of other shit, but I'm not looking for thanks. I did it all for my country and I did it for you. I was a secret agent because I wanted to keep this country safe from the Indians. And if they don't like it, they can go back where they came from.

If you need it, here's Lincoln's Gettysburg address: The Sloan Hotel, 237 West Chestnut Street. Once again, don't forget to tell everybody that this is a secret. Guess Who.

Yup,

Ludlow

9

Hey Grover,

The holiday season is upon us again, and you're naturally eager to hear what's going on out here in Goofy-Ville. As I told you, I'm employed by the "Daily News and Manure Spreader." My work has been thrilling so far, chasing those breaking stories and interviewing the movers and shakers. The big news, though, is the recent trial of a wealthy film producer charged with killing a young, perspiring actress, a sad occurrence. I was assigned to cover the story. The proceedings had me on the edge of my seat, primarily because I shared a chair in the courtroom with another guy. But it was exciting to watch the wheels of justice turn slowly and inexorably in order to arrive at the unvarnished truth or some such crap. I've included parts of the actual transcript. That way, you can get a more accurate picture of the trial as it unfolded.

The defendant was Grymee Buddox, a multi-billionaire and a big Hollywood player. He had already been arrested twice in the past, once for fondling a Presbyterian and another time for offering to provide canine sex to a member of Congress. Corruption at its worst. We all know their job is to screw the public, not various animal species.

The Buddox mansion in Newport Beach was always lit up with wild parties, where the guest list was straight out of celebrity magazines and the police line-up. The victim in this case was Tewreel Biggins, a beautiful, young, large-chested thing from Elk Nuts, Nevada, who was trying to make it in tinsel-town. Young dollies are drawn to Hollywood like a professional athlete to a steroid franchise.

The prosecutor on the case has years of experience bringing killers, felons and unrepentant litterbugs to justice. His name is Gerald Floon, and he's a tiger in the litigation chamber. Floon was responsible last year for putting a dreaded gang of lawless Kindergartners in jail for life. They'll never misuse crayons again. His opponent, for the defense, was Flemmie

Mewkuss, who makes his fortune defending miscreants of all types—from kidnappers, thieves and serial murderers to girl scouts facing cookie-laundering charges. He's a partner in the firm of Mewkuss, Mewkuss, Mildew & Slyme. They're known for handling the toughest cases, such as high-speed mooning and drive-by panty-snatching. There are only two people I don't like in this world, and he's both of them. This guy could qualify as a hemorrhoid substitute.

The jury consisted of six men and six women. Or maybe it was the other way around. Anyway, they represented a cross-segment of the local population. They were all idiots. The prosecutor began with the county medical examiner.

PROSECUTOR
Please state your name for the court, Doctor.
MEDICAL EXAMINER
My name is Dr. Festerd Kaboose. I'm the Chief Medical Examiner for the county since a week ago last Thursday.
PROSECUTOR
And where did you receive your medical training, Doctor?
MEDICAL EXAMINER
At the Wal-Mart Cadaver Crib in Four Skin, Tennessee. I interned at the Moosebutt, Ohio, Slicing Clinic and Burial Grounds. And prior to my present position, I was Chief Embalming Consultant for the American Medical Association—Fatal Episode Committee.
PROSECUTOR
And you performed the autopsy on the victim, Miss Biggins?
MEDICAL EXAMINER
That is correct.
PROSECUTOR
Please tell us your findings, Doctor.
MEDICAL EXAMINER
The victim was brought to the pathology laboratory clothed in a nice, low-cut, blue dress that was soaked with water, alcohol, male saliva and other disgusting masculine fluids. It revealed a lot of her anatomy and made

the procedure very pleasant. She was wearing snow-shoes and had a bicycle clip on her arm, and she was covered with blood, with no visible signs of underwear.

PROSECUTOR

What was her physical condition?

MEDICAL EXAMINER

She was suffering from an advanced case of aggravated deadness.

PROSECUTOR

In what way, Doctor?

MEDICAL EXAMINER

Miss Biggins had been beaten, shot, stabbed, strangled, poisoned, tattooed and stepped on. Possibly mistreated to some degree, as well. Maybe suffering from exposure.

PROSECUTOR

And what was the cause of her death?

MEDICAL EXAMINER

She had a heart attack, perhaps brought on by some kind of trauma.

PROSECUTOR

What causes a heart attack, Doctor?

MEDICAL EXAMINER

It usually occurs when the heart is attacked. Too much cholesterol in the anal passage can also be a contributing factor.

PROSECUTOR

Did that result in the death of the victim?

MEDICAL EXAMINER

No, but I thought it was amusing, so I wanted to mention it.

PROSECUTOR

Hmmm. Did Miss Biggins show signs of sexual abuse?

MEDICAL EXAMINER

Plenty, although not from the night in question. But she was obviously giving it away on a regular basis....

PROSECUTOR

Thank you, Doctor. Now, let's pursue....

MEDICAL EXAMINER

I mean she was getting whomped like you can't imagine. She must have had the lumber thrown to her twenty-four/seven! Somebody was pouring the plunger to her big-time!

PROSECUTOR

Doctor, that's enough! We get the picture! That will be all.

JUDGE

Mr. Mewkuss, do you want to cross examine the witness?

MEWKUSS

No, but I have a few questions. They're for the bailiff.

Assistant District Attorney Floon calls Detective Colin Stite to the stand. He has been with the Newport Beach Department for over twenty years, a serious, hard-case law enforcement person. His nail polish is bright red and his fly is open.

PROSECUTOR

Detective Stite, please put your hammer back in your pants and take us through the occurrences on the night of October 3rd.

STITE

Yes sir. I was taking a leak when I was called to the scene by the responding officers. The officers had found the victim, Miss Biggins, in the swimming pool. They fished her out using a Magnum fiberglass rod and 100-pound-test line. They tried to revive her, but it was no use. After a cursory, or maybe short, examination, they determined she had been stabbed twenty-two times and had over seventeen gunshot wounds in her torso. Piano wire was wrapped around her neck, her teeth had been knocked out, her arms and legs were broken, and a bottle of cyanide was beside her. She refused to answer any questions.

PROSECUTOR

What conclusion did the officers draw?

STITE

That Miss Biggins was a lousy swimmer.

PROSECUTOR

Did you concur with that conclusion?

STITE

At first, yes. But something happened to change my mind.

PROSECUTOR

What was that, Detective?

STITE

Over forty people were standing around, pointing at the defendant and shouting, "He killed her!" I then began to consider other possibilities.

PROSECUTOR

What did an examination of the body reveal?

STITE

The body exhibited characteristics similar to those of a dead person. There were several sets of fingerprints, over thirty to be exact, on the victim's breasts. We also found thirty-seven sets of fingerprints on her keister....er, buttocks.

PROSECUTOR

And were you able to identify those prints, Detective?

STITE

They belonged to the defendant, the male guests, the responding officers, the ambulance crew and a tourist from Omaha.

PROSECUTOR

What did this tell you?

STITE

That a lot of guys were trying to squeeze the water out of the victim's lungs and anal cavity.

PROSECUTOR

Did you recover any slugs from the body?

STITE

Yes sir. They all came from a .31 caliber Snott & Booger.

PROSECUTOR

And did you recover this revolver?

STITE

Yes sir. We found the defendant cowering in the bathroom, holding the revolver. He was covered in blood, some of which had been delivered earlier by the local blood bank, as usual, in case it was needed for the party.

He also had the victim's underwear in his hands. We determined that some of the blood belonged to the victim and we tried to put it back in her. However she was leaking badly through all the holes in her, so it turned out to be impossible. Mr. Buddox also had a large kitchen knife in his possession, a length of piano wire, an Eversharp pencil with a big eraser, and the cap from a cyanide bottle.

PROSECUTOR

Thank you, Detective.

Mewkuss, the defense attorney, rose and walked to the witness stand. As he passed the court stenographer, she tried to kick him in the ass. Nobody likes this guy.

MEWKUSS

Detective, isn't it true that you have been treated for a serious illness in the past year?

STITE

Er ....yes, that's true.

MEWKUSS

And what was the nature of that illness?

STITE

It's called "Grungy Stones." My fingerprints fell off, I developed a rash on my testicles, my appendix had to be replaced, and I couldn't shi ... er, I had trouble completing a satisfactory bowel movement.

MEWKUSS

Ah, but you developed other symptoms too, didn't you?

STITE

Well ....yes.

MEWKUSS

What other problem did you have, Detective?

STITE

I .... I became forgetful.

MEWKUSS

You became forgetful? Your illness affected your memory?

STITE

Yes, it did.

MEWKUSS

Can you give us an example of something you've forgotten?

STITE

I don't recall your question.

MEWKUSS

Nothing further.

Mr. Floon now called Dr. Stobtubb Heiny to the stand.

PROSECUTOR

Dr. Heiny, please state your credentials for the court.

DR. HEINY

I'm a psychiatrist. I received my PhD from the Weehawken, New Jersey College of Psychiatry and Double-Entry Bookkeeping and my training at the Illinois Institute for the Criminally Bloody Nuts. My books include "Insanity for Beginners," "Getting to Know the Demented," and "When Psychotics Are Awarded a Nobel Prize."

PROSECUTOR

Doctor, you examined the defendant, Mr. Buddox. What were your conclusions?

DR. HEINY

After several conversations with Mr. Buddox over a period of three minutes, I concluded that this guy is a certified squirrel.

PROSECUTOR

Thank you, Doctor.

Mewkuss rose to cross-examine, scratching his crotch.

MEWKUSS

Doctor, you just testified that the defendant is mentally unstable.

DR. HEINY

Did I? I don't recall.

MEWKUSS

But didn't he answer your questions in a lucid manner?

DR. HEINY

It's true that he was able to correctly identify the day as Thursday by subtracting twenty-seven from North Carolina.

The next prosecution witness was Lemuel Lippschittz.

PROSECUTOR

Mr. Lippschittz, what is your profession?

LIPPSCHITTZ

I'm a Moil. I p'foim circumcisions.

PROSECUTOR

And you were in attendance at Mr. Buddox's home the evening of June 3rd?

LIPPSCHITTZ

Yass, I vas dere.

PROSECUTOR

Why were you there?

LIPPSCHITTZ

Some friends had arranged a surprise circumcision for him.

PROSECUTOR

I see. Did he agree to undergo the procedure?

LIPPSCHITTZ

Not at foist. He agreed ven I splained how ve vas gonna to do it.

PROSECUTOR

And how was that, Mr. Lippschittz?

LIPPSCHITTZ

Vell, Mr. Buddox is not vot you vould describe as vell-endowed. In fact, it's a little hard to locate his member. He suffers from vot ve call in the business "a bantam blaster."

PROSECUTOR

A "bantam blaster?"

LIPPSCHITTZ

Yass, you know, a "runty rod," a "puny poker."

PROSECUTOR

Yes, I follow you, Mr. ....

LIPPSCHITTZ

Get it? A "dwarfy dangler," a "teeny tapper."

PROSECUTOR

Please, Mr. Lippschittz, I think the court understands ....

LIPPSCHITTZ

He got a "dainty diddler." Lotsa men suffer from dis, a "stunted stabber."

PROSECUTOR

That's enough! We get it! You've described the condition adequately. Now, tell us what your procedure entailed.

LIPPSCHITTZ

Miss Biggins kindly consented to help us locate da object to be sliced and render it operable. She agreed to stimulate Mr.Buddox.

PROSECUTOR

Do you mean she agreed to have sexual intercourse with him?

LIPPSCHITTZ

Yass, in addition to screwing him.

PROSECUTOR

That was extremely generous on her part.

LIPPSCHITTZ

It vasn't soch a big deal. I tink she vas in this vay generous a lot.

PROSECUTOR

So vot ...   I mean, so what happened?

LIPPSCHITTZ

Vell, Miss Biggins pulls up her dress and gets down on a lounge chair by the pool ....

PROSECUTOR

Wait a minute!   You mean in front of all the guests? Where everyone could see?

LIPPSCHITTZ

Dis is how is often done in California. And not everybody vas there. Couple guys rather vatch the Dodgers on the television.

PROSECUTOR

This is highly unusual. But please continue.

LIPPSCHITTZ

So da goil does her part and Mr. Buddox is able to produce a "stunted stiffy."

PROSECUTOR

A what?

LIPPSCHITTZ

You know, a "wobbly wiener." A "half-assed mini-mast."

PROSECUTOR

You mean an erection?

LIPPSCHITTZ

Yeah, not exactly, but similar. Lots smaller.

PROSECUTOR

Go on.

LIPPSCHITTZ

Vell, dey was jumping around and yelling and cursing and I figure dere vas gonna be no snippin' dat evening. So I left.

PROSECUTOR

(Turning to the defense table). Your witness.

MEWKUSS

Mr. Lippschittz, tell us, how do you qualify to be a Moil?

LIPPSCHITTZ

You gotta go through a rigorous training program. Develop a steady hand and a good stroke.

MEWKUSS

And what does the course of study consist of?

LIPPSCHITTZ

Six veeks you study pubic anatomy and couple hours each day you slice carrots and onions. Also practice gift wrapping.

MEWKUSS

No further questions.

That was the testimony that clinched the case. Yes sir, it was the straw that finally pushed the camel onto the freeway. The jury came back with a verdict after watching Oprah for an hour. They acquitted Buddox of murder, but convicted him on four hundred and thirty-five counts of "depraved genital inadequacy." The judge passed sentence immediately. He condemned Buddox to ten years in the electric chair without the possibility of parole and also gave him the finger.

Well, I hope this is a lesson to you, Grover. It was to me. I know I'm cancelling my membership in the National Rifle Association's Hand Grenade Sub-Committee. Until next time, wash under your arms. You might also reconsider your hobby of nose-picking for recreation. Most communities have stringent booger laws. You can check with city hall in the Snot Section. Incidentally, Gretchen and I are going to Europe in the spring to visit the domain of the Hapsburgs (Stan and Edith).

Your constant admirer from a safe distance,

Ludlow

10

Hey Grover,

It's time again for my first annual New Year's greeting. I should report what's going on here in "Psychotic Estates by the Sea." We were on our way the other day to the health-food market, which incidentally has been condemned in the meantime, when we stopped off in the cemetery to deface a few gravestones. We like to chisel extra syllables on the marble, and I seem to have a gift for turning Scandinavian names into obscene Hungarian expressions. After inserting intriguing vulgarities on several granite markers, we modified an entire row of headstones to produce a long and lewd (but pleasingly accurate) description of Eva Peron's backside. I was working from memory in this instance, but I think we got it right. At that point, we noticed that a grave-side service was being held nearby, so we walked over and joined the proceedings to find out where the post-planting buffet was to be served.

There were a lot of expensive dresses and thousand-dollar suits in the crowd. Several people sported broken noses, including the women. The females also displayed impressive vinyl breastwork. I recognized several of those in attendance from newspaper photos. They're connected to the mob in L.A. The pallbearers were about to lower the casket when one of the grave-diggers collapsed and died. He rolled into the grave, dragging a bystander and his shovel with him. They left them where they landed and just pitched the coffin down on top of them. The priest continued as though nothing had happened. He spit up a big hocker and comfortingly intoned, "Spike is not dead. He is only sleeping." A voice in the group remarked, "That ain't what I paid for."

One of the men in attendance, a large, swarthy person with a bulge under his left armpit, a cauliflower ear and a broccoli nose, thanked us for coming and insisted that we meet "the boss" and his wife. He introduced himself as Mugsy. I asked him who had died, and he said it was the guy in the coffin. I then used smaller words to inquire how the deceased had come to find himself the featured figure in the proceedings. Mugsy said, "It was one of them freak accidents. Coulda happened to anybody. Spike was apparently doin' research for his doctorate in quantum physics in a dark alley in the middle of the night when he erroneously backed into a switchblade knife. I assume he needed it to be dark in order to better distinguish them sub-atomic particles he was investigatin'. Then when he fell, he apparently set off a nine-millimeter handgun that was lyin' nearby and oddly pointin' in his direction, which plugged him copiously. He was always kinda uncoordinated. And dat is why he is in the current state of necrosis in which we presently observe him."

Mamie Choke and her husband Artie, the well-known *capo*, accepted our condolences concerning Spike's demise. Artie seemed saddened. He said, "It's takin' a hell of a long time to render one guy subterranean!" Artie is not renowned for good looks or a profound sense of humor. Mamie is much younger than her husband and a woman I would not describe as overly attractive either. Mamie is actually ugly enough to back a mule away from the oat bin, if you know what I mean. Besides that, she has the figure of a pool cue, but without so many curves. Her décolletage was daringly low, but futile. However Artie seems to be enormously fond of her. He asked us about our interests and whether we enjoyed the opera or shooting people. We answered in the affirmative about the opera. "In dat case," he whispered, "In the current performance of La Bohème, the fix is in. Instead of croakin' from consumption, Mimi takes some antibiotics and recovers." I got some money down on that one later in the day.

Artie gave us two tickets to the Hollywood Bowl for the next evening, where Mamie was scheduled to perform several arias from the opera, "A Tutti Non Piace" (Nobody Likes it Very Much). It seems that the lady has taken lessons with the renowned mafioso voice teacher, Skreetcho Intolerabile. We anticipated the evening with the enthusiasm of Custer arranging for a delivery of Indians. But Artie made sure that the Bowl would be full. When Mamie sings, the place is packed because his boys are packing. I thanked him profusely for his generosity, calling him respectfully "Mr. Capo." The guy is a tough number. As we left the grave-site, I heard him conversing with one of his associates:

Hood: I am afraid you are wrong, Boss.

Artie: That is good.

Hood: It is good that you are wrong?

Artie: No, it is good that you are afraid.

We got to the Hollywood Bowl early and had breakfast. Everything was great except the music. The program for the evening was to be a modern work by the untalented but, sadly, prolific composer Hamstrung Picker (whom Artie's boys nicknamed "The Nose"). The Concerto for Piano and One Cymbal by Awefool Noyze was next, and finally Mamie's appearance, singing three arias, followed by an obligatory encore. Artie introduced us to several of his business associates, guys with odd-shaped noses and funny-looking ears. We met Clemente "Little Nuts" Omelletti, Cesare "Drippy Urethra" Pilastro, and Salvatore "Wheezy Dick" Stranezza. They looked as happy as a group of cannibals during a missionary shortage, but they greeted us warmly, then frisked us. "Little Nuts" lingered suspiciously on my ass. I liked it.

Picker's work, "Ne pissez pas sur la table" (We Usually Wipe the Table with a Damp Cloth), was a mess of atonal garbage, performed by an orchestra equipped with dull power tools. The composition is known in cultured classical circles as "excruciatingly decadent rat-shit." This alleged music sounded like a gigantic toilet backing up, set against the howls of a hog being castrated with a cricket bat, and accompanied by the ear-splitting amplification of a series of intestinal malfunctions during a collision between a truck full of chickens and a second conveyance loaded with church bells. It was the type of work that makes you think fatal self-mutilation has its brighter side.

Fortunately, this travesty didn't last too long. Unfortunately, it was followed by the piano piece. The cymbal carried the melody. The soloist was a spastic midget of German-Irish-Chinese descent named Wolfgang O'Reilly Woo, who wore the Mao Iron Cross given him by the IRA. He could have improved his keyboard technique by donning boxing gloves. I know I wanted to. It was clear that two things should have been cut—the second movement and the composer's throat. Nobody risked applause exhaustion.

I actually liked the opera. Somebody should set it to music. Mamie did a reasonable job with her three pieces, considering the fact that her voice had settled in her throat. She missed some of the low notes by a foot or two, but she made up for it by failing to get within striking distance of the higher ones. For her appearance Mamie chose a gown that was virtually transparent. It showed off her lack of any type of figure. The front was cut all the way down to her crotch, and the only parts of her body of any interest were her thumbs. Her bosom was non-existent, though well-nippled.

The first aria was "Non toccare la mia coscia, cafone!" (Get Your Mitts Off My Ass, You Bastard!). Then came "Dov'è la Mia Ropa Interiore?" (When Do I Get My Underwear Back?), and to end the misery she perpetrated "Che Cosa Chiamiamo il Bambino?" (What Shall We Name The Baby?). For her encore, which no one had requested, Mamie finished up with a pop tune, "Pop goes the Weasel." The orchestra was from West Chigger Bite, Vermont, under the direction of Rodrigo Stanislaus Mitsubishi, a one-legged, Bolivian graduate of the Cedar Rapids Conservatory of Rectal Damage Assessment. His conducting technique reminded me of an Elk with his antlers caught in an electrified fence and his nuts in a blender. The members of the orchestra are under the false impression that they qualify as musicians.

We made the appropriate fawning gestures and assured Mamie and Artie that she was the high point of the evening. It's true. She was the least nauseating of all. The other performers would have benefited from large-caliber gunshot wounds. In her case, a two-by-four would have sufficed. In praising Mamie, I admit I groveled a little in the face of all the concealed firepower around us, but it was for a good cause. I wanted to stay alive. She was thrilled with my comments. She did a little dance step, gave me a hug, and jumped right through a harp. Didn't touch a string. We declined the offer to accompany them to church the next morning, where they were to attend a Sacred High Bingo.

Then this weekend, Madge and Earl invited us to their house to suffer through another batch of their friends. I don't know why we keep punishing ourselves like this. We know these two psychos are not going to get any better. I consider myself a pretty good judge of people, which is why I hate the bastards so much. One of my big mistakes in life is to think that a village idiot will always remain at the same level of mental deficiency. Wrong! Everyone at their end of the evolutionary chain continues the unimpeded descent into total cerebral uselessness.

Many people have an aversion to my large-bellied buddy. But I can see something in Earl that no one else can see. I can see that he's absolutely nuts. Old "Great Gut" is thicker than two short planks, but he's actually a good loser. In fact, that's all he does. It must come from the incredible volume of booze he consumes. I guess he likes to drink for revenge because it killed his parents. Technically, I don't consider Earl to be alive. He does fall into the not-quite-deceased category, but only in the sense that he can't be legally interred until the appropriate government agency locates a safe place to dispose of his liver.

Everybody brought a gift for the hosts, of course. It's only polite when you're invited to someone's house. One couple gave them a blackjack. They can take turns using it. Madge received a large supply of duct tape and a nice note with instructions for placing it over her yap. One thoughtful couple presented the love birds with a hand-grenade (pin already pulled). We got Madge a skillet marked "for disagreements only" and an exploding suppository for Earl.

One of the couples was a local businessman, Frazzold Butz, and his wife, Kikken. They looked like they had just been released from a Turkish jail. Frazzold told me he was a leader in the wholesale manure business. You might say he's number one in number two. His wife is a tad on the obese side. She was wearing a Zeppelin designer dress. I couldn't understand what he saw in her until later when I observed her eating corn on the cob. She's had so much cosmetic surgery the only parts left from her original body are her earlobes.

Madge introduced us to Misty and Fuller Krapp. She's a hot chickie, and Madge says she plays around. There's always one in the crowd. Yeah! She had every male crotch in the place tightened in no time. Well, except for Earl, who hasn't seen his weenie since 1969. It seems Misty's idea of being faithful is going to bed with one man at a time. I got into a conversation with her, during which I was able to get an unobstructed look at her over-sized chest possessions (she kept taking them out for easy viewing). The evening was very enjoyable, especially after we left. How do we get mixed up with these goons? Surely it's not because likes attract, is it?

I went to the doctor the other day because I've heard all these warnings about my sphincter. You never know when your sphincter might go bad on you. They check your pucker-string with an "Elasto-Meter" nowadays to test the snap in your gap. It's the last thing in posterior technology. It can confirm that your little rubber band is lined up correctly and banging shut after a good bowel movement. I hesitate to put my butt in the hands of the local health care hoodlums, though. My "springy stringy" may be a little loose, but I've been able to handle the situation so far with a paper clip.

I chose a doctor from the yellow pages (they got that way from lying next to the toilet). Earl warned me about the physician I picked out, but I was foolish enough to ignore his advice. Who wouldn't? This doc's glasses were thicker than the mirrors on the Hubble space telescope. He tried to shake hands with me, missed by a foot and a half and grabbed his nurse's frontal belongings. So did I. Then he stuck a tongue-depressor in my ear. This quack couldn't diagnose a decapitation. Earl said they had once played golf together. It's hard to picture. I don't think either of them could hit a tile floor if they were throwing up. The alleged doctor advised me to have my sphincter replaced, but I'm going to think that one over. I wouldn't trust this slug any farther than I can dribble an anvil through a swamp. I may just get a tune-up. Midas has a deal for $29.95 and they give you a 10,000-mile warranty. I hear there's nothing like having some new life in your *elasticus posterius.* You might consider having yours looked into. Somebody told me that over-the-counter sphincter-replacement kits are currently available and they only require a rudimentary knowledge of embroidery.

On another subject, the investigation of steroid use has prompted a higher level of vigilance in these parts. A physician in Hollywood was indicted this week for giving his patients injections. In his case, he was treating the breasts of women who were not genetically blessed with satisfactory melon size. We met one of these gals at a gala Christmas get-together. It wasn't hard to spot her. She had devices the size of basketballs. Very appealing. In the course of the evening, she sneezed and her bra gave way. It pinned four of us to the wall. We called for help after forty-five minutes, and two guys had to be treated for nipple injuries. They were released, but that's more than I can say for her jugs. A bunch of the male guests hung on to them for the rest of the evening. Harold Bustmawler was especially irritating. He kept shoving everybody around and almost made me lose my grip.

We went to the theater on the 22nd. It was a modern non-denominational version of the holiday story, where the Virgin Mary drives to Bethlehem in an SUV and picks up a group of adoring shepherds on the way. I auditioned for the show a couple of months ago, but the bastards only offered to let me lead a donkey.

Hoping you are the same,

Ludlow

11

Hey Grover,

I feel the urge once again to bombard you with a passel of information about my incomparable life. I just wanted to let you know that I'm engaged in a whole new career. Crime statistics are getting worse, so I decided to get involved and do my part. I am now a licensed private investigator after completing my course work at the California Institute of Criminal Justice and Buttocks Technology. It's a bastion of academic detectiveness, as you can see from the courses I was required to take:

Crime Scene Recognition	Non-Criminal Crime Scenes
Corpse Behavior	Mannerisms of Non-living Persons
Body Outlining with Colored Chalk	Rigor Mortis and its Advantages
Home Autopsy Protocol	Backyard Morgue Construction
Surveillance and Fast Food Choices	Following Suspects (Female)
Female Suspect Anatomy	Frisking Female Suspects
Treating a Kick in the Groin	Returning Suspects' Underwear
Breaking and Entering	Entering Without Breaking
Rectal Thermometer Choices	Rectal Thermometer Extraction
Rectal Thermometer Cleaning	Rectum Cleaning
Treating Self-inflicted Gunshot Wounds	Remedial Review of Firearm Use
Surreptitious Fingerprinting	

My Private Detective office has been open for a couple of months now, and business is not bad. The first day on the job, a tall, willowy blond walked into the place and perched her attractive can on the edge of my desk. She was a knockout! My gaze was naturally drawn to the ten pounds of Grade A Round protruding from the top of her frock. Those honeys were trying to get out of her shirt, and I was thinking about getting in. She crossed her long, gorgeous legs and leaned forward, giving me an unimpeded view of her super-sized beauties. The view was unimpeded, and I almost peeded.

Her name was Wanda Havitt and she told me she was on her way to the mortuary to choose a casket for her husband. I asked her when he had died, and she said, "He starts tomorrow." It seems that Wanda suspected her less-than-better half of catting around and wanted me to get the goods on him before she introduced him to the layaway plan. I could not imagine any guy married to Wanda who would be tempted to look elsewhere for genital comfort, but you know what pigs men are (present company excepted—on occasion).

She agreed to my fee ($500 a day plus expenses, butter cookies and any underwear she cared to discard), and I accepted the assignment of tailing her husband, Kenny, while he was tailing hot numbers looking for tail. It's complicated, I know, but try to stay with me here. I followed Kenny to a rendezvous with one of his lady friends, and took up a position in a tree outside their hotel room. The honey he was using for mattress mashing was even more beautiful than Wanda. At least I think so. My glasses fogged up when she disrobed. Kenny jumped on his paramour and skillfully engaged her para**chute** (clever wordplay there, huh?). I fell out of the tree, but sustained no damage, since their room was on the first floor and I landed on another couple. I managed to get some marvelous photos of this gal's jugs, then came back the next day to take pictures of the lovers together.

The girl's name turned out to be Lotta Boozum. She was well-known in the community for her numerous charitable works while aboard a Sealy Posture-Pedic. I had seen her several times before, handing out advanced copulation badges at Boy Scout meetings and participating in the horizontal sacraments at the Temple of Holy Penetration. Wanda was ecstatic when I showed her the photo evidence, several 8 x 10 glossy prints which I had Lotta autograph for me. She gave me a little kiss on the cheek and also seemed quite happy when I unintentionally got my hand snagged in her undergarments. I don't know how that happens.

That evening, however, while I was watching a reality show in which people were shown sitting around watching a reality show, I got a frantic call from Wanda. She wanted me to come right over to her house. "Something dreadful has happened!" she sobbed hysterically. I jumped in my car and drove straight there, stopping only long enough for a three-course dinner (with entertainment) at a local restaurant, where I was seated after a two-hour wait. The salad was over-cooked.

When I arrived at Wanda's place, I found her standing over her husband's body and covered with blood, a .64 caliber Smith & Wesson-Oil in her hand and powder burns over her entire body. Her eyes were glazed over. She had done a poor job of applying eye-glaze. It was clear that Kenny was in the advanced stages of terminal mortality, since he wasn't breathing. I considered trying to revive him, but didn't want to get my new Dockers soiled. He was leaking too much fuel anyway, lying in a pool of Chardonnay with twenty-two gunshot wounds in his groin. Wanda threw her arms around my neck and sobbed, "I found him like this, you've got to believe me! You do believe me, don't you? Don't you?" I mumbled, "Of course I believe you, my dear. Could you take the gun out of my mouth."

"I don't know why I picked it up," she sobbed. "I was so confused. It was lying beside him and my first reaction was to clean up a little. He obviously committed suicide."

It was certainly not the way I would have chosen to shuffle off this mortal coil, as Hulk Hogan would have phrased it, but her theory made sense. Let's face it, if you're banging two of the sexiest broadies on the planet it's only normal that it would lead to serious depression. I dialed police headquarters to report a car double-parked in front of my house, then added the news of Kenny's demise. A guy I know on the force, Lieutenant Dozer Klapp, told me he would be right there and not to screw up the crime scene. I've had too many doses of that guy. What would I do, other than putting the body in an easy chair, dressing it in a new suit and vacuuming the place?

Klapp arrived with his CSI (Careless Slovenly Incompetents) Unit and began to gather evidence. His side-kick kept kicking him in the side until he was forced to go sit in the car. The head investigator started in the head and worked his way back to the body. He used his chalk like a pro and we got in a quick game of hopscotch while Klapp interviewed Wanda. He asked her to make a statement. She said she would be happy to maintain that the Democrats had no coherent policy and were screwed up in general.

I helped Wanda change into clean clothes (hoping to retain at least one pair of unmentionables) and accompanied the poor grief-stricken widow to police headquarters. Klapp's interrogation was brutal until she began rubbing his crotch under the table, at which time he confessed to murdering the victim himself. After an hour or so and several more confessions, he let her go with a warning to stay within the confines of five major continents until the situation was resolved. I still had some doubts in my mind. I assured Wanda that I would stay with her to make sure she would be all right (and also to get me some of those butter cookies). I helped her undress and get into bed, at which point she told me to get out of the bed.

The police located neighbors who had heard shots, screams, and loud sheep-shearing noises emanating from the house at the time of the shooting. Two witnesses had also seen a black BMW SUV Convertible Sedan Pick-Up Truck speed away a few moments thereafter. They managed to get the license number, since the vehicle had skidded up onto their front porch and run over two cats. Now we only had to locate the car and check for cat hair. I volunteered to canvas cathouses to see what I could find.

Two patrolmen found the abandoned vehicle the next morning in the front row of the County Performing Arts Center, which is converted to an up-scale bordello on Tuesday and Thursday evenings. Interestingly, the car was double-parked next to a camel. Probably a leftover from a performance of Aida or some such nausea-inducing crap. Maybe the camel figures in some of the rented affection activities that take place during the weekdays I mentioned. Anyway, the car was registered to a ninety-year old hooker named Sophie Saggybags and had been stolen the day of the crime (with her and one of her customers in it). The car was full of DNA, but a thorough scrubbing soon got rid of that crud so it could be examined. I observed the procedure.

The technicians found two rocket launchers, several machine pistols, a dozen hand grenades, a five-gallon pail of embalming fluid, four spent shotgun shells, three rolls of toilet paper, and a ticket stub for a performance of the opera "Gli emmoridi mi fanno male" (My Hemorrhoids are Acting up Again) by the great Italian composer Disgusto Repugnosso. I had attended the opera the week before. The aria, "Qualcuno ha fatto una esplosione intestina" (Somebody Choked off a Real Pants-Buster That Time), was especially impressive, sung by the young Sicilian tenor and renowned child molester Droopi Pantaloni. So we were looking for an opera lover who was a pervert and might also be dealing in illegal weapons. That narrowed down the list of potential suspects to all the inhabitants of New Jersey. I checked with Wanda, who was still in bed, suffering from exhaustion, fatigue and a beautiful ass.

I decided to follow Boozum to see if she would lead me to anything suspicious or sexually interesting. A break came in the case when I saw her enter a dark alley late at night. I figured she must be engaged in some criminal undertaking (or fornication procedure in which I might participate), and went after her. I suddenly found myself surrounded by two goons. It was a trap. They were armed with guns, pipes, two-by-fours, blackjacks, brass knuckles, a ball bat and a shopping cart full of waffles. They kicked the resounding shit out of me for half an hour. The fact that they were second-graders didn't make them any less fierce. As I lay there, unable to move anything but my bowels, I looked up and asked Boozum, "Why?" She said, "Oh, I thought you were somebody else. My mistake."

I had several fractures (particularly of my bones), a severed spine, multiple contusions, internal bleeding, black eyes, caved-in ribs, a dislocated dick, a bruise on my left nut, and a loose booger. But I didn't hold it against her. Shit, we all make mistakes. It could happen to anybody. I asked Boozum for a date to show there were no hard feelings. She grasped my rod and assured me that she could feel nothing hard. We made plans to see the new opera, "Il sfintere rilassato" (The Floppy Sphincter). It was composed by Cuccoldo Imbecile, with libretto by Orribile Escremento.

The cops brought Boozum in and tried to sweat her. That is, they sweated while she clowned around and let her prow spheroids hang out. I returned to my office, where I sat thinking about the case. Something was bothering me. There was a nail sticking in my ass from the seat of my chair and I had forgotten to put my pants on that morning. I had to put this murder case to bed. I also wanted to put Wanda to bed. I went to her house and confronted her with my suspicion that she had perpetrated the crime. After hemming and hawing a skirt, she agreed to come clean and stepped into the shower. After drying herself off, she described the events of the fateful evening.

"Kenny came home that night, completely devastated. And his dick was hanging out. He couldn't bear the thought of having me divorce him. He couldn't eat, sleep or take a dump. He begged my forgiveness, he pleaded with me, he cried, but I turned him down. How could I forgive him after he cheated on me so many times? And I had remained completely faithful, except for ten or twelve times during a pick-up basketball game last Wednesday, Thursday and Friday. He grew more despondent each moment and finally told me he wanted to end it all. I tried to talk him out of it, but he was adamant. When Kenny wants to kill himself, he usually does it.

He got a hammer and some nails and put together a frame. His woodworking skills are admirable, although he hit his thumb and his nuts a couple of times. Then he lashed the gun to the frame and ran a cord to the trigger. He yanked on the cord and the gun fired. It blew a hole in the cat. He adjusted for windage, and this time it was set a little low, so it hit him in the privates."

I casually reminded her that he had been shot twenty-two times. "I know," Wanda said. "He had to reload more than three times. He was very determined. When he was done, I dismantled the frame and burned it in the air-conditioning unit. I was about to get rid of the gun when you arrived. That's why I was holding it. I didn't want anyone to know that Kenny had taken his life." It sounded plausible to me. It must have been dreadful for her, standing there and watching the guy plug himself in the balls time and time again. I had a lot of respect for her.

The cops were sympathetic as well. They followed every lead and eventually concluded that Kenny had been murdered by a paraplegic Albanian midget television personality who was subsequently executed for low ratings, exposing himself on camera, making uncalled-for remarks about Hillary Clinton and sexually assaulting poultry.

They closed the file, I got my butter cookies and a pile of Wanda's undies, so everything turned out all right. When I got back to my office, one of the second-graders who had kicked the shit out of me was there. He kicked the shit out of me again, explaining that he enjoyed it a lot. But I didn't care. My wand didn't work too well, but my first case was closed.

Well, that's my report. The important thing is I want to warn you about a dangerous disease going around that affects former baseball players, especially catchers. It's called Passed Balls. See your physician or a licensed genital expert.

Yer lovin' brudder, the nice one,

Ludlow

12

Hey Grover,

It's time to follow up with a report on my work as a private eye and part-time gynecological expert. I know you've been dying to ask me about it. A day after the successful resolution of my first adventure, I was ready to expand my investigative expertise. My preparations were extensive. I polished the desk in my office, put butter cookies in the jar on the credenza and made sure my pants were not on backwards. I didn't have to wait long. In the middle of the morning, a lovely young Asian woman walked into my office. I told her to take a chair and she started to walk out with it, but I got her to bring it back and sit down. She had delicate features, fine porcelain skin, black shiny hair and an attractive can. The top of her green oriental dress was cut low to reveal a seductive New York Yankees sweatshirt. Her skirt had a slit and, I presume, so did she.

"My name Hah-Pawn," she said with a charming accent. "I understand you help people who missing." I told her I might be able to help her and asked her who was missing. She said, "It my husband. He missing." I asked her how long it had been, and she replied, "He missing for years." I was astonished. Her husband is missing for years and she waits until now to report it? She continued, "I too embarrassed to get help before. But no can wait longer. Every night we try have sex, but my husband, he very cross-eyed. He try put it in, but he missing all the time."

I considered the pros and cons of getting involved, but finally chose to tell the lady that I dealt with missing persons, not poorly-aimed dicks. However out of the goodness of my heart I offered to give her a few practical pointers (based on my experience practicing for the Olympic 100-Meter Fornication Event) and told her I would throw in a free inspection of her lingerie for wrinkles or other defects. I went on to explain how bowling for dollars works, but she just shook her head and left with a discouraged look. I shrugged my shoulders and had a butter cookie.

Soon after that, I was visited by another prospective client. Casper Stubbyrod was a mousy-looking guy who worked as a nuclear engineer, crossing guard and toilet repairman for the Acme Rocket and Proctology Tool Corporation. He told me that Acme had been awarded huge contracts by the government to build rocket engines and up-grade their bathrooms. He wanted to blow the whistle on his superiors (he refereed company basketball games after work) and also to report felonious behavior. According to him, the company was padding invoices, charging the government for products they didn't deliver. He said the fraudulent billings represented millions of dollars.

Among the items Acme billed but failed to produce, he alleged, were inflatable urinals, Velcro toilet paper, space suits with built-in self-fondling units, chastity belts with tear-away crotches and X-ray goggles to be used when female astronauts were on board. I was shocked and dismayed at Casper's story (and managed to slip a set of goggles into my desk drawer). He agreed to split the government's reward with me against my fee of $500 a day and a year's subscription to Copulation Digest. I would have to get my usual supply of women's underwear elsewhere.

Together, we worked out a plan for gathering the necessary proof he needed, preferably without incurring any danger to me (or too much work). I obtained credentials that listed me as a state manufacturing-facility and toilet inspector. The documents were originally produced for a one-eyed Bulgarian midget with muscular dystrophy and a bad case of scabby ass, but with clever forgeries and my ability to blend into the role, I was able to pass a cursory examination (and several kidney stones). Armed with an official-looking badge, a clipboard, and my trusty accordion, I affected a bad limp and was given access to Acme's facilities. The company president escorted me around the place herself. I hadn't expected to encounter a female in this position, but Stubbyrod told me that Dr. Ima Hottwunn was a technical wizard, as well as a shrewd businesswoman. She looked stunning, especially from the neck down. I was particularly impressed by the dairy product containers that threatened to burst forth from the front of her wardrobe. She wore thick, horn-rimmed glasses, obviously designed to conceal her feminine attributes. Her business attire consisted of a no-nonsense, see-through blouse cut down to her navel (affording a joyful view of her double burgers) and a business-like skirt maybe four centimeters in length. The whoppers in her shirt, combined with the almost unrestricted view of her crotch inspired major penile enlargement. Her dark hair was pulled back in a severe bun and her buns were pulled back in a severe stance. What a great figure! Miss Hottwunn had a doctorate in theoretical physics and a HOLY SHIT! in physical appeal.

"What kind of inspections do you perform?" she asked. I answered that I specialized in female skivvies and internal organs. She blushed and swatted me in the nuts. We seemed to be connecting well. I told her I wanted to start my inspection tour with the rocket production area. Miss Hottwunn led me out onto the mezzanine overlooking the factory floor. Huge production machines were pounding, stamping, pressing and forming rocket and genital-examination parts. Miss Hottwunn accidentally bumped into me with her large hooters and almost pushed me over the guardrail into a large metal press. It would have made me a lot taller, but infinitely thinner. She apologized. Hey, accidents happen. I spent some time looking over the production lines (and into the front of her blouse), acting as though I knew what the hell I was doing.

I really wanted to get a look at the books. I had seen a set of Booger Malone detective novels and the complete Hardy Boys series when we walked through the front office. Miss Hottwunn led me through the entire production process and explained everything in detail, except for what was going on. Because of the noise, she kept very close to me and (inadvertently, I'm sure) almost knocked me into some massive, wicked-looking machinery several times. If it hadn't been for my well-known agility and ballroom dancing background, I might have become an integral part of a finished space vehicle. I enjoyed the personal contact. I insisted on looking at production documentation, inventory sheets, shipping papers, and a Hustler magazine. Miss Hottwunn readily agreed. She gave me an empty office and had the books brought to me. I spent the next several hours trying to make sense of the complex financial gyrations these documents represented. It was made more difficult by the fact that some sort of vapor seemed to be seeping into the room through a vent near the ceiling. I tried to open the window, but it was sealed. Fortunately, I had the presence of mind to hold my breath for an hour or two.

I had learned this life-saving maneuver in the Far East many years before. It was during a secret mission to collect information concerning Southeast-Asian fornication practices. This was at the same time that Lamont Cranston was developing his hypnotic talent so he could spend more time in women's restrooms. I picked up the breathing technique in Bangkok (named for a guy who used to crack walnuts with his dong), along with two harmonicas, an inflatable dartboard, a Braille driver's manual and a sexually-transmitted head wound.

After comparing production capabilities against shipments and billings, I saw that Acme couldn't possibly have produced all the products for which they billed the government. My analytical skills came in very handy in leading me to this conclusion. That, and a note in the file that read, "We couldn't possibly have produced all the products for which we billed the government." I photocopied the incriminating material. I also asked Miss Hottwunn to sit on the copier so I could preserve her attractive hindquarters for future reference, but she pleaded a heavy schedule and the need to pee just then. So I photocopied my own butt, raced back to my office and called Casper. I expected him to be impressed, but when I showed him the incriminating paperwork, he said, "Sorry, I've changed my mind." I was astounded, as though I had been run over by an astounder. "How can you back out now?" I asked. "We've got Acme's scrotum in the palm of our hand!" He blushed. "Well, while you were screwing around with the books, Miss Hottwunn had my scrotum in the palm of *her* hand," he replied. "She made me an offer I couldn't refuse, so I decided not to pursue the matter any farther."

"Are you talking about copulation?" I asked. I love it when they talk about copulation. "You ain't shittin', Buddy!" Stubbyrod exclaimed. "Miss Sex-Package is gonna let me play 'hit me with the harpoon.' I'm sorry to back out of our project, but I'm gonna get me some of that Momma. How much do I owe you?" I couldn't figure how the sexy lady would have anything to do with Casper. A guy with no arms or legs and scabs all over his body would be more attractive than this ugly hound. But you can never tell when it comes to true love. He said he fell for Ima as soon as she showed him the tattoo on her ass that read, "Use entrance around the corner." We settled on reasonable compensation, plus a photocopy of Miss Hottwunn's splendid backside that he had in his wallet, so we were both satisfied with the deal. Poor Casper didn't get to enjoy his new relationship very long, though. I read the next day that he had somehow fallen into a faulty Acme stamping machine that separated him violently and definitively from his genital area. Didn't even have time to sample the goodies he had been promised. He wound up looking like a radish, confined to a wheelchair in a facility that specializes in treating the victims of genital divestiture (before burial). The prognosis was good, though. The doctors said he would be able to resume his former place in society again for the two days he still had to live.

To my great surprise, Earl showed up a couple of days later. It was a real accomplishment on his part to find my office and then figure out how to open the door. Earl wanted me to help him fight an order from the Division of Motor Vehicles informing him that his driving privileges were being revoked.

It seemed that he had exceeded the acceptable number of accidents in the previous ten days (fourteen). His vehicular transgressions had created vast material damage, including the destruction of a row of eight houses (many set well back from the street), thirteen parked cars, and a billboard advertising pubic hair replacement. A significant loss of life also played a major role in the decision to ban my good buddy from the road. Earl had run over and killed several cats and dogs, four crossing guards, a dozen cheerleaders and a crowd of teenagers. These last two infractions were not held against him. I decided that something had to be done. Earl's second amendment rights were clearly being violated. He had the right to keep and bear arms just like everyone else, even if in his case they consisted of a poorly-aimed 1976 Nash Rambler with a foxtail and a condom hanging from the antenna. I told Earl I was going to go to bat for him. He said, "What?"

I sprang into action, ready to do battle for my feeble-minded comrade. It might cost Earl a bundle, but I wasn't going to let the powers that be push my pal around. Besides, who was going to get rid of those teenagers if he didn't? I mapped out a plan to catch the authorities at the DMV, as well as all the politicos and state appointees I could find, in various compromising positions, then use the evidence in Earl's favor. If you keep up with the news, you realize that our fine authorities and elected officials routinely engage in activities that involve wearing their pants around their ankles, so it was just a question of gathering the appropriate proof. It's not usually difficult. I began following these bums, and it wasn't long before I had photos of them committing vile and reprehensible acts. Sort of like the stuff you do all the time.

I got shots of Faymuss Nummass, the speaker of the California Assembly, practicing carnal dalliance with a number of females, including—but not limited to—humans. It seems he learned his political skills from the Honorable George Ryan of Illinois gubernatorial fame, who in turn simply followed in the tradition of Otto Kerner. Idaho Senator Larry Craig (of Minneapolis Airport washroom renown) continues to hold the banner high, and who can forget the late New England senator when it comes to awards for underwater ballet competition.

After tailing the lieutenant governor, Kloggie Drayne, for a day or two, I recorded some of his sexual shenanigans on film with two strippers. They were paint strippers from a local car shop, but I guess he likes big guys in dirty coveralls. I located the DMV chief, Mrs. Stroka Toff, at a ski resort, where she was attending a conference with her (male) staff, and snapped a great photo of her signing her name in the snow. Interestingly, she was using her assistant's pubic tool to write with. The public would be shocked at her poor penmanship. Perhaps it was caused by the fact that the guy was jumping up and down at the time. I guess she wasn't writing fast enough for him. Armed with my pictures, plus various shots of several movie stars taking a dump, I laid out my proposal to the inmates at city hall. They tried at first to bluff their way out of it. One guy threatened to kick my ass. Pitiful. I laughed and told him to go forth and multiply, but I didn't use those exact words. I then revealed my hole card, a poster-size picture of the entire DMV staff and the full legislature, crapping on the state house lawn (and each other). I had caught them in *fornicatus et defecati flagranti* during a party at which an Ex-Lax casserole had been served. There was no choice for these miserable cretins but to accede to my demands (or invite me to the next party). But my duty was to my good friend, what's-his-name. I considered requesting a signature from Mrs. Toff using my own writing implement, but decided to delay the offer for another occasion. I got Earl's license back, and he was happier than a gang member out on bail. He tried to kiss me, but planted his slobber glands on the coat rack instead. A close call.

There was one restriction on his permit, however. He was limited to his driveway. I could live with that, considering the safety factor, and Earl never knew where he was anyway. He signed the check I wrote out for him and left. By the window. Fell three stories. Luckily, he landed on his head, so no harm was done. Nothing could do any more damage to that piece of squash. Madge was waiting for him in the car. She put him in the trunk.

We attended Earl's birthday party two weeks later, and we had a great time. We didn't invite him. Last year, we allowed him to come to the party, and it was a mistake. We all chipped in to get Earl a present. One guy suggested we buy him a new home and throw it at him one brick at a time. Anyway, now the big guy's car is up on blocks in the driveway. He gives it the gas and the wheels spin, but he doesn't go anywhere. After a few stationary miles, he gets out and knocks on the garage door. When it doesn't open, he bitches that the store is closed. I told him he should leave earlier. He said, "What?"

I intend to leave my appendix to posterity. Harvard has expressed interest in my brain. I hope you've managed to solve your problem of excessive bowel noise. It's good to know you continue to share my respect for high standards. Which reminds me, we had to call the ambulance for Earl last Saturday. He had a mild seizure. Nothing to do with his brain, of course. They found he had smallpox. Then he developed medium pox and, finally, large pox. They cured all of that, but the poor guy was left with a bad case of dirty urine and frothing of the crotch.
Until next time,

Think about the next time.

Ludlow

13

Hey Grover,

Each year I get a bunch of newsletters from people who think I give a rat's ass about the trivial junk that goes on in their crappy little lives. You probably get these excremo-papers too. I never read that ____, but it gave me an idea. I decided to send a newsletter of my own about something that's really noteworthy, namely what's going on in *my* life. Now, that's interesting. But I'm going to change things a little. I plan to write one of these things every week and send it to everybody I know or ever met.

To begin with the most uninteresting news, our good friends Madge and Earl, who thankfully live some distance from us (although a foreign country would be better), decided to redecorate their residence, since it was completely destroyed by an earthquake a few weeks ago. We were all surprised by the magnitude of the geo-ripple that shook its way through the area, but that's part of living here in dreamland. We're routinely kept busy trying to elude the earth-shakes, the annual floods and the mud slides that follow hard on the heels of the massive forest fires.

The quake spread like cow dung on a hot sidewalk. I understand the epicenter was located near a bathroom in Paris Hilton's house. It's hard to understand how these natural disasters continue to wipe out homes that are built, destroyed and re-built numerous times, especially since the owners have put them in such safe locations as hanging on the edges of cliffs, in flood planes, and nestled in potential wild-fire regions. The earthquake was a Richter-Scale 14 affair. We're talking real butt-puckering violence here. That force is equivalent to the kinetic energy of two-thirds of the horseshit let loose in a single political speech, so you can imagine what Madge and Earl's humble abode looked like. For more than twenty minutes, Madge was unaware that an earthquake was occurring. Earl was attempting his morning bowel ritual, and the little woman (a figure of speech) figured the thunder and destruction were routine.

The devastation turned out to be significant. Bricks, mortar and toilet seats were flying everywhere. Chubby and Dubby (Madge and Earl) managed to catch some of the floating debris, thankfully saving the first-edition Guttenberg Bible they had bought by mail in 1992 from Stan Guttenberg in Teaneck, New Jersey. Quick thinking on their part (well, not on Earl's part, actually) also enabled them to rescue their 78-rpm record collection that featured Andy Devine in concert at Carnegie Hall, with an appearance by Louis Armstrong reciting some crap from Shakespeare. But the household was otherwise reduced to absolute rubble, which wasn't that easy to distinguish from the rubble they were living in before the vibrations began.

The rest of their neighborhood suffered even worse damage than they did. Just about every trailer in the community was affected. Earl, especially, is going to miss the rusted pick-up that had a place of distinction on cinder blocks in his front yard, though most of it was hidden by the tall grass. The estimable vehicle disappeared in a large crevice that opened in the ground. I told him how sorry I was, but he was busy with his reptile collection and only said, "What?" Another earthquake that rattled through here some years ago struck Madge and Earl's town and inflicted $11 million worth of improvements. Fortunately, our buddies were covered by the Enron Insurance Company under an umbrella policy that primarily insures umbrellas, so they figure their claim will be settled in full one of these days. God bless that industry. There is a note of optimism in all of this, though. In spite of the danger caused by raging fires, shifting tectonic plates, murderously high water levels and mountains of sliding mud that have wiped out entire towns, we here in California cling to the hope that if significant loss of life occurs, at least a few movie stars will be killed.

Our residence was spared, thanks to the fact that I spray regularly around our area with Quake-Stop®. It's a mixture I patented myself, made up of equal parts of tri-tremor-goosy-sulfate and hydro-stinkdung-perchloride. I have a guy in Hog Dong, Tennessee, manufacturing this stuff with a Bunsen burner or something and I'm marketing it through high-end outlets like Nordstrom's, Abercrombie and Futch, and Sewers 'R' Us. The stench is potent enough to stop any natural disaster. Everyone has to wear gas masks when we sit on the patio, but it adds a note of mystery to any gathering and it greatly improves appearances if Madge and Earl are present. Earl wants to take charge of rebuilding their home himself. That's how bright he is. I don't know how you rebuild a 15-foot trailer. Allowing Earl in the vicinity of any tool, including a paper clip, is probably prohibited by law, and if it isn't, it should be. I can just picture him trying to construct something. He has trouble operating the refrigerator. The success he achieves in any project is similar to shoving shit back up a goose's ass. But Earl insisted to us the other day that he was qualified for the job. It was at an outdoor barbecue party down the road, thrown by a couple of their acquaintances, Dewitt and Gedditt Knightly. You can imagine the dimness of anybody who invites Madge and Earl anywhere. I don't know how we got on the guest list.

Anyway, Earl showed us the plans he had drawn up, or rather scratched on a cocktail napkin with a leaky ball-point pen. It looked like something extracted from an Egyptian tomb, which is where Earl would be if we all had our wish. I fail to see how he's going to get a pool (complete with diving board) in the trailer, but reality is nothing Earl has ever been immersed in. Madge just shakes her head and slaps his from time to time. Fortunately, her hubby usually forgets what the hell he was doing after focusing for a moment or two on a stray thought. In the end, the city zoning board will probably decide to tear their neighborhood down and erect a new one in the swamp.

Our hosts have known Madge and Earl for years, since they all spent time in the same detention center. Madge did a short stretch for attempted hooking (unsuccessful, naturally) and Gedditt was brought in for double-parking on the 405-Freeway in the nude. Dewitt and Earl were arrested for exposing themselves to a Salvation Army Brass Quartet. The usual suspects were in attendance at the barbecue. Aiken Ballz and his wife Grabbya were there, as were Puzzy Pimpells and her husband Skweezie. The food was interesting, if not exactly edible. Dewitt served charcoal-broiled sow's snouts, dumpster pudding and black-eyed bananas. I hope the potted plants survived where I deposited my portion. Gretchen and I spent most of the time talking to each other as the host couple gulped down high-octane cocktails and offered us vodka spiked with diesel fuel.

Pastor Givette Toomy, from his church in Las Vegas, was also in attendance, along with his wife Sockette. His congregation is Saint Herbie's Ministry of Carnal Fulfillment and Jackpot Worship, a fusion chapel that combines portions of several casino beliefs, including the admonition in First Corinthians to fold if you don't have three's or better. Their baptismal ceremonies are held on a roulette table (sans garments). The good pastor was called to the cloth after receiving a vision of Saint Mitzi losing her clothing in a crap game. Sockettte is a former Vegas showgirl and part-time love merchant who converted to the faith following a life-changing experience involving four guys with chains. She brought them along to the chapel when it opened.

My detective work is expanding nicely, you'll be pleased to learn. I'm frequently busy with situations involving corruption, infidelity and adultery. Sometimes they involve other people. But the masses just don't have our values anymore, Grover. I mean, my values. I forgot for a minute about the crap you pull. I was hired two weeks ago to follow a woman to the East Coast. Her hubby suspected her of infidelity, and I substantiated his suspicions. In New York, I was able to witness several of her escapades, many of them taking place simultaneously. This gal had a busy butt. Of course, with my well-known sensitivity I was able to cushion the impact of my findings by using poetic language in my final report, as follows:

"Your Missus has shown her volition
To grapple young men with a mission.
She rolls on the floor
With two, three of four,
And it ain't just a yoga position."

However my most interesting case this week was the death of a wealthy insurance executive in Beverly Hills. Everybody wants to kill one of these guys. I accompanied the police to his residence, where we viewed the body. He had apparently died of natural causes, since there were no indications of foul play, other than the fact that he had a ski-pole protruding from his anus. His young, well-built wife was discovered in an upstairs bedroom, with multiple self-abuse wounds and a wistful smile on her face. Three of us spent a compassionate twenty minutes with the widow, offering to massage her injured areas and straighten her garment, which consisted of a see-through nightgown,

The autopsy report, to our surprise, declared the case a homicide and called those of us who responded to the scene "dumber than dog-poop." Faced with these unfounded statements, we nevertheless sprang into action. Fingerprints on the ski-pole were found to match those of the family gardener, a handsome guy in his late twenties. But the grief-stricken widow explained that the young man had often handed her late husband the pole during dinner so he could spear a sausage. The gardener was released in the custody of the lovely widow, and they were seen entering a room at the Beverly Hills Hotel, where she obviously planned to help the fellow deal with the stress of his recent interrogation. I'm sorry to say that charitable acts like this never make the headlines.

Our investigation, during which members of the gendarmerie playfully kept telling me to "stay the hell out of the way," soon led to a ski resort, where we arrested a college student who was brandishing a solitary ski-pole on the slopes. He tried to wiggle out of the situation by pointing out that he only had one arm, but that didn't cut any crap with us. We're too clever for stupid excuses.

Our one-armed suspect was tried and convicted, in spite of a trumped-up alibi offered by ninety thousand people who perjured themselves by claiming he was at a football game several hundred miles away when the crime was committed. I hope they rot in Pasadena. I'm happy to report that the victim's widow and the former gardener are doing their best to deal with their sorrow. They left on a three-month cruise together, and I was gratified to learn that, for obvious budgetary reasons, they booked only one cabin. Sacrifices like these often go unheeded in our society.

I hope you've been able to get the holes plugged in your shorts. It's often embarrassing when they whistle during bouts of flatulence, and it seems to attract packs of unwanted dogs.

Ton frère du jour,

Ludlow

14

Hey Grover,

In my capacity as a private eye and copulation consultant, law enforcement agencies frequently seek my help. This is also true of the criminal class, with whom I come into contact in the course of my good works. One of my acquaintances, Vito "Bubble-Hammer" Pazzo, is a client of mine who lives in Bel-Air. Vito is "capo di tutti capi," or "boss of all bosses" (except for Mrs. Pazzo, who takes no crap from the ferocious Sicilian). Bel-Air is about as up-scale as you can get. A large number of landscape workers there have their own maids.

In my line of investigative work, I've seen some fascinating cases. One that stands out is the following: I was listening to a ping pong game on the radio and leafing through the latest issue of Rectal Hydraulics when the call came in. Thelma van Merde, a wealthy socialite with homes in Beverly Hills and Lagos, Nigeria, asked me to come to her palatial estate nestled next to the railroad tracks right off the 5-Freeway. As I walked the last couple of blocks to her place, I saw two guys trying to steal an old lady's purse. She was putting up a real fight. I decided to help, and it didn't take the three of us very long to get the damn thing away from her.

Mrs. van Merde is heir to the van Merde fortune. Her late husband became incredibly successful with his invention of the polyester two-way rectum, used by cosmetic surgeons the world over and some other countries too. Although she is past fifty, the lady retains much of the compelling beauty of her youth, including a really nice ass. My hostess offered me a chair, but I declined, explaining that my home was already adequately furnished. The front of her cream silk blouse revealed two eye-catching examples of voluptuous female topography (with appealing nipple adornment). Several parts of her anatomy deserved game points.

She crossed her attractive legs, accidentally landing a glancing blow to my crotch, and described the ordeal in which she found herself. It seems that her son, Throckmorton van Merde III, had not been heard from lately. "I last spoke with him several weeks ago," she said, "so naturally I'm worried. He usually keeps in touch, but he hasn't contacted me for a while, not even to bitch about money. But I want to see him again. I'm trying to get him to develop some mechanical skills, like getting his ass out of bed." I asked her if she knew of anyone who might want to hurt her son. "In addition to me," she replied, "maybe everyone in the Western United States, Canada and parts of the Canary Islands. Canaries, especially, have an aversion to the little prick. I hate to consider the possibility of foul play, particularly if I'm not present."

Mrs. van Merde agreed to my usual fee—$500 a day, butter cookies and unrestricted access to her lingerie drawer—and I accepted the task of locating her offspring. I asked her for any object that might have Throckmorton's fingerprints on it. "The only thing I can think of is his dick," she answered, "but I guess you'd have to find him first."

I made do with a couple of her son's baby pictures and began my quest. My first move was trying to get out of the house. My client was no help. She picked up a book on fornicational yoga and ignored me. I finally left by an upstairs window, then returned to my office to work out a plan of action and gift-wrap some garter belts. I began calling some of my informants from the shady edges of the city and after fifty-two tries, I hit pay-dirt. But I swept it up and kept calling, finally locating someone who had recently seen the missing person.

Tony "Smelly-Shorts" Flatulenza had helped me in the past. He runs a boarding Kindergarten for sixteen-year-old girls in Malibu, providing gifted candidates a classical education involving twelve-step hooker lessons. The man is an anchor of selfless charity in a stormy sea. Tony recalled spotting Throckmorton at an art gallery in the Valley a few days earlier. He thought the exhibition was still open, a showing of pornographic religious works by the emerging Syrian artist, Sayve-Mee Asseet.

This painter's method is to position himself in a toll booth on the 241 and toss cat shit onto the side of U-Haul vehicles traveling at full speed, leaving the finished product in the hands of the gods (and cat shit in the hands of the artist). I had seen his work a couple of times. It looks like cat shit on a truck to me, but perhaps I don't understand modern art that well. I went to the gallery and looked around, hoping to locate the object of my search. The gallery owner, a slim young man with a shaved head and a groin to match (displayed in his open fly), told me that he expected to see Throckmorton again soon. It seems that Mrs. van Merde's boy knows his cat shit. I watched the place from my car, which I had parked unobtrusively just inside the front door of the gallery, hoping to catch a glimpse of the missing heir.

Later that day Throckmorton showed up. A redhead was with him. Her hair was jet-black, but her head was red. She was wearing a seductive sheet-metal blouse, a thick army-blanket skirt, and hip-length firemen's boots that appeared to chafe her crotch as she walked. Throckmorton had his hand in one of her boots. He looked like his baby pictures. Fat and bald. They didn't stay long, and when they left I put my car in gear to follow them. I foolishly dropped it in reverse and shot backwards at 50 mph through three walls of the gallery, dispersing art lovers and destroying over twenty paintings and four large pots of cat shit, including one into which a cat was shitting at the time. The crowd cheered. As luck would have it, I ended up in the alley and was able to speed to the street at the moment my two subjects got into a Rolls-Royce driven by Stevie Wonder. They sped to a secluded spot on the median strip of Wilshire Boulevard. Throckmorton and his companion climbed onto the hood of the car, where he proceeded to violate her in plain view of six lanes of traffic. The expression of affection never fails to move me. It brought to mind some lines from Robert Browning's beautiful poem: "How do I love thee? Let me count the strokes." Call me sentimental.

I was so engrossed in their activities as I drove past, that I crashed into Saint Ralph's Church of the Blessed Holy Mackerel, where a wedding was reaching its conclusion. My brakes failed, and I continued all the way up to the altar, raking pews full of screaming guests onto their asses. I rolled down the window and kissed the bride, squeezing her ample frontal parts with one hand as I signaled for a left turn with the other. She stuck her tongue in my mouth. Yuck! I drove out a side door, ignoring the collection plate, but passing close to the baptismal font for a quick gargle. At the main entrance, I hung around to watch the newly-betrothed pair exit the church, where everyone threw rice, most of it cooked and some still in the pot.

I made it back to the scene of Throckmorton's lewd outdoors exhibition just as they finished. It was getting dark, and I trailed the Rolls-Royce to a popular night spot. The recent copulators disappeared inside, but when I attempted to follow, a bouncer barred my way. It was Kobe Bryant, bouncing a basketball and lining up another shot. We were three miles from the arena where the game was being played, but that doesn't mean anything to Kobe. I flashed my badge and my decoding ring, and after he threw up another air ball, I entered the club. Sole music was blasting from the loudsqueaker ("Shoe Fly Pie," get it?). In the eerie darkness, I could see my quarry at the bar, sucking on Shirley Temple cocktails and throwing down sulfuric acid chasers. I managed to insert myself between them and we struck up a conversation. I asked them if they had screwed anybody interesting lately. They seemed to like the direction of our talk, and I soon felt someone rubbing my ass. I hoped it wasn't Throckmorton.

Fortunately, it turned out to be the young lady (who told me her name was Shirley Doowannitt). I returned the favor. She said, "I love what you're doing. Where did you learn to hold a girl like that?" I replied, "I used to play the French horn." I hadn't used that particular move for a while, but I like to keep my hand in. Shirley is not precisely unattractive, but if you want to evaluate her features in terms of ugliness, I would say they veered toward the high side of average. She held out a closed fist and told me that if I guessed what she was holding, I could have sex with her. I ventured, "Two giraffes and a warthog?" She said, "Close enough, Lover!" They invited me back to her apartment, but when we arrived I told them I didn't feel well and took my leave. I shook Throckmorton's hand and Shirley's boobs, confident that I could find those big, round, er .... I mean, him, whenever I wanted. I went home to change my shorts and came back the next day, only to find that Shirley and Throckmorton had moved out. What a fiasco!

My duty was to report to Mrs. van Merde. She took it well and only called me a "stupid prick" a couple of dozen times. I acknowledged my lack of good judgement and told her I would understand if she kept her blouse buttoned during my visit, but assured her I would be satisfied with a lengthy look at her exemplary rear. That seemed to mollify her. I tell you, that butt was fine. It belongs in the Museum of Fine Arts. Or at least the Keister Hall of Fame. I took ten percent off my daily fee and scaled my undie requirements way back.

Now I had to start my search all over again. Fortunately, I had recorded the license number from the Rolls-Royce, but it turned out to be a rental from Hump-Mobile, Inc. The firm specializes in providing luxury vehicles for sexual events like post-communion cherry busting and intra-mural date rapes. All their cars are outfitted with a multiple-speed Handy-Dandy Dashboard Doucher, a condom vending machine, extra underwear in various colors and sizes (including long-johns), a dildo rack and a well-appointed crapper. I reserved a mid-size model for the following weekend.

Through the car-rental records, I located the house where Throckmorton was staying with another Floozie. I made sure that he was inside and then enlisted Earl to block the only exit by lying down in the driveway. If my prey wanted to escape, he would have to run my buddy over (no big loss there), and in that case maybe we could get tire tracks off the dimwit's ass that would allow us to identify the vehicle. But my precautions were unnecessary. When Throckmorton came out of the house, I was ready. I slapped a set of handcuffs on him. Regrettably, my aim was low and I clamped them on his nuts, but that rendered him helpless anyway (though not especially quiet). I was pretty proud of myself as I escorted Junior back to the van Merde residence. It would probably be heart-rendering, I thought, to see the reunion between mother and son.

We were led into the family room and the matriarch entered regally, one hand clutching her heart. She opened her arms to the lad. Throckmorton sobbed, "Mother!" and rushed to her. She hauled off and swung a wide-arc roundhouse right to his beezer. Clocked that kid slicker than snot. The blow was rendered more effective by the use of brass knuckles. It sent him sprawling into a stack of glass figurines that were arranged to depict some sort of artistically pleasing gang bang. The poor guy tried to get up, but his loving mom used an expensive vase to put a new part where his hair would have been if he had any. Cold-Cocksky, as they say in high-class Russian circles. He was out like a paraplegic base-runner.

"Get that idiot out of here," she told me with a cool smile. "That's all I've wanted to do for years." With that, I turned the kid over to the butler, who patted Mrs. van Merde's exquisite butt and pitched Throckie III out on his flabby ass, taking the opportunity to relieve him of his wallet and kick him in the nuts too. Mrs. van Merde was extremely pleased with the way things had worked out and gave me a bonus (a leisurely view of both exciting regions of her torso). I was so grateful, I agreed to forego the butter cookies. Earl asked me a couple of days later why I had told him to lie down in the driveway. It took that long for the idea to seep down from his squash. I gave him some story about air raid drills. Guess what he said.

Listen Grover, I want to give you another heads-up about your tendency to fish around in your nose when you don't have anything else to do. I see on the Internet that your town has recently issued more stringent booger regulations, so it's possible you may need a license now. Check with your Nostril By-Products Department at City Hall (second floor, next to the Dingle-Berry Office).

The frère in your hair

15

Hey Grover,

I thought you'd be interested to know that I recently won a roll of linoleum by guessing the number of marbles in a toilet bowl. I wish someone had flushed it prior to the contest, but still, it's nice to know that my luck is holding. I figured you'd be worried, so you'll be relieved to know that Earl has made a miraculous recovery. In fact, he's improving every day, so it shouldn't be long until he comes down with some other exotic disease. We'll just have to live with the disappointment of his improvement, even though it means we're forced to associate with our two prize-winning simpletons again from time to time. Hanging out with these people produces the same pleasure as wiping your ass with roofing materials.

I may have mentioned that Madge is a little on the chubby side. In fact, she has an advanced case of chronic hogginess. The fat meter goes right off the scale in her case. Madge suffers from advanced reverse bulimia, but she's managed to deceive herself into thinking that she's still young and svelte. Gives you an idea of how poorly her cranial vacuum-tube works. Madge was a swimmer in her youth, though I don't know how they found a pool that she couldn't empty when she dived in. Anyway, she entered the state breast-stroke competition a couple of weeks ago. The poor woman came in dead last and then bitched that the other girls were using their arms. The only consolation for those of us who attended the meet was an impressive exhibition of female flesh (excluding Madge, of course). Male tools in the spectator section were substantially distended.

Earl's brush with mortality has apparently made him philosophical. That is, when a flicker of thought actually occurs to him. Instead of "what?" he often remarks, "What the hell?" Their daughter, Adultera, gives them a lot to worry about. The girl is eighteen and dumber than a lobotomized ox. Not much in the outward physical area either. She has Madge's looks and Earl's brains, so you can put the evidence together for yourself. The only thing physically attractive about this girl is when she closes the door behind her.

She came home late last night and asked her mother, "Would you like to hear about the car or would you rather read about it in the paper?"

My detective agency is thriving, you'll be pleased to know. I'm involved almost daily with repugnant occurrences and disgusting sexual practices. And my clients have problems too. One of my successful high-profile cases is currently being used by the FBI in their training program. It's an example of how a crime can be solved by the patient application of classic deductive reasoning and the fact that even a blind chicken can find a kernel of corn on occasion. The case concerned a kidnapping that demanded all of my law enforcement and prevaricating skills. You may have seen it on the news, although it's easy for you to miss when you're watching the Jewelry Network.

I was listening to a recording of Mozart's 39th Symphony with Arturo Toscanini conducting the Sons of the Pioneers when the call came in. Misty Gapp, the teenage daughter of Drippun and Squeakee Gapp, was snatched by assailants unknown as she exited her parents' stately home in Newport Beach. I was called to their imposing estate near the water (oops, just had a mudslide there. Now it's *in* the water).

The missing girl was well-known in the community. She attended a religious school run by the Charitable Sisters of Fiendish Abdominal Rumbling, founded by Saint Spree-Service (I'll give you a little time with that one) in the year of the great hooker uprising—the first one. We've had several. Misty was a beautiful, obedient child, with a pious demeanor, a low two-digit IQ and large chest decorations. Her parents were naturally distraught, but I was able to use tact and diplomacy to calm them until they were traught once again. Her mother wept non-stop until I batted her one in the mouth and told her to shut up. "Do you think you're the only person whose daughter has ever been kidnapped, probably raped and beaten and eventually murdered, dismembered and dumped in a landfill?!" I screamed at her. You have to put these things in perspective. We sat by the phone, waiting for a ransom call, playing pinochle, pig's knuckle and pony express (that's post office with a little horsing around) and trying to pass time and gas as noiselessly as possible.

The call came four days later. The caller tried to disguise his voice, but I recognized one of the Lee brothers, Ugg. He was a convicted felon—a thief, murderer, rapist and current member of the state legislature who had served two terms in the penitentiary for posing as a prison inmate. He instructed Misty's father to put two million dollars in a cloaky-sack and mail it to a specific address. I was amazed that the kidnappers could be so dumb. I merely had to lead the police to the address, wait for the mail delivery, recover the money and free the girl. A cinch. Drippun asked to speak to his daughter to be certain that she was still alive. She came on the line and said, "I'm okay, Daddy. This is actually kinda cool. Oh, could you like put some clean underwear in the ransom sack for me? Mine have got some icky white stains in them."

I was at the abandoned house the next day with a swat team (who were there to keep the flies away). We waited for several hours, but the mailman never showed up. We finally found him in an alley nearby with a torn fingernail and a badly fractured mail bag. The blackguards had intercepted him before he completed his delivery. They had took the money (They had "taken" the money? Still sounds right.) and scrammed, taking the lovely, innocent child with them.

Over the course of the next few months, we received postcards from Misty that had been mailed from various exotic locations in Europe and the Caribbean. They usually showed pictures of the poor girl in revealing bikinis and other skimpy clothing, drinking wine or elaborate island concoctions, large male hands covering her butt so it couldn't be traced. The message assured her parents that she was being treated well. I had my suspicions. I asked myself what Elvis would do.

Inspired by my desire to free the young damsel (or the damn youngsel—I can never keep them straight), plus a large fee from the Gapps, I worked backwards from the postmarks on the cards to establish a pattern that might pinpoint Misty's whereabouts. I fed the information into my computer, where I had prepared a model based on data from other kidnappings in the same block over a period of the previous two weeks. The computer searched its memory banks and the bottom drawer of my desk. After an hour, the screen produced the message: "Are you nuts?" I resorted to another approach. I examined the last postcard and saw that it contained the name of a desert island ski resort just outside Tombstone, Arizona. Why not take a chance?

I asked Misty's mother for some of her daughter's clothing (preferably underpants) for DNA comparison (DNA = Damn Nifty Ass). I also asked her mother for some of her own undies. She gave me the ones she was wearing. A quick Greyhound bus ride deposited me at the resort, where I spent a couple of hours peeking in windows and getting the shit kicked out of me by people who didn't want me peeking in their windows. But I finally caught a glimpse of the kidnap victim lying in bed. One young guy was pouring the sausage to her, and six or seven others were standing in line, fairly well-spaced apart. I stealthily entered the room and took my place at the end of the line.

When at last it was my turn, Misty yawned and announced that she was starved. "This jumping around really makes me hungry," she said. Curses. The boys went out to get some food, and I acted quickly, throwing handcuffs on Misty. Then, carrying her outside over my shoulder, I managed to jump-start a high-speed riding mower. I set her on my knee and looped her cuffed hands around my neck. With one arm around her waist (felt good!!), I took off like a rocket. Her frontal accoutrements hung in my face, partially obstructing my view, but providing a welcome diversion.

We blazed a swath through the well-manicured lawn, spewing rocks, bits of cactus and hotel guests everywhere. I made a wrong turn into the lobby and cut another path through the thick carpet. In other words, the mower took a nap (Ha-ha-ha!). Several security people started off after us in hot pursuit. The revolving door wasn't easy to negotiate, but I made it through on the third try and found myself in the pool area. Standing on the other side of the pool, Misty's buddies spotted us. They started around to block our progress, but we were on a big mower, moving fast, and they fanned out in all directions as I bore down on them.

The guests lying around the pool scattered as I knocked over lounge chairs, tables, people and lots of other junk. I was fortunate enough to grab a young lady by the rack as we zoomed past. One guy proffered his dong, which I ignored. A well-dressed woman carrying a Chihuahua leaped out of the way and dropped her pet. I swerved gracefully and ran the little bastard over. No harm done. We should not confuse animals with humans, except in some parts of Alabama. Finally, I was able to maim a large segment of those present and steer us out the main gate. Then it was onto Route 10, headed for the airport. Miss Gapp pleaded with me to release her. Her gloriously substantial udders bounced pleasingly against my face as we lumbered down the highway. "I'm naked!" she wailed. So I covered her crotch with my hand.

I won't tell you of the obstacles I had to negotiate in order to get Misty back to her parents. Let's just say it's not easy to sneak a screaming, naked, handcuffed, big-breasted girl through the boarding area of an airport anymore. It took every skill in my quiver, including the procurement of a minor-league bat-rack, a surfboard and the bridle for a Shetland pony. I need hardly mention the stepladder and the arc-welding machine, nor will I bore you describing the clever way I fed four cats into an ATM.

But it was all worthwhile, and when I entered the Gapp home with Misty slung over my shoulder, the joy was profound. Everyone gathered with the family cheered like mad (the police, the FBI, five sheriff's deputies, half a dozen sewer workers and four members of the Los Angeles Lakers—who were there because Kobe Bryant had the ball and they didn't have a chance in hell of getting it). I guess they were all delighted because the kid's bare ass was hanging out in the breeze. I know it made me happy.

It does my heart good to perform services like this. I can sense the warmth and pride flowing through you, as well. Well, that's how I handled it, in my usual heroic manner. I was paid generously for my services and got to keep a pile of the family underwear. Misty's father included some of his, but I'm going to throw those away unless you want them.

The brother in your life.

er ..., *You remember*

16

Hey Grover,

Greetings from Northern Italy. We're here at lovely *Lago di Como* (the White Cliffs of Dover). I want to keep you abreast of my exciting activities with a detailed description of our trip, because you'd pester the hell out of me if I didn't. We arrived in Milan and I rented a car. I wanted to reach the city before all the McDonalds were closed, so I was in a hurry. The guy at the counter tried to give me some safety instructions, but hey, I don't tell these pepperonis how to make lasagne, they don't tell me how to drive. Right off the bat, there was a red-and-white wooden barrier blocking my way at the garage exit, but I got out of the car and ripped that damn thing right off. Then to avoid traffic I cut across a large expanse of manicured lawn in front of the terminal. Saved a lot of time. It made some deep gashes in the grass and plowed up some flower beds. But what the hell, they'll grow back.

I admit I could have slowed down a little when I drove through the baggage claim area, but the signs should be more explicit and passengers need to stay loose. Especially the nuns. Love to see 'em sprint. A couple of those pricky little police cars (seven or eight) got on my tail with their lights flashing and sirens screaming. Cool. I faked them out by taking the first entrance onto the freeway. I don't know what that sign meant with the big red "X" on it, but the upside was that there were no cars in my direction to slow me down. I floored it. The downside was that there were a lot of cars coming at me from the other direction. You should have seen them scatter, though. How could all those drivers take a wrong turn like that?

The cops were some distance behind me when I rammed through the guardrail and down the slope onto a parallel street. That thing was hard to get off the hood. I hit a few people a glancing blow and flattened a cat. Cut through the front room of a small villa. I hate it when people become hysterical at the sight of a speeding car in their home, but we got a good look at some nice statuary and I was able to seize a satisfactory feel from one of the residents. I wish it had been a female. After a minute or so, I pulled in behind a *ristorante* (gas station) and ran over two more cats. Also a guy in a white apron. I took out a big terrace where people were eating, and they dived in every direction to get out of the way. Tables, food and lots of other crap flew all over. It was fun to see. Leave it to foreigners to have people eat dinner at a gas station. We're running into a lot of stupid stuff like this.

I saw the **polizia** go whizzing by out front. Those olive-munchers didn't have a clue where we were. I waited for things to settle down (except for the mob pounding on the car with rocks and pipes), then got back on the highway and headed for town. I kept telling Gretchen to take photos, but she's useless when she's screaming. I'm going to talk to the car rental people about the flimsy glass and other poor materials they put in their vehicles. It was getting dark as we reached the outskirts of Milan. I had a general idea where our hotel was (likely within the confines of the city), but these narrow-minded clowns insist on posting their signs in Italian. Nevertheless, I had prepared for encounters with the natives, having memorized several set phrases to help me get by, such as *"Come sta?"* (How they hangin?). I pulled to the curb in front of a guy on the corner and said, *"Cerco l'Albergo Centrale"* (I'm looking for the Centrale Hotel). He said, *"Va bene, continuate,"* (Okay, go ahead). This was going to require another approach.

I asked him, *"Sa dov'è l'Albergo Centrale?"* (Do you know where the Centrale Hotel is?). He said, *"Si"* and walked away. Where did I go wrong? Okay, I would have to rely on my path-finding expertise. I consulted my guide book and determined that the Number 19 bus stopped in front of our hotel. Now all I had to do was find a bus stop for the Number 19 and follow it. Sometimes I even surprise myself. I turned the corner, and as luck would have it, the bus we wanted was right in front of us. I started to follow it and when I had gone three blocks, Gretchen pointed out that the bus had been stopped in front of our hotel. I knew that.

I backed up three blocks and parked on the sidewalk. Screw the elderly couple that got pinned against the building. Didn't they see me signal that I was leaving the street? These people could learn to hustle a little. We entered the lobby and I approached the guy at the desk. In the hotel industry people usually speak a little English, but here is how my conversation went with this guy:

"Buona sera. I'm Smutt."

"I no responsive for this."

"No, that's my name."

"Oh, yes Mister. You name Smoot. You room is really."

"My room is really what?"

 Is really for you."

"That's what I assumed."

"Yes sir, Mister. We fix it room and now is really."

"Oh, the room is ready."

"I think I talk too fast for you. I gonna slow down."

"Where is the room?"

"Is right between couple other rooms."

"What's the number, you idiot?"

"Is no lumber. Furniture all finish. Paint is maybe little wet."

"Look, can you just give me the key?"

"Sure, Mister. First please you feel around this card."

"You mean fill out the card."

"You English not so good. You want pie now?"

"No, I don't want any pie."

"But you got to pie."

"Oh, I have to pay."

"I sure I talk too fast for you. You pie with cricket card?"

I gave him my cricket card and he motioned the bellboy over. We had five enormous suitcases filled to the brim and weighing a ton each. Gretchen always takes every object she owns when we travel. My stuff is in my jacket pocket. The bell-person was at least ninety years old and barely four feet tall. He weighed fifty pounds, soaking wet with a cracker in his pants. He put a bag under each arm and took two others in his hands, wheezing like a Clydesdale. He looked down at the fifth bag and then at me with a pleading expression on his face. I said, "Here, let me help you." I took the last suitcase and stuck the handle between his teeth.

We followed the poor guy as he dragged the luggage up three flights of stairs, beet-red and hyper-ventilating. I took one look at the room and sighed. I said, "You call this a hotel room? That wall is so thin I can almost see right through it!" He panted, "Is the window." I went around checking to make sure that everything worked. I yanked on a handle and nothing happened. Disgusted, I said, *"Il gabinetto non funziona"* (The shitter's busted). He said, "Is the mini-bar." I tipped him a peso and kicked his ass. It's Mexican, but it's still cash, right?

Gretchen decided to take a bath, and I went downstairs for a walk. At the desk, I asked the clerk, "Where's the square?" Without looking up he said, "Outside." I left the hotel and a group of children laughed and pointed at me. *"Brutto americano!"* (Good-looking Yankee guy), they said. The Italians repeat this everywhere I go. They call Gretchen *la bella signora* and I'm the *brutto americano*. At least these Italian folks know a handsome devil when they see one. Even the kids. I went into a bar and ordered a Shirley Temple cocktail (two parts ginger ale, the other part ginger ale too—with an umbrella). The bartender gave me a glass of wine. The stuff tasted like rat piss. It couldn't have been worse if he had soaked it up off the floor with a bar rag and squeezed it into the glass. I never got splinters in my tongue from a drink before. The place was crowded, and I heard the friendly greeting, *"Brutto americano,"* several times. One young man came over and said, "You Americano, no?" I asked him how he knew. "Is easy," he said. "Bottom of you pants six inches above you shoes and you got yellow stains around you fly—which is open." I think it's nice when the locals try to converse with visitors. It's enlightening for them to encounter us sophisticated Yankees and find out what real worldliness is.

The next morning I went to the front desk and endured another conversation:

"What's the fastest way to get to Lake Como?"

"You have car?"

"Yes."

"Good, Mister. Is fastest way."

"Let's make it simple, dorkie. Which street do I take to get to the A21?"

"No sir, Mister. You don't should take street. We need street here."

"Never mind, you stupid cluck!"

"Thank you for kindness. I here for helping you."

I took out my map and plotted the route for myself. We left the hotel at 6:00 AM and by noon we were in France. Oops. Well, no big deal. The frogs have got nice scenery too and they're okay, even though they insist on speaking French when tourists are around. Seven hours after that, we pulled into our hotel, *Albergo Horribile* (The Grand), on the lake. Gretchen was quiet the whole trip. The proprietors are Putrido and Corpulenta Posteriore, a jolly couple. They welcomed us heartily, laughing and cuffing each other playfully, and showed us to our suite. This is my kind of hotel, spacious, pleasant, and the bathroom is not far from the main building. Our balcony overlooked the lake, and we spent a lot of time there shouting obscenities, giving tourist boats the finger, grabbing our crotch and spitting on anybody who came close to the shore. When I say "we," I use the plural form of the pronoun in the sense that I did it when Gretchen wasn't around.

Signora Posteriore has what Gray's anatomy textbook calls "a big ass." The host couple threw a little party for their guests the first evening so we could all get acquainted. It's a small hotel and there were only three other couples. Anya and Lars Söderström were from Upsala, Sweden. Trevor and Miriam Pail-White hailed from the quaint little town of Biddleswade-on-the-Thrumpinghamshire in England. Marcello and Breastissima Rossano came from Naples. The proprietor had hired Antonio Fistula and his mildly retarded, all-Italian orchestra (mandolin and trombone) for the evening. Their repertoire consisted of traditional Italian love songs like *The Muskrat Ramble, Deutschland über Alles* and *Moscow is the Shits*. They only played until eight-thirty because the trombone was rented.

Major Pail-White is a scrawny little runt with the typical British moustache and tweeds. He's a retired army officer. The guy's not bad-looking if you can stomach people who have a face like a butt soaked in vinegar. During the evening, he regaled us with tales of his worthless campaigns in the Raj, having served in India for over twenty years. He should have stayed there. The most boring twit I ever fell asleep listening to. I panicked at one point when I realized I'd rather be listening to Earl. Trevor's handsome little woman, Miriam, is at least still very attractive. As they would say in Russia, "Π&%ΓΡ∀ΣΧΦ"(Swella Buttsky). Come to think of it, the Russians said that about me too. Anyway, Miriam made insightful comments about the customs of India and, when her husband's attention was elsewhere, what a dumb shit he was.

Breastissima Rossano is a big flirt, but what a Momma! Her hair is thick and dark, her figure is nifty and her immense frontal knobs get the old pubic blood pumping. I admired her posture, which consisted of bending forward and giving us a solid look at her jutters. Marcello is good-looking, witty, courteous and a little rumpled. They described their home town, sharing anecdotes about the cultural advantages and pickpockets of Naples, along with statistics on the latest murders and Mafia assassinations, how much protection money they pay, and the lack of garbage removal (which goes unnoticed for several months).

The only thing the Soderströms could talk about was snow and sled dogs—and nude bathing in the snow with sled dogs. Lars Soderström seemed oblivious to his wife. I caught him looking at Signora Posteriore's ass more than a couple of times. Anya is exactly what most guys picture when they think of a Swedish woman—tall, blond and a serious piece of carcass. She has elaborate hooters and the propensity to fondle crotches under the table. In the course of the evening, she offered herself to each of the men on more than one occasion. But I have my standards. I'll make a final decision tomorrow.

Here it is the next day, and what do you know? At breakfast we learned some interesting news. It seems that Major Pail-White and Anya Soderström had taken off together for parts unknown during the night. I was really surprised. At the table, Miriam remarked casually, "I don't know how he intends to satisfy a young woman like that. Maybe he'll wiggle his ears." Lars commented dryly, "Good idea. She likes it that way." So now we were down to three couples. The next morning, there were more revelations. It seems that Marcello Rossano and Miriam Pail-White had headed for the hills just before the sun went down. Signore Posteriore had seen them in a rowboat on the lake, with Marcello pulling for the opposite shore and Miriam pulling on Marcello. I turned to Lars and said jokingly, "Well, I suppose you and Breastissima will be next." He said, "We are," and took out one of her melons to give it a squeeze. She smiled and stuck her hand in his fly. I tell you, love is grand. I patted Signora Posteriore's ass.

Breakfast at the hotel is a buffet with coffee that's so strong it takes both hands to dunk a donut. Reminds me of the coffee we had in the army. They boil it until it looks like mud, then they put a horseshoe on it and if the horseshoe sinks it's not done yet. We take lunch each day on the road as we tour the area and run over the locals who are too slow to get out of the way. I love to sneak up on them and honk the horn. They shit their pants. We follow the signs that indicate good places to visit, like *Vista Scenica* (Trees Block This View) or *Villaggio Pittoresco* (No Indoor Plumbing In This Dump). We were able to attend the local Manure Festival one afternoon. I'm sending you samples by separate post. Dinner is at the hotel each evening, and here's the daily menu so you can see the large selection we had to choose from.

Minestrone

----

1. Spaghetti

2. Spaghetti con Tomate

3. Spaghetti senza Tomate

4. Tomate

5. Tomate con Spaghetti

6. Tomate senza Spaghetti

Vino del supermercato

Gelato con Spaghetti

Yesterday we saw a sign at the side of the road that proclaimed *"Esibizione d'arte per Turisti non molto Intelligente"* (Art Show for Well-Informed Tourists). I stopped despite Gretchen's admonitions. My cultural side always shows, as you recall. Man, you never saw such a display of originals. There were pictures by Michelangelo, Leonardo da Vinci, Titian and Botticelli. Hundreds of them, and only about forty bucks apiece. I bought ten works by da Vinci. Also some of his "paint by numbers" stuff. No one can capture Times Square on canvas like Lenny could. I would have bought more if he had done something in green.

After eight days on Lake Como, we motored east across the country toward Venice. We were to pass close to Verona, and I read in the paper, *La Stampa* (the Stamps), about a special production of Aida to be presented this year. They do this opera annually on several consecutive days in the large Roman arena and it's a mammoth spectacle with a cast of hundreds. The article in the paper described the current production as one of the most daring in history. In an attempt at more realism and to spice up the story, the celebrated opera director, Odioso Erexione, had been brought in to handle the staging.

As you know, in the final scene Radames is sealed in a tomb, but his love Aida has previously hidden herself there in order to die with him. Erexione hired two of the most popular singers in the country. Molto Masculino is a big, handsome stud with a reputedly hefty wand and Statueska Sexualli is not only drop-dead gorgeous, but is outfitted with the largest lactation devices in Italy and most of its neighboring countries. In this version, as the tomb is lit, the two lovers sing their final duet with the tenor giving it to Statueska doggie-style. The reviews were positive, despite a few cracked notes on some of the more intense strokes. I scanned the paper for photos.

We often go to the opera (Gretchen persuades me to attend by using time-tested Prussian methods). My favorites are *La Bohème* (You Mean That Fat Broad is Dying of Consumption?), *Turandot* (Dottie Takes Her Turn), *Der Fliegende Holländer* (The Flying Dutchman, or Joop Gets His Single-Engine License), and *Rigoletto* (The Letto Has Been Rigged).

I just had to get tickets to Aida for the next night. Gretchen likes the music, but I'm much more well-rounded in my tastes, able to appreciate the associated fornication too. Signore Posteriore helped me, and we were able to buy front-row seats. I looked forward to the opera with the enthusiasm of any lover of the arts (and skin). We drove to Verona and parked near the train station. As we got out of the car, we heard over the loudspeaker: "Attention Please. The passengers who took the train bound for Rome are kindly requested to return it."

At the arena, we were in our seats early. The woman next to me was breast-feeding her son. The kid looked to be about nineteen. But curses! Wouldn't you know it? Masculino and Sexualli weren't on the program. They were unable to go on, having spent the afternoon in a dressing room rehearsing their final scene. Over and over again. Drat. At the last minute, they were replaced by two large artists, Beama Montonoso and Bira Belli. Those acquainted with the opera world are aware that these artists are two of the finest voices (and largest editions) in the game. We're talking Moby singers here. Together, they wouldn't fit in a Sumo ring. When their bellies are touching, their mouths are seven feet apart. So in the final act, instead of reproducing the desperate carnal passion of the previous evening, they ended their duet and shook hands.

While we were in the Veneto region, we spent a day in Venice. We've been here many times and can't get enough of it, although the authorities tell us they've had enough. At one point, while Gretchen was stocking up on worthless junk as usual (no shop shall be left behind), I really had to take a whiz. High-tension bladder pressure. There are always a lot of people on the tiny streets, so I figured no one would notice me as I stood on a small bridge in the crowd. I eased it over the balustrade and drained it. These audacious Italians are so excitable, and plenty humorous. People immediately started screaming things like *"Brutto americano!"* (Movie-star type Yankee person!), *"Con lo strumento piccolo!"* (You with the mighty cudgel!) and *"Non urinare nel canale, cafone!"* (Way to go, Buddy!). I smiled and waved back. Soaked a passing gondola.

This is by no means the end of our trip. We still have a couple of weeks to go, but I'll save the remainder for my next letter. Don't be impatient. Even though I'm on the road, I keep up with Earl's situation, and you'll be happy to learn that his condition has improved since the last time I wrote. The doctors were able to treat his last illnesses with massive injections of some kind of wonder drug. I think it was based on curare or some cyanide derivative. That cleared up the events I described previously. The problem is that he keeps developing new afflictions. Now he seems to be suffering from an instance of "bent baton." This caused a punctured pudd, which in turn led to painful convulsions of the ass. On top of all that, he picked up a bad case of slobber-dick. If we're not careful, it could develop into weasel-wand. I'll keep you posted.

Your devoted Brudder,

I. Remayne

17

Hey Grover,

We're back!!! It was an exhausting sojourn in the land of *la dolce vita* (ravioli and cheese) and I must say the hospitality was not especially consistent. I've seen better jails. I had planned to describe everything in exhaustive detail, but suffice it to say it consisted mainly of wild accusations and a lot of ass-kicking. Sadly, most of it was mine. But it would have been worse if Gretchen hadn't been along. The close-combat portion of her primary education paid off on more than one occasion. I hope you got the stuff we sent you. Don't open it indoors. In the meantime, to keep you in the loop, here is another newspaper column I filed before we left.

April 4. Today's column is devoted to the social event of the year. Beautiful Newport Beach and Saint Ernie's Church of the Blessed Siphon-Job were the setting for the gala affair, where Buffy Putts and Dr. Mortimer Shortshaft were joined in holy matrimony. I was fortunate enough to cover the proceedings. The bride is the daughter of Mrs. Vera Putts and the late Hiram Putts. He's always late, so he missed the nuptials. Of course he managed to show up for the subsequent food and booze portion of the proceedings.

The father of the bride is the well-known real estate developer, community benefactor and acknowledged municipal chiseler responsible for many outstanding construction projects, including high-end condominiums in many slums of Africa, as well as the recent Neiman-Marcus store perched on the slopes of Nepal's second highest mountain and an entire residential community for the homeless built along the tracks in the New York subway (close to the third rail).

The bride's mother, the former Vera Neiss, of the Slophole, Montana, Neisses, was Miss Regional Landfill of 1970 and not bad. Nice prow extensions. She comes from a large family of no-good jerks who make their money in squirrel-ranching. The clan's fortune is derived from their automated production methods for de-nutting and squashing the bushy-tailed pests and shipping them to caterers throughout the Third World. Now that I think about it, a lot of that stuff wound up on my plate in Italy.

The glowing bride (perhaps from some form of radiation sickness) recently completed her education at Madame Snootmeister's Academy of Slutology in Armadillo Mucous, Texas, where she graduated second in her class of two. After eight years, she finally received her degree in rudimentary arithmetic (without emphasis on fractions), passing on a technicality. She was nosed out of valedictorian honors by Mary Lee Weerowe-Lallong of Nutsack, New Mexico. Buffy's remark at the grad ceremony was, "I'd rather graduate second than next-to-last like Mary Lee."

The groom is the handsome and slightly retarded son of Mr. and Mrs. Wendell Shortshaft, formerly of Camden, New Jersey, one of the garden spots of the planet, if you don't count large stretches of Nigeria or the shantytown in Rio de Janiero. The elder Mr. Shortshaft is a partner in the law firm of Stompitt, Bangitt, Dingitt & Skrewitt, where he specializes in venereal disease litigation (and sometimes contraction). Young Dr. Shortshaft's limited intellectual capacity did not prevent him from becoming a cosmetic surgeon in Beverly Hills, specializing in rectal alignment, keister tucks and wand-shortening procedures. His practice has become one of the most sought-after subjects of litigation in the area.

A few narrow-minded clients have chosen to take issue with the good doctor's whimsical habit of adding cleverly-placed tattoos during surgical procedures. One of his more light-hearted ink-ons was, "If you can read this, you're close enough to kiss it." Another humorous addition was, "For best results, pull lever in front." One lawsuit concerns the inconsequential mistake Dr. Shortshaft made when re-positioning an off-center rectum. After the operation, the patient complained of severe diarrhea, claiming that the discharge shoots through his trousers and squirts several feet into the surrounding area. This is alleged to disturb the guests at social events and crowded retail outlets. My reaction to the complaint is, "Put a cork in it!" Geez! Dr. Shortshaft was fortunate enough to make bail in time to pledge his troth.

The bride's gown was lovely, fashioned entirely of see-through lace, cut low and held up exclusively by her nipples. The garment consequently allowed a view of virtually all of Buffy's physical charms, especially her magnificent and extensive anterior construction, which we have often referred to in the past as HOLY SHIT!! as you may recall from previous columns. My readers know me well enough to be sure that I would never engage in crude generalizations based on gender, even if I were referring to women, but I can only describe this babe as "Slobber-Incitement."

The bride's mother was clad in an understated Christian Back-Dior creation, designed to show off her nifty ass to the best advantage without detracting from her copious hooter area. I want to tell you, she displays a magnificent portion of slinky buttness. A large number of the male guests (twenty-two, not counting me) took advantage of the occasion to squeeze her can. One guy squeezed mine. At the other end of the spectrum, the groom's mother, Mrs. Shortshaft, had obviously found her beastly rags at a Big Lots clearance sale in Dubuque—or maybe behind the store. They consisted of two king-size bed covers sewn together at the last moment. And the colors were appalling. The only saving grace in her choice of clothing is that it gave her the opportunity to display her massive chest. The downside, though, is that almost any choice of duds would show it off. Her frontal real estate is freakin' huge. There's not enough firepower in an artillery battalion to blow those babies off.

A long red carpet was laid out from the gravel in the parking lot to the chapel, similar to the carpet that one sees at the Academy Awards, only this one came from Wal-Mart and had a few bathroom stains on it. The glamorous bridal party and lucky guests made their way past a large gathering of enthusiastic onlookers, including paparazzi and perverts, who were eager for a glimpse of the members of the wedding. As the lovely future Mrs. Shortshaft floated by, one disgusting brute whispered loudly to her, "I've got a stiff one right here for you, Toots. Let's see your ass." Without faltering, Buffy whispered in reply, "I'm looking, but I don't see it, Dwarf-Dong!!!" It was so embarrassing. I put it back in my pants. You would have been mortified.

A large contingent from the entertainment industry graced the gathering. The women who lined the path to the church screamed for one male actor to give them an autograph and open his fly. I offered the girl next to me a view into mine, but she brushed me off, claiming she had left her reading glasses at home.

The groom appeared and waved to friends and neighbors, unaware that his pants were falling down and his shorts didn't match his socks. His father hurried along behind the darling little flower girl and was about to grab the young tyke by the heinie when he stepped in some dog poop. Falling heavily, he grabbed the skirt of the woman beside him and ripped it off as he pulled her down. It was the popular actress, Kuppla Rypewunns, and she was now unclothed from the waist down. But the good woman maintained her poise and continued waving to the crowd, flashing her boobies to draw attention away from the spectacle of her undraped backside. The mishap precipitated a chain-reaction. An attendant rushed up and hit her with a chain. A couple of thoughtful gentlemen ran from the crowd and covered her exposed rear with their hands, eliciting a coy smile from the lady and a hasty exchange of phone numbers.

Then several other members of the procession, failing to watch where they were going as usual and already half in the bag, tripped over the fallen couple and plowed up several yards of carpet with their honkers. The masses cheered. Lots of asses were exposed, most of them unfortunately belonging to the men. However we did get fleeting, but nevertheless satisfying glimpses of some fine female breast-feeding gear.

The bride's fat-assed sister, Regurgitayta, was the maid of honor. This is a gal who is without a doubt the caloric-intake champion of America, the lower provinces of Canada and the crummiest regions of New Jersey (all of it). Church workers had thankfully moved the pews several feet toward the wall so she could waddle down the aisle, but it wasn't enough. She still knocked dozens of guests from their perches, chewing on a ham sandwich. By the time she made it to the front she had eaten all of her giant bouquet and was eyeing the flower girl's arrangement.

The guest list was *très* exclusive. Paris Hilton's cousin, Brussels Marriott, was there. Her cream-colored, trashy mini-dress was chic, simple and unencumbered by recent cleaning or underwear. The young Miss Marriott chose a daring, unbuttoned frock in checked pastels that afforded a perfect view of her vital organs, including a tattoo on her pubis that proclaimed: "Put it here if it doesn't fit in the overhead luggage compartment." Catchy.

The sports world was well-represented. Barry Bonds brought an old bat. The Right Reverend Mowlestyer Childe officiated, reading from the holy paperwork. It was a high mass, so communion was included. Thankfully, someone had seen fit to substitute beef tacos for the traditional wafers. At one point, there was a bit of a commotion at the railing, while they instructed me that the appropriate position as a communicant was not flat on my back under the ladies as they knelt. A distant cousin sang "Oh, Promise Me (And Leave A Fifty On The Dresser)." She wasn't distant enough, since we could still hear her, which wasn't the worst part. We could see her too. When the reverend said, "You may now kiss the bride," eight guys moved forward to comply. The groom managed to block the last two, stepping in front of Buffy while she tried to push him out of the way. I lost my concentration and missed most of the vows, because the young lady seated next to me was struggling to pull the hem of her skirt down. She was unsuccessful, mainly because I kept pushing it up again.

Following the ceremony, the reception was held outdoors on the wide grounds of the Newport Incinerator Center and Homeless Shelter (opposite the toxic waste dump and two doors down from the solvent recycling plant). Hundreds of guests milled around, conversing, dancing, and consuming the franks and beans catered by Al's Foot-Long Hot Dog Stand (the stand is a foot long, not the hot dogs). Speaking of dogs, there were some real woofers present among the groom's female relatives, but most of the ladies were pretty hot. It led to a lot of ass-grabbing, but I quit when a couple of guys told me they didn't like me touching them. The three-piece orchestra (bass drum, triangle and dust-buster) was made up of members of the Los Angeles Symphony percussion and janitorial section, who specialize in Levi Strauss waltzes and some Latin numbers, the most popular of which was XXVIII. The event would have been more pleasant if the maintenance crew had not chosen that particular afternoon to mow the lawn, cut down some dead trees, and bury a septic tank.

In a side room during the reception, Buffy, the new Mrs. Shortshaft, was observed showing some of her wedding presents to the groom's brother, in this case her underwear, which she had removed to give him a better view. It's not clear why she had to shed the rest of her clothes too. Anyway, her brother-in-law was apparently so thrilled to welcome Buffy into the family that he spent more than twenty minutes embracing her (while on the floor). The best man and two ushers also expressed an interest in the bride's gifts, patiently standing in line. I had kind of figured Buffy to be a little loose when I saw her French-kissing everybody in the receiving line at the church, including the women.

I was lucky enough to be awarded a dance with Mrs. Putts. Buffy's mother is exceedingly attractive for her age. Let's modify that. She could produce a stiffy on Millard Fillmore, and you know how long he's been dead. I especially like the part of her that I examined while peering down the front of her clothing. I could look in and see the floor between her super-sized beauties. She laughed and flirted and ground her pelvis against mine while we danced, which was extremely arousing but not easy, since we were in a Conga line at the time.

We were directed to the auditorium, where a piano was at the center of the stage and risers were set up for a large orchestra. The elder Shortshaft called for attention. "This is a surprise for my daughter," he said. "First, it's my pleasure to introduce the brilliant young pianist, Tay Gaschott, who will play three pieces by the Bulgarian composer, Gowna Waye, who starved to death just this week. He wrote the Sonata in D, the Nocturne in F and the Mazurka in Cleveland." At this point, everyone rushed out of the room and swarmed to the bar. They didn't want to miss the intermission. When they returned, Gaschott played his final chord. As the pianist took a bow, the crowd shouted, "Bravo! Bravo!" In response, Enrico Bravo bolted from the wings and threw him off the stage—to thunderous applause.

Mr. Shortshaft then announced that he had flown in the entire Vienna Symphony Orchestra, a trained bear, and two stars from the Bolshoi Ballet to perform for us. The dancers were Igor Tewpleezyoo and Katya Mityapanzoff. The crowd leaned forward in anticipation. The orchestra, eighty musicians, quickly took their places and the conductor motioned to the dancers, who were standing at opposite ends of the stage. The ballet stars raced toward each other for the *pas de deux* (Charleston), with their arms outstretched. Igor slipped on some doggy dew that old man Shortshaft had tracked in on his shoes. He hit the floor and slid into Katya, knocking her legs out from under her and propelling her into the air, where she completed a full gainer and landed smack on her kisser. She slid along the stage, leaving a trail of recently completed dental work behind her. Out like a third srike.

Igor continued his own slide and banged into a plaster column that supported a large bust of Beethoven. It toppled over, and as he attempted to rise the fifty-pound sculpture beaned the poor bastard right on his long-haired gourd. Lights out. Next stop: the deck. He hit the boards like a barrel of lug nuts. The orchestra left the stage, followed by the bear shaking his head. A couple of landscapers drove a garden wagon up and piled the unconscious hoofers aboard. End of Act One and Finale, all in one.

The guests celebrated into the wee hours of the morning. Several sweet young ladies were on their knees in the restroom, cranking out most of their recent food intake. Someone pointed to the little flower girl and the ring-bearer, six or seven years old, who were dancing together just like the adults. It was such a sweet picture. They were naked. Earl had been invited in order to make the other people look good, so I spent a pleasant hour or two lighting firecrackers and slipping them into his fly. The newlyweds are now on their way to the Desert Inn Spa and Rattlesnake Farm just outside Duluth, Minnesota, where by a freak coincidence the groom's brother, his best man and two ushers are registered in the room next door.

I don't want to end without commenting on Earl's present condition. It seems he contracts a new malady almost daily. The latest tests show that the guy now has a nasty case of rusty anus, compounded by shrivel-dick and a scabby can. Madge is not doing so well either. She developed mild ass failure just this week, but it seems to be getting worse. The medics are considering euthanasia, if only to make things more tolerable for the rest of us. We're hoping for the best.

The brother of your brother's brother,

That's right, you! Wait a minute ....

18

Hey Grover,

To give you the chuckle of the month, we got back from Italy and I promptly pitched off my bike while trying to smooth out a spot of concrete with my arm. Cement isn't that flexible when you hit it with some speed. Broke two bones around the elbow. They operated that afternoon, put two screws in one bone and pulled the other one back together with pins and wires. Good thing they had some hardware from an old lawnmower lying around. They used the operating room at Home Depot. Kept me overnight in the hospital (the surgeon didn't want me to get any rest). He was concerned about infection, but said it would be all right if confined to the brain. I'm looking forward to physical therapy for my hammer, which was scuffed in the process.

But to more important things. I'm sending you some additional important stories from my newspaper column. I know you like to keep informed about the crucial events of our times. My work will probably be syndicated soon, so you'll be able to read the stuff in all the big newspapers, like the "Baltimore Bugle and Saxophone" and the "Newark Daily Diarrhea." Until then, our local paper has the honor of publishing my stuff and here are some re-prints.

April 16. **Heroic Police Rescue Pet.**

A panicked Mrs. Tiddzer Hewge of Frecklepecker Lane called 911 yesterday to report that her cat was lodged high up in a tree on her neighbor's property. Officers Ayness and Bung responded quickly and spied said feline in a sturdy oak on the adjacent estate. The owner of the tree, Lettin Fardz, was observed pitching rocks at the offending animal. "I'm tired of that little bastard perching in my tree and shitting all over my oleanders," he was kind enough to inform the gathering.

Officer Bung, in the best tradition of our men in blue, took control of the situation. In an admirable display of quick thinking, he grabbed a shotgun and blew the furry pest clean out of the tree. Smithereensville. He was later mildly rebuked by the department for damaging a fine botanical specimen, but the reprimand will not go into his permanent file. When interviewed, Mrs. Hewge said, "Gee, I kind of wanted the cat back."

May 17. **Car Thefts on the Rise.**

The city council announced at their meeting today that the incidence of car theft in our city is on the rise. Last year one stolen car was reported, and this year the number has sky-rocketed to two, a percentage increase of ... er, let's see ... lots more. The number would have been three, but was reduced to two, because I had reported my car stolen and then realized that I just forgot where I parked the damn thing. In a future column I will deal with the lack of responsibility on the part of establishments where alcoholic beverages are allowed to be consumed in large volumes. Police Chief Fawlty Flapp assured the council that his officers have undergone comprehensive additional training to instill in them the knowledge of just exactly what constitutes a stolen car. He reports that the majority of them have grasped the concept that it concerns automobiles. Our gendarmes, ever vigilant.

April 18. **Local Team Wins Crown.**

Congratulations are in order. The finals of the National High School Copulation Tournament were held this weekend at Roxie McHooter's sprawling estate in Hollywood, and the "Rutting Rodents" of Slimeway, California, came away with the championship, out-pointing a determined bunch of future perverts from Coe-Kane High in Sacramento. Team captain, Hardy Plunger, and his lovely young partner, Sadie Prears, sealed the victory when they executed an impressive series of dribble-dunks and topped the whole thing off with a difficult half-twist during their final stroke. A complaint was lodged, claiming that the move debased the high cultural level of the sport, but the instant-replay review failed to show any violations of the rules of competitive violation.

The only untoward occurrence came when a member of the fourth-place team from the Jacksonville "Jumpers" was disqualified for a gaseous infraction. At the moment he brought his cargo home, the young man emitted a ripe, smoky-blue stinger that rattled several doorknobs and incited a call to open the windows. Coach Maykham Grunt was elated with the victory. "These kids put everything they had into the game," he said, his eyes moist with emotion. When asked to compare this activity with other team sports, he replied, "Well, in football the play ends when a person is tackled. In our game, that's when the play begins."

April 19. **Calm Restored in Domestic Dispute.**

The bobbies were assigned yet again to investigate a loud quarrel taking place after midnight in the Manuel Tortilla residence, located on Dumpster Street behind a billboard and just under the 5-Freeway overpass. Residents in the neighborhood had called to report loud activity and passage of wind involving Señor Tortilla, the victim of an extensive tequila celebration, and his lovely but somewhat corpulent wife, Maria-Gorda. Witnesses painted a picture of an enraged Señora Tortilla, who took issue with her husband's late-night wish to introduce two partially-dressed and somewhat inebriated young women into his bed (in which the good Señora was already in residence and trying to log some shut-eye).

Officers Kowalski and Pudd arrived on the scene to find Señora Tortilla brandishing a frightening choice of cutlery and attempting a testicle-ectomy on her spouse. The master of the house was suffering from massive cuts to his buttocks, as well as swollen nuts and a fractured groin. His *mujer* had booted him several times in the *cajones*, her feet shod in relatively large sizes for a female. The missus was screaming, "Voy matar al hijo de puta!" at full volume as the policemen restrained her. The verbatim translation of her statement ("I'll kill the son of a bitch!") may not sufficiently reflect the underlying note of affection which we are all sure the agitated lady meant to include.

Officer Pudd arranged to have the Mister transported to the nearest emergency room, and later reports have him resting comfortably in the Ass-Management Ward. The two young ladies whom Señor Tortilla wanted to host for the night were caught by Officer Kowalski as they hurried down the street with the major portion of their anatomy displayed due to the lack of adequate attire. After a struggle, he managed to get them into his patrol car and remove them from the scene. Citizens with information regarding Officer Kowalski's whereabouts are asked to kindly contact police headquarters.

April 20.   **New Fashion Line Introduced.**

Miss Lottie Krapp inaugurated her personal clothing line yesterday in the presence of numerous well-wishers (and several people who didn't give a a parrot's posterior) at the Downtown Mall, which as you readers know, is situated between the tire plant and Miss Daisy's Retail Love Emporium. The new line of revealing women's wear is aimed at teenage females, upwardly-mobile career gals and adventurous housewives, whereas Miss Daisy's curvaceous and warm-blooded salesgirls target downwardly-mobile teenage boys, horny career guys and husbands whose wives don't understand them.

The new Krapp fashions feature seductive designs that will allow you ladies to get in touch with your sexy side and are meant to be worn sans underwear. They will also prompt guys to get in touch with you (and when I say "touch," I mean "touch"), so instructions that come with the clothes suggest keeping your legs crossed. Miss Krapp's garments come in many sizes, except for you dogs with elaborate behinds. So if you happen to be one of those giant waddlers considering a visit to the boutique, forget it. You might not fit through the door anyway, grease-bucket! Why don't you just order a couple more cheeseburgers with fries and keep munching your way to total bathroom-scale destruction. But take your lard-laden butts elsewhere and don't stand in front of the store.

April 21.   **Fire Destroys Bathroom.**

At dawn this morning, smoke was seen billowing from a bathroom in Ayatollah Drive. When the fire trucks arrived, flames were shooting skyward and the chances of saving the excrementorium were minimal. The odds were reduced even further by the fact that the idiots from Firehouse 9 had forgotten the damn hoses. Luckily, the blaze didn't reach the house. A cursory investigation showed that the fire had been started by Mahmood Rezni, the owner of the property. He had apparently fallen asleep while squatting on the growler, smoking and reading his favorite comic strip, "The Completely Clothed Motorcycle Virgins of Baghdad." The two-seated structure was declared a complete loss. This same evaluation had been applied to Mister Rezni on numerous occasions in the past, most often by his grieving widow.

At the scene, Mrs. Rezni fought back tears and murmured, "I suppose I'll miss the prick." Rezni was the proprietor of a successful secondhand waffle outlet that he had converted from an abandoned hog trough. His daughters, Maya, Hoznami and Ginger, helped out from time to time when hooking duties permitted. The shop will now be run by his son Hakeem, a graduate of UCLA'S snake-charming curriculum. The family is considering selling the business and returning to their ancestral home in Fort Wayne, Indiana, as soon as the sixteen tenants presently renting one of the bedrooms in their house can find other accommodations.

April 22. **A Life Ends Tragically.**

The authorities were faced yesterday with a grim task, obliged to inform Mr. and Mrs. Piper Rentsch of Gooseneck Court that their son, Kressunt, had taken his life. Shortly before noon, the young man threw himself in front of a speeding train and therewith snuffed out his promising adolescent existence. It appears that various icky body parts remain stuck to the front of the train. For that reason, the timing of funeral arrangements depends on getting these items returned, although they may not be able to flag the express down before it reaches Fort Lauderdale. Friends, relatives and neighbors continue to ask themselves why the boy chose to terminate his life in this manner. It is known that he suffered from occasional mental problems, so it might have been simply a loco motive that drove him to such an extreme act. Loco motive!! Get it, folks? Ha-ha-ha!

April 23. **Good Works Recognized.**

I want to end this report with an uplifting story. Most of us know Miss Elsie Gunderson. She is now seventy years young and retired, but the inhabitants of our fair city remember her for her dedicated and unstinting work as Community Services Manager for almost four decades. Elsie never married, but chose to devote her life and energies to the development of charitable programs for those in need. And now this reporter has learned of a harrowing contretemps that Elsie experienced in the confines of her home.

In the middle of the night some weeks ago, the good woman was awakened by noises emanating from the downstairs area of her small but charming abode. Clad only in her nightgown, she descended the stairs and approached the source of the commotion. To her great surprise, she discerned the form of a young man who was going through the drawers of her prized sideboard, a piece bequeathed to her by her late Uncle Cole Kuttz of Fargo, North Dakota. Despite her age, Elsie is still in remarkable physical condition, descended from sturdy Scandinavian stock, those dull-witted hoodlums who settled the Northern Plains of our great country. We also know that she has a "can-do" attitude and a heart as big as her imposing breastwork.

With the fury of a tiger defending her cave, Elsie pounced on the intruder's back, knocking him to the floor, and the ensuing struggle is difficult to describe, but suffice it to say it was ferocious. The two figures were locked in a vicious duel, wrestling, biting and choking one another as they rolled around on the rug (the one with the fruit-tree pattern in attractively muted colors). As they fought desperately with each other, Elsie's nightgown was pushed gradually upward until a significant portion of her well-preserved figure was displayed. The struggle continued, and in the melee the burglar's fly was caught on the corner of an overturned table. As a result, his pants were somehow pulled open and slowly stripped to his knees, disclosing an appendage that had become impressively rigid in the heat of battle. Further clawing, grasping and fighting inadvertently led to the unintentional insertion of said appendage in Miss Gunderson's most precious orifice, and at that point the scuffle took on a distinctly different tone.

The young man continued his attempts to subdue our friend, but his efforts were now altered to accomplish this objective by strong thrusts of his new weapon of choice. Elsie, for her part, though little experienced in the activity in which she found herself participating, immediately felt the flush of a newfound sense of receptivity for her opponent. Though she had been beating on the interloper only seconds before, our heroine's heart quickly warmed to the modified encounter. The relationship that had begun as an adversarial arrangement took on increasingly collaborative characteristics, lasting a considerable length of time and punctuated by determined grinding, grunting and loud cries of approval.

After pushing themselves to exhaustion, the pleasantly surprised and entangled pair subsequently fell into a deep slumber that lasted until early morning. Then, in their refusal to believe that such a thing had really occurred between them, the former adversaries repeated the episode just to make certain that they had not been hallucinating. This led to an invitation from Elsie for the happy trespasser to stay a couple of weeks, which he gladly accepted. Her young companion (Studly Stanchion by name) remains a routine visitor to the Gunderson residence to this day, a steady admirer of Elsie's generous nature.

In the course of their subsequent meetings, Elsie learned from Studly (among other things!) that several of his acquaintances were also in danger of following a criminal path and Elsie recognized at this juncture the opportunity to continue her charitable work beyond retirement. She quickly created one of her most altruistic programs, "The Social Club for Wayward Young Men," now a fixture of our community and located in her home. Elsie recruited a select group of her friends (attractive widows and female retirees) to help her make the project a success. Our thanks go out to Elsie Gunderson for getting young males off the streets and providing a location where they can really fit in.

That's my report for this time, guy. How elated you must be to receive my letters. I can only imagine the child-like joy on your face. Incidentally, the last column reminds me of the time in France when I plucked a half-drowned young thing from the high waves at Deauville and proceeded with mouth-to-mouth resuscitation. My personal technique involves free use of the tongue while massaging the victim's chest. This method proved so popular in Frogland that it was included in the next edition of the French Red Cross Manual under the heading, "L'Utilisation de la Bouche Pour Commencer des Relations Sexuelles" ("Saving Girls from Drowning"). This really doesn't have anything to do with the subject, but I like to share pleasant memories as they occur to me.

I was recently asked to address the senior class at the local high school on the occasion of Career Day. It was touching to see the vacuous, but eager faces and exposed crotches of the youngsters before me. I touched on the various vocations that might be of interest and warned that some of those present may be, like Michael Jackson's cosmetic surgery, doomed to failure.

I cautioned the young people to avoid politics, likening it to prostitution, but with less dignity. One of my suggestions was to pursue a career in the field of roadside fireworks sales. For those who contemplated traveling abroad after graduation, my advice was to take along enough money for food, hotels, transportation, bribes, surgery, antibiotics and ransom payments (reminding them that traveler's checks are not usually accepted for this last item) and to always carry their cash in their underwear. Not all the countries in Europe have adopted the Euro, so they will need to have pesos and kilometers in their possession.

I hesitate to close my letter without letting you know how Madge is doing. We were recently at a neighborhood event and though there's always a certain amount of friction at our gatherings, often resulting in excessive gunplay, it was otherwise a pleasant evening. I hid from Madge most of the time by secreting myself in the bathroom, but we were unable to avoid Earl. Physically he seems to be normal, if you consider it normal to trip over the pattern in a rug and suffer unwanted anal events at social functions. But his intellectual capacity has not improved markedly. He still has the cranial horsepower of a small rodent. Squirrels continue to best Earl in the area of tactical thinking. But try not to let it get you down, Grover. It didn't bother you when I exhibited the same symptoms, seeing as how you didn't send a card.

Don't get up. I'll turn off the lights.

Ludlow

19

Hey Grover,

I just finished a couple of screenplays, and I'd appreciate your critical opinion and keen praise, as always.

1. The first film will be the long-awaited sequel to "Lassie, Come Home" and is entitled "Lassie, Get Your Ass Out of Here." The story takes place on the family farm, where the wide porch of the attractive white farmhouse is fronted by flower beds. The plot follows Lassie's life from the beginning and shows little Johnny playing with her as a puppy. The precious little animal develops the habit of running full-speed into the side of the barn and as a result grows up cross-eyed and a little disoriented. Although the family tries to housebreak the dog, Lassie continues to soil the rug and jump up on the dining room table during meals, where she often plants her keister in one of the vegetable bowls. Finally tiring of the antics of their cherished pet, the family kicks Lassie's ass soundly and chases her away from the farm. As the dog runs across the road, it's struck by a sixteen-wheeler and flattened like a tortilla. The final scene shows the family at this tragic juncture standing on the porch, watching the truck disappear over the hill. Little Johnny is scratching his crotch as his father urinates on the petunias.

2. This film is set in the English countryside of the early twentieth century and constitutes a study of country manners of that period. The story opens in 1914 at the family estate of Sir Edmund Bollocks, who is no longer among the living, having been unfortunately decapitated at the knighting ceremony. King George VII (he of the shaky alcoholic hand) was heard to mutter "Oh shit!" at the time. Guests move casually about the house, some of them passing through the large library, where Reginald Stiffrod is dressed in evening clothes, from the front of which protrudes his male member. Although Reginald likes to air his thingy out, he is not a hardened pervert and always asks the ladies present if he may unsheathe his tool before doing so. I hope you take some instruction from this approach, Grover. Luckily, the guests are spared the sight of this particular

embarrassing display, since Lady Bollocks has the thing covered by her frock.

The butler announces dinner and the guests file into the dining room, led by the lady of the house and leaving Reginald alone with his twitching plunger. A quick-thinker, the young man rings for Molly, the upstairs maid, who upon entering the room immediately comprehends the situation. Using several effective and well-practiced gyrations of her delightfully tempting physique, she rapidly reduces Reginald's wand to trouser-tucking size and at the same time demonstrates her appreciation of masculine anatomy. As Molly leaves the room, she is intercepted by the gardener, Wilton Softwunn, a pleasant but intellectually challenged dork who blurts out his love for the young girl. She tells him to go screw himself. Following her departure, Wilton remains stationary for a moment, trying to figure out how to follow her instructions.

Among the guests at Bollocks Manor are Mrs. Amanda Ochs and her husband Bud. She is from old money and new cosmetic surgery. The couple is accompanied by Chester Drors and his lovely spouse, Drew-Pea. Chester inherited his money from a favorite uncle, who was Assistant Deputy Second Secretary to Something or Other in the government. The great Irish poet, Paddy Rump, is also present. His most famous lines are known to every Irish child:

> "As gratefully in Dublin now I stand
> With Maggie Riley's mitts upon my gland,
> My feelings plumb the depths, her motions sweet
> Make me forget we're on a crowded street."

During the meal, Henry, the handsome but addled son of Lady Bollocks, tells the gathering that he intends to join the army and fight the Hun in what will become known as World War One the First. None of the guests pay much attention to him, since they don't know who the Hun are and are only barely aware of who the hell Henry is. Besides, they're busy stoking in the grub and trying to figure out how to get laid. One of the women politely asks who the combatants will be in the coming struggle, and the wealthy, large-bellied barrister, Sir Bumpy Reer, informs her that Uruguay will match their might against Tibet, but only until Guam fields an army in the fray.

The butler, Meadows, listens to every word with a stone face (the result of being pasted in the kisser with a stone). Unbeknownst to the assembled group, he is in reality the treacherous German spy, Krotchkiss von Damenhumper, a major in the dreaded SS (Slobber Studs). His mission is to collect vital military information for whatever Reich is in power at the moment (he does not retain ordinal numbers well), but his personal objective is to dip the old Bratwurst in as many of His Majesty's female subjects as possible.

Miss Lillian Hoggpuss, the daughter of Sir James and Lady Emily (of the regrettably retarded Hoggpusses) is secretly in love with Henry. The young Lillian is blessed with splendid health, which is reflected in the size of her admirable hooters. But her passion for Henry is so secret, she herself is not even aware of it. The script might need a little tightening at this point. Sir James, her father, has built a financial empire manufacturing flyswatters, which were of course not as technically advanced as the electronic versions we presently have at our disposal.

The film achieves its dénouement as the relationships are resolved one by one. Henry goes off to war and as he descends from the truck that delivers him to the front lines, gets his ass shot off. Check him off. Miss Lillian opens a home for orphans, some of whom are without parents. She piously rejects the pleasures of the body to devote herself to her work, except for a couple of times a week when she trolls for pecker at a local pub.

After the armistice, Molly marries von Damenhumper, whom she had known as the butler, Meadows. He reveals to her his Teutonic origins, but she doesn't care because he has a super hammer. They move to Germany, where she becomes a member of the emerging Nazty Party and helps a silly-looking, sexually-dysfunctional retard with a comical moustache come to power. Her husband is killed a short time later in a duel after insulting a female member of German high society, telling her that her breasts taste like Polish sausages. The affronted woman plugs von Damenhumper right through the heart. It's a fine shot that is made a bit easier by special German dueling rules that allow her to tie him to a chair before the choice of weapons is made.

Reginald Stiffrod emigrates to Kenya, achieving the rank of Lord High Flunky of the Bloody Colony. The young man continues his disgusting but harmless pastime of allowing his Willie to flap around and marries a native (Reginald is color-blind). He is therefore accorded citizenship in the local tribe. You may someday also achieve this honor. Some years later, while he is on safari, a charging rhinoceros takes off Reginald's buttocks and most of his pubic section, just as he is about to bag a lion. No one knows why he insists on luring wild game into a sack. With his dying breath, Reginald utters the words that make him famous in the annals of British colonial history: "The beggar got me nuts that time."

For several months, Lady Bollocks dallies almost daily in the sack (no connection to Reginald's safari equipment) with Wilton, the gardener, and after pledging him her eternal devotion, fires his ass and marries a wealthy old squire from Dorset by the name of Master Clive Bayshun. Master Bayshun has made his fortune in the hog-manure market, which is evident from his obvious fondness for porkers and his pungent fragrance. If he had wheels he'd be a garbage truck. But he has more money than scabs on a bronco-buster's ass, so she's able to overlook his shortcomings, which include the size of his Johnson. The new Mrs. Bayshun then re-hires Wilton and the three of them live happily ever after until her hubby commits suicide by plugging himself in the noggin thirty-six times with a shotgun. This method raises no suspicions, since he is known as an excellent marksman. This flick might be a winner. I'm thinking Amanda Luv as the female lead if she's still around.

3. In my third film, an adventure-thriller, two teenage boys find a suitcase full of money that has been carelessly left at a Lincoln, Nebraska, bus-stop. The courier who originally had the bag started to get on the bus, but the door closed on his dork and he dropped it (the suitcase, not the dork). Harley and Jake, the two clever science standouts from Lowen High, take the bag home and shit their pants when they find it contains millions of dollars in large-denomination Bolivian currency. This film *genre* has been done before, but if we get into production we plan to make it a top-quality vehicle (the broads will have really huge chest accoutrements).

The boys rack their brains trying to think of the worthiest charity to which they can donate the money, then hit on the magnificent idea of getting laid. Screw charity, they rightly decide, they're going to get them some female carcass. Unfortunately, while Harley is locked in nut-vacuuming carnal activity with a rented Momma, he casually blurts out the story of the cash. Because of her connection to members of the underworld (through the most charming part of her torso), the lovely lust merchant spills their secret and our young heroes soon find themselves the subjects of lethal pursuit. The mob is after their cans. They are chased, threatened, stomped, beaten, shot at, cursed, and become the butt of lewd comments.

In one harrowing scene, in which a harrow is preparing a field for cultivation, they elude their pursuers by constructing a two-man helicopter using baling wire, aluminum piping, a used circuit-board, some toilet-paper and a three-man helicopter. Lugging two backpacks full of money with them, Harley and Jake make for the Canadian border, which as you know is somewhere in the vicinity of Canada. It's anybody's guess why they choose that objective, since we all know Canada is closed for lunch most of the time. The pals are great science students, but they don't know squat about geography and wind up in Bayonne, New Jersey, where neither of them speaks the language (nor does anyone in Bayonne).

Finally cornered by a group of large, mortality-motivated and tattooed hoodlums in a warehouse on the Albuquerque docks, Harley and Jake use their technical skills to escape withering gunfire by fashioning an explosive device from a bottle of shampoo, a small dog and a condom (which Jake has been wearing). They cleverly manufacture disguises that allow them to pass as Romanian flamenco dancers and escape to a Caribbean island, where they are able to assume further new identities. Harley changes his name to Jake and Jake changes his name to Harley. This throws their pursuers completely off the trail.

The final ending has not been decided yet. On one hand, we can have the young men live happily ever after, sunning themselves and copulating with the local honeys. This would send an uplifting moral message. On the other hand, the kids could tire of the pleasures of the flesh and join the church, where they can copulate with members of the congregation. I've tried it both ways, so I can honestly say I don't give a shit what they do, as long as we can screw the cast out of points in the final contract and the actresses have whopping great fore-sections.

4. This film could be a candidate for the Oscar. It follows the life of Durbisch Pyookski, who is a child from Exkretia Falls, a small town in Estonythuania. Its one saving grace is that part of the toxic waste dump contains a children's playground. Durbisch lives with his widowed mother, who supports the two of them by selling re-tread contraceptive devices and copies of Fortune magazine in the miserable town market. The boy grows up with the determination to leave home and make something of himself. One day when he is fifteen, he realizes that he is twelve and decides to strike out on his own. He tells his mother he is leaving, that he loves her deeply, and that he will return some day to take her away from the poverty of her surroundings. They embrace and she steals his wallet.

Durbisch makes it across the border to the Soviet Union, where soldiers kick the meticulous shit out of him and throw him back into Estonythuania. But the boy is undeterred (and obviously not too bright). He eventually finds his way to Poland. There, soldiers kick the methodical shit out of him and throw him back into Estonythuania. On his third try, he finally makes it all the way to East Germany, where soldiers kick the unqualified shit out of him and throw him back into Poland. Durbisch is getting tired of this crap, but he is not one to give up. He conceals himself in an oxcart full of manure and traverses East Germany. Upon his arrival in the West, some soldiers kick the shit out of him just for the hell of it. They must don gas masks for this project.

Durbisch eventually gets work shoveling manure in the stables on a small farm, where he falls in love with the daughter of the owner, Brunhilde Dorkschneider. After many months, Durbisch gets up the courage to tell her of his feelings, but the poor bastard only speaks an Estonythuanian dialect that is a cross between vile nostril discharge and a sore throat brought on by pubic-gland swelling, so she kicks the unmitigated shit out of him. Durbisch, however, is blessed with great determination (and poor cerebral circulation), so he has come to expect this kind of treatment.

His hard work finally enables him to escape his demeaning condition. He steals some money and Brunhilda's panties (while she's wearing them) and takes off again, heading West. Regrettably, Durbisch has a miserable sense of direction, so he winds up back in Poland, where soldiers capture him. He tells them to spare themselves the effort this time and kicks the shit out of himself, pounding his head several times with a rifle butt and banging his nuts against a metal post. Now he has to start all over again, but this time, he is successful in reaching the Munich waterfront. He sneaks aboard a ship just before it embarks, and in five days finds himself back in Estonythuania. His mother kicks the shit out of him.

The next time, though, Durbisch is not to be denied. He builds a raft out of short lengths of railway track, lashed together with chains, and paddles across the bay to Helsinki, where soldiers help him ashore and welcome him to their free country. The local administrators give him a room in the reception center, provide him with a little money, find a job for him in a hotel kitchen, and arrange for a group of Finns to kick the proper shit out of him.

Durbisch works hard and earns passage on a freighter headed for the States. He is given quarters in the cattle hold (where the cattle avoid him), and after a difficult crossing arrives in New York harbor, where the passengers, many of them refugees like himself, stand in awe at the sight of the Statue of Liberty. Unfortunately, Durbisch misses the spectacle because his ass itches and since he is more than a little disoriented from having this part of his frame pummeled so frequently, he has trouble finding his ass on the first try. Therefore, in his attempt to alleviate the irritating sensation, he inadvertently scratches the ass of the sturdy Siberian peasant woman standing next to him at the rail, who proceeds to kick the resounding shit out of him.

By this time, Durbisch is thirty-seven and has learned a few words of English. The first phrase he commits to memory is, "Please not kick shit out of me!" which is spoken while cowering under the nearest piece of furniture. The young man, still full of promise, obtains labor of the most menial kind, filling public restrooms with human waste, but he saves enough money to enroll in night school. It's hard to believe, but by sheer will, Durbisch overcomes every obstacle and graduates several years later from Columbia University, achieving the highest honors with an advanced degree in

Estonythuanian with a minor in cowering. Our hero receives his diploma at the commencement exercises and elatedly runs out of the university grounds shouting, "I did it!" In modern Estonythuanian, this is rendered by "Winnsheeld foggin opp!"

As he stands on the sidewalk, a passing jogger knocks him into the gutter of West End Avenue and he is run over and mashed extensively by an uptown bus. Durbisch dies two hours later in the hospital. He might have survived, but the medical staff preferred to kick the shit out of him. The film's message is eminently clear: "Keep your Estonythuanian ass out of our neighborhood. We have enough trouble with members of Congress." I'm toying with possible titles. I kind of like "Manure Without a Cause," but I'm also receptive to "How Green Was My Lunchmeat."

Let me know which of these projects appeals to you the most. I can cut you in on some of the profits if you let me decide how the points are awarded.

Your next of kin
(kin you imagine that?)

Ludlow

20

Hey Grover,

Thanks for the DVD of your singing group. It's amazing how modern technology can make you guys seem almost average. I don't know what sound you were aiming for, but if it involved chickens and exposed wiring, I'd say you were successful. Ha, ha, ha! I wanted to let you know that my arm has healed well. I can now scratch my crotch with my right hand, although I get a lot of funny looks in the supermarket when I take my pants down to do it. Otherwise, I've had a busy time. Because of my in-depth experience in the world of espionage and washroom sanitation, I was asked by a secret government agency to do consulting work for them. I can't tell you the name of the organization, but I'll give you a hint. Their initials are the "Central Intelligence Agency." Keep that under your hat. The agency asked me to review their procedures and also develop new codes to replace those they were using based on the Peanuts comic strip.

Contrary to popular belief, it's possible to construct codes that are unbreakable. One well-known approach is where two people have access to a copy of the same book. The message consists of digits which refer to the page of the book and the number of the word on that page. This method is completely secure, one drawback being that it's necessary to have the book with you at all times, which is cumbersome when you're on the toilet. The choice of the book is also important. One should avoid encyclopedias of more than 1,000 pages, any references to Donald Trump, and Romanian agricultural novels.

The code I invented is number-oriented, but merely requires two people to memorize a single sentence containing all the letters of the alphabet. Each number in the message then refers to a specific letter. An example is: "**I caught the quick brown fox jumping that lazy dog, Rover**." But my favorite is: "**The quick-witted Jerry Boxer has a fairly vile and mean-looking zit on his pecker**." You get the idea, I'm sure. I've used a variation of this code for several years to communicate with Monika Broadstern, who appreciates any reference to peckers, although she originally wanted the key sentence to include the word "large."

I also told the agency to abandon the use of a "dead-drop" for passing information and replace it with a "drop-dead." This procedure entails implanting an encoded message (using a dart gun) in the anal passage of a person who has been shot and placed in an agreed-upon location. The individual retrieving the body removes the message from the deceased, using rubber gloves or a long-handled rake. Naturally, one should avoid recruiting friends or close relatives for this operation, except for special circumstances. Someone like Earl would be a perfect candidate.

Since "e-mail" messages can be easily intercepted by satellite, I developed a new process that I call "S-mail." This method makes use of a slingshot. One simply beans the recipient in the gourd with a hollowed-out ball containing the message. It also works if you get him in the nuts. One real advantage is that the shooter can fire from an open window high up in any building and therefore doesn't have to wear pants. Cell phone messages are vulnerable to interception. For that reason, when two people need to converse on these devices, they should meet in close quarters and remain a maximum of two feet apart. The back seat of a car is a good place. One can use a closet or a bathtub equally as well.

The agency asked me to look into their use of lie-detectors too. No lie. It became immediately obvious that their procedures were woefully inadequate. As you know from your numerous indictments, technicians place electrodes and blood-pressure cuffs on the subject—arranged on the chest, arm, palm of the hand, and sometimes the scrotum. There are several other anatomical areas that also betray an attempt to bullshit. Sphincter flutter is one of the most reliable indicators of fibbing, so a long thermocouple needs to be inserted in the tailpipe ("bunghole" to you technophiles). About two feet should be sufficient. Regrettably, it also announces the fact that one must take a powerful dump, but it's still worth inclusion. In addition, a simple door-bell buzzer should be attached to the nuts. The tests I have run show that the testicles swell up when bragging about getting laid, but tend to shrink significantly when lying. With most guys, these two indicators are invariably connected. Lastly, the operator should be armed with a ball-peen hammer to clock the lying bastard when the needles start jumping.

We discussed the issue of recruiting foreign agents, and after three minutes I submitted a clever plan to supersede the procedures that were in place. Drawing on my own successful experience in the field, I showed those present at the meeting (a security guard, two mail-boys and a guy from the boiler room) my sure-fire approach. During my operative days, I used to place harmless ads in the local newspapers, such as "How would you like to become a spy and rat on your government?" The responses rolled in, and after sending the majority of the applicants back to the institution from which they had escaped, I put together a crack team of real bird-brains. That was the strength of my plan. Nobody would suspect these turnips. Of course, it wasn't easy to read their reports, which invariably contained references to household detergents.

One of the more sensitive items on any agenda is the method for funding agents in place. Here is an opportunity to improve the case officer's financial situation. My personal preference was to haggle for an enormous amount, allow the agency to negotiate a lower figure, and then betray my agents and keep the cash. It often interrupted the flow of information, but I received awards for the best-furnished safe houses in my operating area, including well-stocked liquor cabinets and dirty magazines. I admit it took a lot of courage on my part to send a couple of our relatives to an uncertain fate, but sometimes sacrifices are called for.

In the meantime, I can fill you in on the news from our humble slum. We're in the midst of celebrating the city's 20th anniversary. In order to escape the festivities, which consist of open city-council sessions, a street fair, concerts by the town brass band, an ass-kicking tournament and small-firearms events for the kiddies, we decided to get away for a few days. We heard the band once by mistake a couple of years ago. It consists of a saxophone, three mandolins, twenty-six tambourines, and a proctologist's tool. The only song they know is the Albanian national anthem. If you ever need thirty simpletons to rid the neighborhood of unwanted animal life, you might want to book them. You'd have to stay indoors. Another reason to take the trip was that a gigantic mudslide swept through our town a couple of days ago and washed away several hundred residences. So now the streets are blocked while they clear up the mud and put it in Earl's driveway.

We booked ourselves on a bus tour to the north, with stops at some McDonalds restrooms and a body shop in East Badger Butt. The drawback was that several of our neighbors were on the same bus, including guess who? Yup, Madge and Earl. During the excursion, Madge cornered us and told us the story of their lives. You can imagine how thrilling that was. Earl's family originally came from West Virginia. His father ran the local feed store back there in the early part of the 20th century, played the organ in the Lutheran church and helped keep the local whorehouse out of financial difficulty. Earl was encouraged to take music lessons and chose the clarinet, but he gave it up after he caught his wiener between the reed and the ligature and the fire department had to come and cut the instrument out of his pants. To this day, Earl is frightened by double-reed instruments. He switched to the bassoon, but the family made him quit when the neighbors complained that he was goosing all the girls with it. I can testify to the fact that a bassoon is excellent for this type of activity.

The family moved to California and the old man got a job in an airplane factory as a welder and never looked back. He was enamored with welding and welded wherever he went, often while driving. He had the habit of welding various household articles together (like the couch and the toilet, or the floor lamp and the stove), which made some aspects of housework difficult for his wife and embarrassed visitors who found themselves seated next to bowel-related appliances.

Earl didn't quite distinguish himself in school. On more than one occasion he was sent home from grammar school for fondling himself under his desk. The teacher is reading a poem to the class and Earl's got his mitts down below, choking the gopher. There's also a class picture that was taken when he was ten, showing him with a finger about five inches up his nose and his other hand in his fly. He hasn't managed to break either of these disgusting habits, although the digit in his nose-hole is the lesser of the two evils. Earl's wand tends to protrude at social functions, stubby as it is, and it was especially humiliating for the Ladies of Salvation Club at the church supper last Friday.

I explained before that Earl has gradually lost cerebral traction over the course of his life, but he really started to go downhill about six years ago, according to Madge. One day, he was trying to dress after stepping out of the shower and he got his big toe caught in the elastic band of his shorts. He hopped a couple of steps, then fell and dinged his noggin a hard one on the edge of the bathtub. Hasn't been the same since. The tub either. He became instantly devout and likes to listen to the Hour of Prayer on the radio. Now he talks about the Christian responsibility to save the polar bears and wets his pants a lot.

Madge comes from Syracuse, where her parents owned a sewage recovery business and they wanted her to take it over so they could retire to Anadarko, Oklahoma, where they had distant relatives. But somehow she became drawn to surfing, which is not overly popular in Syracuse. She took off for California and met Earl at a surfer mission in Santa Monica called "The Chapel of the Cool Wave, Man." They were both skunked out of their gourds from drinking pumpkin juice laced with Mr. Clean and when they sobered up were somehow convinced that they had performed several kinds of sex on each other—or somebody. Not that either of them knew what it was. Anyway, Earl proposed because he thought it was the moral thing to do, so you can see that his cranial switch has been stuck in neutral for a long time. Madge had never been touched by man or animal up to that point, and she shed her common sense in one superior rush of idiocy.

A couple of years later, she had a near-death experience during breast-reduction surgery, which still left her with one of the largest set of balloons in the hemisphere, only slightly smaller than her ass. A vision of Saint Elvira wiping her butt with a preferred-stock certificate convinced her that her future lay in the financial markets, so following a crash course at the brokerage firm of Dewey Kiepyer Cash, Madge was turned loose on an unsuspecting public. She never shuts up, and she got people to invest just to get out of the wind. Madge's voice sounds like a snow plow being dragged down a blackboard and has been known to make quadriplegics try to sprint for the hills.

Most of the dolts on this trip could be used for purging your intestines. The couple sitting in front of us was Piston DePanz and his wife Pearl-Down. They brought their son Krapptun, who played Dvorak on the tuba the whole way. The lovely Mrs. DePanz is seldom disheveled and she looked reasonably sheveled on this occasion, as well. If I leaned forward at the right angle I could peer into the front of her blouse and count her bust barrels. Piston gives off a strong fragrance that suggests he passed away several days ago, and he spent a lot of the trip giving his nose a liquid honk. He told me that he was trying to decide what to have done with his remains when he finally goes to that big snot-ranch in the sky. Most of my Christian charity was used up by that time, so I suggested that he consider doing the community some good by having his remains cremated and used to fill a pothole.

Lena Genstawahl sat behind us and practiced non-stop flatulence during the entire safari. The air turns chartreuse when she lets a ripe one loose. These were genuine badger shots that could necessitate the evacuation of entire cities. I don't know how she does it without major hemorrhaging. She squeezed off a hisser, a ripper, a croaker, and a cheek-flapper, and then capped off the program with a monumental cargo blast, the kind with real solids in it. It's actually pretty impressive if you appreciate that sort of thing. Lena and Polly Shurshooze always travel together. They're two widows whose late hubbies volunteered for a euthanasia study last year, and it's easy to understand why.

Holdiss Pleeze sat across from me wearing his green seed corn cap (he's not what you would call keenly sensitive to fashion rules). He sat there raking his crotch the entire time. He scratched his stones so hard I'd be surprised if he still has two of them left. Stepford Sludge signed up for the trip at the last minute. We pulled into San Luis Abysmal about noon and learned that our motel had been condemned while we were on the road. The tour guide, a little blond named Fawn del Pekkurz, got us rooms in another place not too far away. It looked as if it were next on the list to be condemned, along with Earl. They had a lutefisk buffet lunch laid out for us that looked like desiccated squirrel cadavers that had been run over by a truck. I heard that sometimes this stuff doesn't taste too bad, but the statistics are not on your side. The only alternative was "poulet alla cacciatore de jardinière à la piña Rodriquez con testosterone." I declined the food and confined myself to liquid nourishment.

We took this trip partly for entertainment, most of which takes place on the bus. At one stop, a guy from our group, Chunky Dumper, had a few too many vats of barley juice and got into a contest of fisticuffs with a small child on the corner of "Walk" and "Don't Walk" near the penal compound. Chunky has a short temper and always tries to pick a fight no matter where he is. Talking to him is like interrupting a bear taking a shit. He's the type of guy who'll sit in Soldier Field in Chicago rooting for the Green Bay Packers and then wake up in the hospital and wonder why a dozen tubes have been inserted in disgusting parts of his physiology. Chunky's biggest problem is that he loses every fight he starts. The kid he picked on this time was only seven, but managed to knock Chunky loose from several teeth and his jock strap too. Some of us carried him to his room and took the occasion to pound his ass some more. As we left, one of the maids came in and walloped him in the nuts herself.

We stopped in the city by the bay for a day. Gretchen and I had a room to ourselves, but everybody else had to bunk together because they were on the cheapskate plan. Forty-eight people in a double room. We tried to elude the group, but most of them stuck to us like bird crap to a windshield. A bunch of us wound up on the terrace of a Fisherman's Wharf restaurant, where Earl stood up to give a toast and fell over the railing. It took about twenty minutes for the gathering to finish the vote on whether to have him rescued, but first we decided to order dessert. A couple of fishermen finally snagged him by the scrotum with a gaff and pulled him out of the briny. He complained the rest of the night about the excessive humidity.

We made it to wine country the next day, but the revelry went downhill just south of Sonoma. We were approaching a country intersection and could see a big truck barreling toward the highway. It didn't slow down as our bus came to the crossroads. Stepford Sludge said, "Ya know, it looks like that truck's gonna hit us." Holdiss said, "Yup." And at that moment the two vehicles met, illustrating a number of interesting laws of physics, the main one being that a high-speed collision between a truck and a bus produces a pot-load of sparks.

Thankfully, the front of the bus received the major portion of the impact. It spun around a couple of times and finished up about a hundred yards into a bean field. Lena soiled her pants, but I think that was well before we sighted the truck. Ellen Emmopee wound up flat on her back in the aisle with her dress up over her head, exposing her best feature (I think she pulled it up herself), and Earl dropped his Johnson, which he had fetched into the open to check for signs of rust. He has to use the Braille method. He can't see the thing over his gut. The truck driver honked his horn, waved once or twice, and continued on his way. It's a California driving pattern.

I'll let you know how it all worked out. Right now, I'm late for my autopsy class. You'd relish the excitement here, but it might be too much for your sensitive nature. You were always so soft-hearted. I remember how you had to fight nausea whenever I caught my genitals in a door and it raised blisters. Looking back, I always felt you were suspiciously close to the door when it happened. Fortunately, blisters don't form anymore when I do that. Earl's doing reasonably well, although with so much medication he's experienced massive sphincter shrinkage, along with butt swelling. It made him cross-eyed, but the high-voltage shock treatments could clear it up. If that doesn't work, they'll probably dunk him in sheep-dip and perform an ass transplant.

The eternal fraternal,

Yo

21

Hey Grover,

I realize I left you in suspense with my last missive, so I want to clear that up. After the wreckage from the collision between our bus and the truck had been cleared away, we finally made it to our destination in the wine country. The bus was still operable. Only part of the top was ripped off. Our driver suffered a badly scuffed ass and a dislocated ear, so he had to be replaced. A couple of his fingers were also broken, because he had them wrapped around his tool at the moment of impact (perhaps a considerable time before that).

Stepford Sludge got behind the wheel, gave his crotch a healthy scratch and tromped on the gas. The old Stepper does not have what you would call a keen feel for steering dynamics. After wiping out a couple of billboards, several mailboxes and a cat, he took off and sideswiped a row of parked cars, along with a baby carriage. The child cursed us profoundly. We pulled away with the assumption that somebody would come along and find the driver lying beside the road and take him to the appropriate medical center. Tried to get his mitts off his Johnson, but he had that thing in a death grip.

Our group was booked into one of the foremost luxury resorts in the area, Uncle Irv's Grape Ranch, a combination winery, slag-disposal heap and sewage-treatment facility just outside Genital Junction, California. This is the heart of the wine country, packed with free-loading scumbags who crowd the tasting rooms, pushing and shoving, to sample the effluent. No one can accuse me of that behavior, but I'm glad you weren't there. Uncle Irv himself welcomed us as we fell out of the bus. He's an unsightly gentleman of advanced years, a few rungs above Earl on the beauty-meter. He wore one cowboy boot, a seven-gallon hat and jeans with the ass ripped out. His fly was open as well, which struck a sympathetic chord with Earl.

Irv's wife is the former Miss Dee Spott, who is pretty rough on the eyes too. If I had to choose between spending time alone with her or an overflowing bedpan, I'd opt for the stainless-steel edition. Her father is the tyrannical Des Spott, a certified all-around viper from West Palm Beach, Georgia and Mule-Snot, Idaho, where he's still wanted on an ass-scratching warrant. It wasn't his. You may have heard of him. His favorite trick is to pass the collection plate at church and when members of the congregation reach for it, he yanks it away to reveal a pretty darn good stiffy. The sheriff's wife especially wants to get hold of him. Some of the more brazen older ladies take up to a quarter of an hour to let his tuber loose, so during the service two organs are being played at the same time.

Irv and Dee ran into each other at a Perverts Anonymous meeting in Elk-Stool, Arizona. They had each been trying to sneak across the border into Mexico, but the authorities kept kicking their asses and throwing them back into the U.S. Those folks have standards too. At the meeting, the theme for the evening was "International Bathroom Etiquette." It's a subject you might want to pursue now that your nostril-drilling is under control. I've been to a couple of meetings and came away with some solid information concerning drive-by sexual practices. We also heard lectures on how to start a rectal inspection business, the production and enjoyment of geriatric pornography, and do-it-yourself catheter insertion. A well-known author, Holyer Noze, read from his recent book, "Letting Go: Drop Your Wand and Take up Knitting." Another writer presented two of his latest releases, "Responses to the Passing of Gas: How to Cope With a Posterior Muzzle-Blast, a Point-Blank Partial-Pooper and Other Ear-Popping Eruptions" and "Genital Extrication: Penis-Dislodging Techniques and the Use of Firecrackers." I send this information to a deviate of your stature, because you share my appreciation for sophisticated aberrations.

Uncle Irv wants to expand his wine business. His product is made from grapes that have been left to rot by other wineries and are thus already well along in the fermentation process. Once you get past the burning sensation in your mouth, the searing fire in the throat and the high-voltage wallop in your belly, I find it rather cheeky, with a subtle overtone of muskrat droppings and hand-grenade fragments. The finished stuff may not appeal to the masses, but as you know, there is a specific repugnant segment in this country that will consume anything if it's cheap or free. Test markets in Rahway, New Jersey, and the prostitute quarter here in town point to fair potential sales. A side-feature of Irv's product is that it does a good job of removing warts and rust, along with discolorations that sandblasting can't touch. It's best to drink it slowly, otherwise it gives you jock itch. Uncle Irv uses it to run his tractor too.

He threw a lunch reception for our crowd and served some of his vintage dry-cleaning fluid, cautioning us to avoid spilling it on the furniture. I figured it would improve the decor, which had obviously been designed by a pack of legally blind, escaped transvestite convicts. Irv's missus was wearing a fashionable outfit made from a beaver's foreskin, and Earl let a few drops fall on her dress. She was naked in no time. Not an inspiring sight. Lena Genstawahl thought it was a signal to play, so she began to disrobe, but Stepford and Holdiss put her duds back on her as fast as she took them off. Dee quickly recovered from the mishap and donned another garment, then entertained us with a pleasant Beethoven composition on the snare drum. Her dress this time was made entirely of shells (artillery shells). I looked around as she performed several rim-shots on the drum and saw Piston DePanz in a corner doing the same thing to Fawn, the tour guide.

The buffet featured stuffed cabbage (stuffed with more cabbage) and the finger food didn't look overly appetizing, since our host had his fingers in it. That's the technique Piston was using with Fawn too. Gretchen and I had wisely packed our own lunch. In his usual manner, characterized by a lack of cerebellum-particle motion, Earl chugged down fourteen glasses of Irv's select concoction in just a couple of minutes, subsequently consigning himself to a spot next to a potted plant and the beverage to the pot.

The Prussian Princess and I had laid out some cash, so we got the presidential suite, which was nicely appointed with all the comforts of a first-class hotel (most of the stuff had been stolen from one). The rest of the unfortunates were on the "Shanty-Town Plan" and were shown to the bunkhouse, where several travelers complained about the loud snoring and belching. And they hadn't even turned in for the night yet. The next day we were bused on a tour of local wineries. When I say "tour" I mean everybody skipped the guided portion of the visit and rushed to the tasting room, where they proceeded to sample all the slop they could get their beaks around. They even emptied a dozen bottles of Windex and a mop bucket. Earl got excited and messed his pants. None of these wizards is mildly conversant with the intricacies of the thinking process. When we returned from the fifth winery, nobody could get off the bus, so one of the high points of the trip was watching the staff haul the drunks off and stack them in the yard. You recall my exemplary reserve and admirable good taste, so you will not be surprised to learn that at every stop I first sniffed the rich bouquet of each offering and swished a small mouthful around to separate the various taste notes before downing a five-gallon pail of whatever the hell it was.

Our entire bunch ate together on the veranda in the evening. It was a merry time, with most of us flinging pieces of deep-fried flounder at each other and playing grab-ass. I got in a few good gooses on Irv. The cook was a one-eyed, left-handed former Irish hunchback jockey with a hare-lip and no hair. We later learned that he was wanted in Ohio for stealing painted lines from the Interstate. The guy had previously been kicked out of the racing business for using his whip on the horse's privates in the home stretch. The first time he resorted to this maneuver his mount won the race by seven lengths, but unfortunately at an adjoining track.

The food was served in a raccoon sauce, some portions with the raccoon still in it (and an unhappy animal at that). Gretchen and I passed on the chow and unwrapped our sandwiches. Our waitress was the former Mamie Sikk, a pleasant, large-chested woman from Sri Lanka who suffers from some kind of sexually transmitted limp. Earl thought he recognized the symptoms and took out his wand to check for sure, even though the only organ he's seen since 1961 is the Wurlitzer in his family room. To check his crotch, Earl requires a mirror or the help of innocent bystanders. But they have to have good eyesight. The last time we were at their home, Madge played a medley of Buddhist fight songs on the organ. Also an A Cappella arrangement of Stravinsky's "*Mon amour est profond*" (You Gave Me This Rash).

The waitress had her blouse open down to her belly button and she kept shoving one breast in Chunky Dumper's ear as she served the baloney casserole. He bitched about it, as he does about everything, but we noticed that he didn't let go of it right away. Under some conditions the woman might have been erotic, but it turned me off when I saw her whoppers dangling in the soup (two bowls on opposite sides of the table). Her globes did give the porridge a pleasantly nippy flavor, though.

Irv confided to me that he likes to sit out on the veranda and shoot cats when they come into the yard. When things are slow he drives around the neighborhood and plugs the little bastards wherever he can find them, even entering private homes. Good for Irv. I got the impression that he goes for overkill when I saw him camp in a rocker with a twelve-gage shotgun and a box of hand-grenades. Dee said his score was up to 25 (that week) and he'd also managed to take the starch out of a few passing cars while he was at it. That explained the automotive parts I saw strewn along the highway when we pulled into the complex.

Somebody must have called the coppers, though. A sheriff's deputy drove up, got out and handed Irv a sack full of cats. One old broad in our tour named Wilhelmina Skunkthumper screamed at Irv, something about the barbarity involved in murdering cats, and he turned the shotgun on her. He pulled the trigger, but the weapon jammed and the woman was miraculously spared. I kicked her in the ass. She shouted to her husband, who was standing nearby, "Are you going to let a perfect stranger do that to me?" He said, "Not when I can do it myself!" And he kicked her in the ass.

Now, you wouldn't expect to see a lot of moose here in the wine country or most parts of California, but according to the natives there's been an incursion of the brutes recently. They're not so unique in Maine or North Dakota, but tend to stand out pretty much in more populated areas like Miami or Los Angeles, and they can play havoc with the local industry. They roam around and wipe out acres of grapes and fencing at a time, perhaps attracted by the high sugar content in the grapes and the aroma of outhouses. Most people don't realize that sometimes a moose can suffer from mental problems, just like humans. It causes them to do peculiar things that you and I might not notice, but would be immediately obvious to another moose. For instance, they roam around at night and look in bedroom windows, then issue a high-pitched laugh when they see some guy with his ass hanging out or porking a babe. They also like to scratch their asses on automobile mirrors and urinate on front porches. In case you want to learn more about this phenomenon, there's an excellent book on the subject by Dr. Tyne E. Wattsiss of the Carnegie Water-Mellon Institute entitled "Our

Friends, the Moose: What you Should Know About These Mangy Bastards." You may have already come across this information in the course of your moose research.

Anyway, the next day we all went out on a moose-sighting expedition. Irv and Dee came along, since they know where the best animals hang out and have a smell that attracts them. Chunky Dumper started bitching as soon as we alighted from the bus, which made sense because he stepped in a huge pile of moose dung. He grabbed the first moose he could find and belted it one in the snoot, but the animal won the match by kicking him in the nuts. It elicited loud cheers from our group. Chunky never learns. We found a seat in the bleachers, and a couple of Irv's employees chased a herd of moose past the seats. I had never been close enough to smell one of those things before, but I can't say I want to include it in my daily schedule. I'm having enough trouble with Irv and Dee (let's not even talk about Lena). We soon tired of the whole thing, especially the part where some of the shaggy creatures stopped and took a crap right in front of us. When we trudged back to the parking lot, we found a moose on the bus. It didn't bother me, but Earl had to sit next to it and the moose seemed irritated.

That evening we all sat around a big fire and listened to some of the staff sing fermenting songs. It was sort of an amateur talent night. Polly and Lena did a little tap dance on the gravel while stark naked, and Chunky tried to juggle three fence posts. He got them up in the air all right, but he missed them when they came down and they crowned the dimwit. All three of them right on the gourd. You should have heard him whine. He shut up when Stepford popped him in the snoot with a statue of the Baby Jesus he carries around. Dee played a few up-beat numbers on the French Horn by the little-known composer of "Melodies To Urinate By" that you hear now and then in public restrooms. Not the ones you frequent. I'm talking about indoor facilities. Dee handled the fugue portion of the composition fairly well, but one of her jugs got stuck in the spit valve and that lent a squishy shading to the coda.

We learned later that the bonfire was actually a conflagration that began in the bunkhouse and consumed several other outbuildings, but that didn't dim the merriment. We kept drinking and goosing Lena. Ellen Emmopee said Bliss Terdass started the fire when she tried to dry her diaphragm by holding a match to it. It must have been painful. She failed to remove it before commencing the operation. The bunkhouse burned to the ground and it meant that everyone had to sleep on our tour vehicle except us. A couple of the folks asked us to share our lodgings with them. We told them to get their asses on the bus. Uncle Irv put them up in the barn for the next couple of nights. He didn't have to remove the livestock. They got one look at our bunch and exited the structure in an orderly fashion.

Stepford did a pretty good job of driving on the way back, which wasn't easy for him, because Polly kept trying to sit on the gear shift. We stopped for an overnight in Bung Canyon, just outside of Bakersfield. It's pretty desolate. The list of attractions is limited. This is the place you'd head for if somebody told you to go pound sand. They hold the international garbage-removal competitions in Bakersfield every year and it's doubtful that they get rid of any of it after the prizes have been awarded. I understand that a team of rubbish wranglers from Oxford, Alabama, came away with top honors in the finals this year, beating out a squad from Lagos, Nigeria, who had brought their own refuse.

We all had rooms in a local boarding house. I had booked the presidential suite, so our stay was pleasant. The others were given keys to the remaining habitations and our host left it to the group to decide who slept where. By this time they had gotten to know each other pretty well and decided to all bunk in the same room.

It's good to be back after having our cultural horizons expanded. I'll let you know when the next trip is planned, but I'm not sure you could take all this refinement in one dose, especially if Lena is on the bus again and her rumble seat is in good working order. On the health front, a call just came in from Madge. Earl is in the hospital again. It seems his latest illness, probably aggravated by the consumption of Uncle Irv's top-of-the-line, progressed to a malady known as Drippy Dungbox. This condition often produces defecation arrest, along with pooper pimples and a warped wiener, so he has to be monitored closely. We visited him yesterday, and he was alert, playing with a toilet paper tube. Earl may be in the final percentile on the IQ list (just before some strains of bacteria), but in his defense I should mention that he was disadvantaged by the gene pool that was available from his relatives. Earl's maternal grandfather, Mumford Smerd, was imprisoned at an early age, I think it was eleven, for urinating in church during a high mass. It might have gone unnoticed if he had not been standing on the altar at the time. The priest, who was trying to celebrate communion, had a hell of a job getting the kid's foot out of the wafer dish. When you take this into consideration, Earl didn't have much of a chance, so let's show a little tolerance for the dimwit loser.

Not everyone is as fortunate as you are to have had a positive example like me. You recall that I developed quickly and was changing my own diapers at the age of three months, whereas you lagged behind and were only occasionally publishing short stories. Rather than refer to you as retarded in the family, we preferred to use words like "limited" and always thought of you as well-meaning in a kind of useless way. I can now confess that I was frequently annoyed by your trick of surreptitiously soiling my diaper, but I forgave you long ago and, anyway, they're easier for me to change now.

Thy Scribbling Sibling,

Ludlow

22

Hey Grover,

I never sit still for a moment, a trait you undoubtedly admire, so I've opened an adjunct business to my detective agency. I recently received my on-line PhD in Psychotherapy from the South Hampshire Institute of Technology. I'll send you a sweatshirt with the school letters on the front. Now I can combine my ace investigative experience with my understanding of the human psyche, cerebral cognition, perceptual receptivity and local nut cases. I went through a period of intense study, immersing myself in the deepest subjects of the unconscious, such as:

The Unsound Mind
How the Mind Sounds
Other People's Unsound Minds
The Mind's Influence on Bowel Trajectory
Workings of the Mind
Workings of a Mind That Isn't Working
Abnormal Psychology
Normal Abnormal Psychology
Abnormal Abnormalities
Normal Deviation from Abnormality
Madness and its Applications
Therapeutic Use of Rodents
Restraining the Demented
Being Restrained by the Demented
History of Whacky Folks
Diagnosing Sex Offenders
Diagnosing Female Sex Offenders
Advertising for Female Sex Offenders
Cocktails with Female Sex Offender
Female Sex Offenders and Clothing Removal

Armed with my diploma, I began my career in Medicine, Psychotherapy, Marriage Counseling and Foundry Work. It's easy to find a ready clientele of serious psychos. In California, you can yank them off the street by the dozens. Anyway, it wasn't long before my business was booming. My very first clients were a couple considering divorce who wanted to make one last try at reconciling their differences. Phil Trayshun was a short, thin man with a weak chin, a protruding hairline and a receding butt. His wife Penny was a nice-looking piece of womanhood, dressed to show off her charms, the front two of which were exceptionally extensive. I asked Phil to describe their problem. "My wife is a big flirt," he said. "I know she's not serious and she doesn't mean anything by it, but it bothers me when she's so suggestive. She says she's just having a little fun. I wish she'd stop." During her husband's speech, the young Mrs. Trayshun ran her tongue over her lips, smiled at me, and mouthed the words, "Wanna do it?"

"Can you help us?" Phil asked. I suggested a twelve-step program that included meditation, frank discussions between the two of them, and frequent follow-up solo visits on Penny's part. Phil thanked me for my input, and the two of them left my office hand in hand. As she followed her husband to the door, Penny squeezed my heinie, slipped the top of her dress off one shoulder, and gave me an inspiring view of an appetizing piece of breastwork.

My next appointment was with Bud Leit and his wife Donzerly. He was an unattractive male in his sixties and she was a real dog. Woofer to the 3rd power. She explained that their marriage was in jeopardy because of the voluminous, putrid gas that Bud randomly released in copious quantities. His cannon-like colon explosions prevented them from enjoying any kind of social life. Their friends and acquaintances had put up with Bud's mustard shots as long as they could, but eventually found it impossible to ignore them. I hoped he could hold it in for the duration of our consultation. "I can't help it," Bud protested. "I have to detonate or I'll faint." The Missus allowed that when Bud detonates, everybody else faints.

My challenge was to alter Bud's vapor trail to something more substantial, morphing it into a product he could eject without insulting the environment. Drawing on my extensive technical background, I prescribed a compound I had developed some years ago for weighting down corpses that tended to inconveniently rise to the surface. This is a concoction consisting of large chunks of gravel, concrete blocks and splinters from old bowling balls suspended in rat mucous, to be drizzled into the offending orifice with a turkey baster. The total solids of the mixture exert a gravitational force that results in massive intestinal stimulation, producing a prodigious manure festival.

Of course every medical application has its side effects (in this case massive cardiac stoppage), but the gas is substantially reduced either way. The major drawback is that "toilet back-up" sometimes occurs and clogs the porcelain. The advantage is that it gets the final product into a form you can get your hands on. Another marriage saved through chemistry.

My next meeting was in my capacity of private investigator. The attractive, middle-aged lady's name was Fridgitte Krevuss, and she asked me to find her husband, Buster, who had recently run off with his secretary, Melonie Frunt. "He's been cheating on me with her for more than six months," she told me, "and I decided to confront him. He admitted everything. Men are such bastards!" I cleared my throat and the good woman reddened. "I'm sorry," she said. "I'm so embarrassed. I don't mean all men are bastards. Probably just you and Buster." I took no offense and asked her if she knew where the fugitive fornicators might have gone. "I have no idea," she admitted. "He cashed in a big insurance policy, cleaned out our safe deposit box, sold several million shares of fertilizer stock and left with the last roll of toilet paper." I asked her if she were financially able to get by on her own (trying to determine if she could afford the butter cookies I so desperately needed). A quick peek up her skirt convinced me that she could handle the underwear portion of my requirements.

"I'm lucky in that regard," she said. "My father was Peter Zlimp, the head of Girlie Products Corporation. He made a fortune importing plastic insertional objects and other sex aids from a third-world country (New Jersey) for women on the go. His biggest seller was the 'Power-Poker,' a ten-inch model with a harness that allows it to be used all day while moving around. I'm wearing one now. I have the mansion in Brentwood, a *résidence secondaire* in the south of France, and a portable potty in Romania."

I assured the good Mrs. Krevuss that I would locate her wandering spouse (I always tell them that), explained my fee schedule and butter cookie requirements, and added an offer of assistance whenever she wanted her Girlie instrument changed. She blushed, kicked me in the shins, unwrapped a fresh "Power-Poker" and handed it to me. My cookie jar runneth over. I got a description of Buster Krevuss and his adulterous piece of buttocks and put the word out on the street that I was looking for them. This was accomplished by drawing the information with chalk on the sidewalk in front of the local pizza joint. I indicated that a big reward was offered.

To my great surprise, Buster's secretary, Miss Frunt herself, called me the next day. "I want to claim the reward," she said, "because I know where we are." I surmised that I was not dealing with a post-doctoral student here. I kept her on the line so I could trace the call. Sure enough, it was coming from my phone. I asked her to meet me at an abandoned warehouse next to the Senate Office Building in Washington D.C. She hesitated and suggested we get together at a Starbucks in Bang-Her, Maine. We finally settled on "The Tortilla Trench," a dubious eatery in the slums of South L.A. I arrived early and found a seat in the back of the restaurant near a dumpster.

I knew it was her the moment she walked in the door. As I rose to greet her, I stumbled and was able to break my fall by grabbing her chest jewels. She giggled and said, "You men are so clumsy. Everybody does that." I asked Melonie why she was after the reward. I was under the impression that she was in love with Buster. "Are you kidding?" she laughed. "He's a dim-witted jerk, just like all men." Then she blushed and said, "That was indelicate. I mean just you and Buster."

She went on to tell me she had worked her scam many times. First she got a job working for a rich man. Then she started doling out her pubic goodies to him, and the guy parted with large amounts of cash while stoking her full of the product of his excitement. After a few weeks, Melonie got the chump to buy her an apartment, spent a few days wearing him out, and then left him quicker than you can say "*Donauschiffarhrtsgesellschaftskapitän*" ("later"). She sold the apartment, collected whatever reward was available and started the cycle all over again. Now she didn't seem so dumb. "How about you?" she asked me, "Do you have a lot of money?" I admitted that I was just a working stiff. "How stiff?" she inquired. She told me where Buster was hiding, and I gave her my card:

Confidential Investigations, Marriage Counseling,
Internal Medicine, Professional Underwear Research

When I told Mrs. Krevuss where she could find her hubby, she was delighted. She made arrangements to visit him herself and began sharpening large knives. The good woman paid me off (adding a nice pile of under-clothing) and told me to give my informer the reward. It was just a few thousand bucks, but Melonie took the reward and gave me half. A nice gesture. She also let me stumble against her chest again. I hung on for about ten minutes until she told me she had to go.

I've described some difficult challenges, but one of my most frustrating cases was just a week or so ago. The police were hot on the trail of a repugnant cretin who was exposing himself in local shopping malls. In a brilliant sleight-of-hand display, he whipped his antenna out, and when a crowd of women formed around him, he stole their underwear. I should try that. I was at the stationhouse when the cops brought in several dozen shocked and pantyless ladies to go through the mug book. None of them could identify the perpetrator. They had all been concentrating on his equipment, which they described as "engaging." A couple of them asked. "Do you have any Johnson shots?" I handed them some of mine (I carry them with me for situations like this), but it only elicited snide comments.

I recognized this guy's M.O. (Mangy Organ). I figured the culprit was Virile Wiener, a real hard case and a person not to be trifled with in a game of "Simon Says." Wiener had an extensive rap sheet. Starting when he was very young, he had been arrested for consorting with cocker spaniels, urinating in a stolen bucket, and flattening cats with a hammer. The fuzz currently wanted to talk to him about his role in making long-distance calls and passing gas into the telephone. Wiener's early life had been a real mess. His father was still in prison, serving a sentence for counterfeiting one-dollar bills by erasing the zero from tens. His sister sold crack (of the anatomical variety), then got her act together and was admitted to MIT, where she received an advanced degree in erectional studies. With a substantial amount of capital, mostly in small coins, she was able to open a successful chain of embroidery franchises. There was one thing the family was too ashamed to admit, however—the fact that Rush Limbaugh was a distant relative.

We decided to check out some bars in the seediest section of town, so I wound up in a strip joint with a couple of the cops. The girls were doing their best to reel in tips by sticking their mostly naked butts in our faces. When one of them danced by, my buddies tucked some twenties in her G-String. She plopped her can in front of me, and I ran my credit card down the crack of her butt. An hour later, I was staked out in a vacant lot. The jokers at the stationhouse are always pulling stuff like this on me. Luckily, a group of kids came by and untied me from the stakes so I could begin my vigil. I was located across the street from Wiener's old Boy Scout Lodge. It was a long shot, but lo and behold (or hold on below), I saw Wiener come out of an alley and approach the front door. He had changed his wardrobe. He now wore pants. By coincidence, so did I.

I considered catching up with Wiener and holding his hand, but discarded that option, since it might have made him suspicious. In a few moments I knew where he was headed—to the mall. Thank goodness. Now I could get some last-minute shopping done. I've been looking everywhere to buy camouflage clothing, but I can't seem to find it. When we were inside, I saw that he was headed to an area with high female traffic density. Women of every age were rushing about, determined to get to the dildo sale. I beat Wiener to the spot and, in a selfless effort to save these fine examples of womanhood from embarrassment, cranked out my own Johnson and slashed it proudly around in the air. The women continued to hurry past me, some of them laughing out loud. I turned and spied the object of my pursuit standing on an escalator with his dong pointing due north. Females rushed from every part of the mall, screaming and cheering and holding their underwear out to him, many of them running right by me and giggling. One older woman sneered.

On the second floor, he leaped into an elevator, but I was quick enough to dart into it before it began its descent. There I was, alone with one of the nastiest, most dangerous wand-wavers in the country (or at least my neighborhood). In your town he would have gone unnoticed. We eyed each other threateningly, but before he could throw a punch the doors opened, so I was able to get up out of the fetal position. As he lunged to exit the elevator, a large crowd of women pressed forward and asked for his autograph. But you remember my incredible quickness. I grabbed Wiener by the collar (or did I collar him by the wiener?) and the doors slammed shut on his hog, which was still full-masted. His reaction was fairly subdued. He screamed and messed his pants. He almost messed mine. I pushed the button to keep the door closed. Slapping the cuffs on him, I kicked his ass a few times, then dragged my prisoner (with a badly scuffed dong) to a waiting patrol car. That was the end of it. Except for thirty or forty women who attacked me and called me vile names, kicking, swinging purses, shopping bags and, in one case, a small dog.

I may not have told you that we were at Earl and Madge's place for Sunday dinner. The food is always breath-taking and it gives us a chance to experience a world of pathetically low IQ's (not always mine). Madge's voice would knock the rivets out of the Brooklyn Bridge and Earl now believes he's a bunny. At one point he interrupted Madge to tell her he wanted to say something and then asked her what it was. And damned if he isn't sick again. I don't know how one guy can come down with so many symptoms at the same time. He sprained his scrotum getting up from the crapper on Tuesday and his testicles swelled up like softballs. Earl subsequently went through a period of freckle loss. We rushed the big guy to the emergency room (stopping for burgers and fries on the way) and tests indicated a chronic rectal twitch and convulsions of the sphincter, caused by a crusty anus. My good buddy's health has been vulnerable since he was a kid. As a teenager he suffered from premature ejaculation and then late ejaculation, which finally resulted in premature lateness. It's a wonder he's still alive and I wonder if he is.

Your good neighbor, not geographically speaking,

Ludlow

23

Hey Grover,

My freelance research into technical issues continues, as you would expect, and I have several projects underway that could change the course of scientific history—or at least the flow of sewage. My laboratory is in a former twelve-hole outdoor toilet facility outfitted with the latest scientific equipment, including a solar-powered ass buffer. The most important undertaking on the agenda will be to determine how abnormally high underwear temperature is related to sex-gland enlargement and a sudden craving for pastry. This study is funded in part by the Pancake Church and Cosmetic Surgery Spa (Las Vegas Synod) and the International House of Plastic Marital Aids.

Before going into detail, I should inform you that Earl has passed on. We chipped in to buy him a shotgun and a suicide manual, but he passed on it. He refuses to condone the indoor discharge of firearms unless squirrels have made their way into his home. We wish he would be as resolute in the area of unwarranted intestinal discharges. A bushy-tailed invader actually got into his place a few days ago, so Earl grabbed a ball-bat (34" Andy Pafko model) and knocked down one entire living room wall trying to clock the little darling. Also took out two bookcases, Madge's patio lounger and the growler. She was perched on the latter apparatus at the time, so you won't be surprised to hear that she suffered massive fractures to her pride and her heinie.

The adventure unfolded when, after trying for ten minutes or so to nail the furry creature in the living room, Earl spied it slinking into the dumper-compartment where Madge had installed herself. He wiped the living-room plaster off his face, swung his Louisville Slugger, missed the beast completely and pasted Madge a good one where the sun don't shine. When the cast comes off, she's going to rip him a pretty painful replacement. The squirrel was observed raising its tail disdainfully and pointing its hindquarters in Earl's direction while smirking.

At any rate, my work has created a whole new dimension in my life (and my shorts). I feel that I'm contributing to the overall knowledge of the world at the same time that I get a gander at some really nice butt-region (my research subjects are women who are engaged in the field of horizontal commerce). I regret that you live so far away, otherwise I could use your assistance. Your keen sense of order would be a welcome contribution to our work. I need someone for thermometer duty, involving their insertion in long rows of keisters and recording the readings, which are sometimes difficult to decipher because of what we call "excrement cling." If you decide to come and help me, you can sleep in the lab. We'll rig up a bed for you in the latrine and make sure it's high enough so the rats can't get at you.

There's a lot for you to do on weekends too. The local Condom Museum is worth a visit, as well as the community sinkhole that opened up a couple of years ago and swallowed a bus that was headed for the cathouse. Fortunately, only members of the city council were riding it that day. The new town fathers haven't gotten around to funding repairs, so buses keep disappearing in the damn thing. You'll have a skateboard at your disposal so you don't have to worry about transportation as you take in the sights. Naturally, you will want to attend church while you're here, and I've made arrangements for you to get a good place in line at the drive-through (in your case, skate-through) sacrament window. If you choose to enter the sanctuary, watch out for ladies who like to goose the male worshipers. The older women are especially aggressive. They grab you by the rear and try to yank your pants down. I attend all three weekend services and try to catch a weekday mass as well.

There are plenty of tortilla joints around here where you can take your meals, a couple of them outside the slum areas. We can talk about compensation when you arrive. Bring toilet paper and rubber gloves. If you can't find them, boxing gloves will be okay. It would be great to collaborate with you again. Speaking of your steady hand, I always meant to ask you about your propensity as a catcher to give me the signs with your middle finger. But no matter now.

I subsequently refined the move you taught me when you showed me how to exit a moving vehicle, and this allowed me to create the powerful hook-slide that I used with such great success in my baseball career. That maneuver, combined with the quickness of a greased weasel, made me the head-first base-stealing scourge of the prison team. That is, unless my wand fell out in mid-flop (or flopped out in mid-fall). If that happened, which was all too often, I repeatedly came up about eight feet short of the bag. You get the picture. As for my stealing skills, they began in the locker room before the game when nobody was looking, but I excelled on the field too, as I said, tearing up the base-paths. I was pretty upset, though, when they told me I couldn't keep a base after I had stolen it. It was kind of embarrassing, standing there on third with the second sack under my arm. I asked them to show me that regulation in the rule book, but they were adamant.

My sliding ability also contributed a lot to my popularity later on, after I was kicked out of Boston for urinating in the mayor's golf bag. It was my bad luck that he was carrying it at the time, but it still stands as a record in New England for urinating from a speeding golf cart while putting. As you would expect, my ability to leap from respectable heights and land with uncanny accuracy assured my entrance into a desirable level of European society, although it wrecked a lot of furniture and put a definite bend in my Johnson. It's hardly noticeable. I'll show it to you the next time I see you. Many of the young sweeties I associated with had the cute habit of switching off the lights when I was in full flight, but the uncertainty of the landing added a rather furtive excitement to the exercise. Sometimes I was alone when the lights came on again.

It was especially dangerous if the woman was married, but it's hard to get it out of your blood once you get started. You may want to reconsider your position on that policy. One particular scene stands out in my mind. I was hard at work on Manuela in Barcelona one night (my vote for "nifty butt" of the year) and just about ready to fetch my freight into the barn (if you get my meaning), when we heard a key in the door and she announced, "*Dios mio! Es mi esposo!*" Freely translated, this is rendered as "Holy shit! It's my old man!" or it could be "I think you should get off!" Depends on which dialect one employs. Either way, it's not what you want to hear when the train's about to leave the station, if I may use a graphic Spanish idiom. The situation was fraught with bowel-gripping uncertainty. Only my lightning-fast thinking, supersonic speed and extraordinary ability to disguise myself as a floor lamp saved my can (but deprived me of Manuela's).

One other difficulty occurred the time I was parked with Collette (a clear second place in the nifty butt category) not too far from her home in a suburb of Paris. In my haste to ground my club, so to speak, I somehow got one foot entangled in the elastic band of her undergarment and shoved it all the way through the leg-hole, introducing it into the steering wheel and causing the horn to start honking. Due to an elevated level of adrenaline, I had forgotten to shut off the ignition, and my warm-blooded partner's gyrations managed to knock the vehicle into gear. I tried to extricate my foot from her unmentionables, while attempting the opposite procedure with what I will modestly describe as an imposing erectile event, when the conveyance began moving and somehow rolled down the lane, coming to a jolting stop against Collette's front door. Can you imagine?

At that precise moment, a sudden cramp caused my free leg to stiffen and my foot made contact with the doorbell. Collette's hubby answered the door, and he erroneously assumed the worst, just because she was sitting on my mid-section with her bloomers down around her knees. This type of thing can befall anyone. I don't know why some men jump to conclusions with minimal evidence. Anyway, he disappeared for a split-second and returned brandishing a hunting rifle that incited sphincter-tightening anxiety on my part. In the course of my travels, I have had various weapons pointed at me, primarily for reasons of mistaken identity, so it is with some level of expertise that I judged this particular armament capable of significantly curtailing some of my vital functions. The sight of the firearm did not, however, limit the workings of my bowels.

Occurrences like this can ruin an otherwise fine day. Collette's spouse pulled her from the car, at which time I took the opportunity to give her tail a good-bye pat. The guy raised his rifle. I found myself looking down the barrel of that menacing musket and couldn't help but admire the stellar condition in which he maintained it. I was about to ask him what brand of oil he used, but decided to shelve the question for later (if there was a later). Collette thought fast (disrobing and thinking were always speed talents in her case) and threw her arms around monsieur's neck, thus preventing a clear shot. He threw her aside, but it allowed me the few seconds I needed to jam the car into reverse and back down the lane at full speed, taking out fifty yards of fence and an outdoor excretion shed. I also crushed a row of mailboxes and two cats, so the evening wasn't a complete waste. It's funny how these two episodes stick in my mind when there were so many others that didn't go as well. But you have to be philosophical about such setbacks. There's an old Norwegian expression that's very appropriate here. *"Demm Rayndeers allatyme skrewin onna frun steppes"* ("The hell with it!").

But back to the matter at hand. If you don't want to come out here, I understand. Your toilet brush collection demands a lot of your time, I know. Earl has asked several times if you could send pictures. But you should really consider using paper. Your duties as a crossing guard must keep you busy too. Incidentally, you may want to check your fly before installing yourself on the corner. The front page of your local newspaper had a picture of you pointing the way for children with a rather nasty-looking appendage. The caption reads, "Look, no hands!" Things like that are welcome news here. In the event that you can't free yourself, I will be forced to make other arrangements, although it will be disappointing. I've lined up Slamm Dunque, one of Earl's pals, as a fall-back position. The only drawback is that he wants to keep the thermometers. The Slammer is as bright as you would expect. In fact, he has an IQ only slightly higher than a rutabaga, meaning he does Earl's tax returns.

Earl plays poker every Friday night with Slamm, Ivanhoe Innkling and Duncan "Pitcher" Kookeeze, the former Dodger hurler. If somebody remembers to bring the cards. "Pitcher" started one ballgame back in the sixties, beginning and ending his career on the same magnificent afternoon. His best pitch was a knuckle-ball. It was referred to that way, because he invariably threw it inside and managed to paste the batter on the knuckles. He hit the first fourteen batters he faced, walked the next twenty-two, and then served up a grand slam. The manager was so pissed he left the poor bastard in for six innings just for spite, which lasted five and a half hours. His spite lasted much longer.

Members of the grounds crew were the only ones who stuck around to see the visitors pull out a close one by the score of 214 to 1. The only run scored by the home team was when "Pitcher" came up, swung at a change-up that bounced four feet in front of the plate and took a hard one in the pubic section. The ball caromed over the first baseman's head and the official scorer marked down one run, although nobody was on base. He was later advised of his error, but said he didn't give a shit.

Ivan was also involved in the baseball business. He's a former sportscaster, having received his sportscaster's certificate from the Underbrush, Mississippi, School for the Cranially Maimed. He used to broadcast night games on the radio for the Evansville, Indiana, "Bananas" back before the installation of stadium lights. Nobody could see much of the contest, but it didn't make any difference because nobody came to the games (or tuned in either). Ivan made it up as he went along while downing copious brewskys, never actually attempting to observe the contest. Anyone listening to his description would assume that the team knew which end of a bat to grip, which was a dangerous assumption.

Their best hitter on the team drew two walks during the year and was the only one to reach base all season. He was promptly picked off first base both times, mainly because he didn't know where second was. The Bananas once went through an entire season with only one win, their most successful year, when the opposing team came down with a monumental case of the runs and had to forfeit, but not before contaminating the visitor's locker room with a foot-high layer of diarrhea happenings.

Pitcher and Ivan ran into each other at a Losers Anonymous meeting in Jersey City, North Carolina. At the time, Ivan was collecting unemployment checks from neighborhood mailboxes and Pitcher was earning a meager living as a professional target for nuclear weapons engineers (the same guys who invented the 8-Track cassette). The two new friends started hanging out together, drawn to each other by a common low level of belfry current. They decided to start a business together supplying fertilizer to landscaping firms, but had to give it up after a few months because they couldn't shit fast enough and were spending way too much money on Ex-Lax. It makes sense that they somehow gravitated to Earl. You know the old saying, "Birds of a feather crap in the same hatbox." Or something like that.

Earl was working for the city at the time, cleaning flagpoles and other Eastern European immigrants. His poker games with the gang are a little different, as you can imagine. Earl bets the house if he has a three, but it works out because if anybody bets at all, the other two usually fold. They frequently forget to ante up before a hand anyway. What a bunch of losers. I sat in on one of their games once and only lost two hundred bucks. I later tried to teach them to play bridge, but they wouldn't jump.

Your ever-loving $#*& in the @+%,

Ludlow

24

Hey Grover,

I may tend to be loose with the facts on rare occasions, but sometimes a little inaccuracy avoids the need for a detailed explanation. In Russia, they obviously had me confused with a popular ballet star, because everybody called me a Bolshoi artist. My grace and lightness have always been recognized. We're off to the United Kingdom tomorrow, the home of the Queen, with whom we will probably have tea at Buckingass Palham or Windsel Castor. The invitation should come through any minute now. I used to fly from Paris to London about once a month, and during my many forays to the island realm I aspired to a knighthood as a reward for not being caught nicking merchandise or merchandising knickers. But I didn't even receive a dayhood.

During one of my visits to the royal shack, as I knelt before Her Majesty, I thought she was going to knight me. But instead of a sword, she grabbed a long-handled mace and raised it above her head. Holy Shit! She was going to bust me a serious rap in me noodle. With some effort, her guards wrested it from her and kicked me in the ass. Then she kicked them in the ass. Lizzie obviously never forgave me for advising her to pull up her socks at a reception back in the seventies. Anyway, there could be a little problem getting into the country, but my usual backup plan will have a submarine drop us off the coast and we'll land by rubber dinghy. Before you panic, I want to assure you that I won't forget to fill you in on every exciting moment of our trip. Your undying interest in my activities goes back to our childhood, when you used to betray your curiosity with cute expressions like "Shut up!" It warmed my heart, I don't mind telling you. It's still great to hear from you. Or about you (on the police frequency). There are many magnificent sights in England. I just can't think of any right now, but I'll describe them to you in my next communication. I plan to check out the fish and chips shops (buffalo type).

Before we leave, I want to tell you about an exciting new project. In my capacity of film writer, actor and producer, I'm bringing a wonderful movie to the screen, and filming has already started. I managed to get funding by talking Earl into signing over his house and his car to me, in addition to his pension, his savings and his Social Security checks. When Madge finds out she's going to extrude a flagstone or two. I hope we can show a little profit before they throw her out in the street.

I had to promise Earl a part in the film to get the money, so I altered the screenplay to include a horseshit character who gets thrown off a cliff in the first three minutes. We've already shot his part, and he wasn't completely satisfied with his lines, which consisted of a loud scream on the way down and a healthy grunt when he hit the rocks. I told him he could holler, "Oh, shit!" too. That seemed to placate him and we were able to finish his scene with only eleven takes. I wanted to get it just right, with the Earlster landing face-first. He kept complaining— something about multiple fractures, but I made him keep at it. We wrapped the last take in just four hours and somebody lent him a bicycle so he could get to the emergency room.

One of the hurdles to getting this thing into the theaters is the rating board's decision, those bastards. They're a little hesitant to give it a family rating, one of the reasons being that my organ is prominently featured in most of the scenes. Their main objection is that it has a bend in it. You know, the one I mentioned last time. I keep telling them that it lends character to a colossal but otherwise boring appendage. The board also expressed concern about the use of full-frontal nudity at the wedding ceremony and in the open casket at the wake. I offered to deflect attention from the bare anatomy in both scenes (which are vital to the development of the plot) by requiring the congregation at the church and the mourners at the viewing to be naked too. It also saves on dry-cleaning costs.

The film basically stars me and two less significant characters. I was successful in signing Slug Ishkohlun and Pyoobik Rasch, a couple of future stars who have already made their names in the sex-education and kinda naughty film business. These flicks are used in California to teach pre-schoolers about the pitfalls of having sex with people who are not family members. My story follows the life of a handsome young physician (you can already picture me in the role). The hero, Sawlid Horrsmeet, is from Mule Sack, Oregon, who becomes interested in a surgical career while dissecting live cats as a young boy, often sewing them back together again in interesting but abstract combinations. After completing his medical education at Harvard (the Harvard, North Dakota School for the Testicular Deprived), he builds a successful breast-shaping franchise in New York, while also off-loading trucks at the Fulton Fish Market. At the same time, he conducts research into the consequences of massively backed-up public toilets, for which he is awarded the prestigious No-Bell Prize for "Achievement in the Field of Excretion." The award consists of the implantation of an explosive device in an acquaintance of his choice and a certificate suitable for framing.

Sawlid realizes after a few years that he is burned out, suffering from booby-overload and a rancid mackerel smell, so he is determined to change direction and give something back to society. He intends to devote his selfless energies and cat-slicing skills to the disenfranchised, and maybe score some butt at the same time. Therefore he leaves his lucrative practice on Central Park West to bring hope to the forgotten lower classes—the poverty-stricken natives of Peoria, Illinois. I thought about choosing our town here, but I didn't want a lot of homeless people getting in the way. Little does Sawlid realize that the level of female beauty in Peoria (and your neighborhood) is several notches below that of unwashed donkeys. He's lucky he didn't set up shop in New Jersey.

But Sawlid is not deterred (I think deterred means "too bright"). He opens a clinic on the third fairway of the Slapaway Golf Course, placing it right in the middle of the dogleg so golfers are forced to hit a low, shanked, chunked, hooked, slicing roller around the building. Nobody has been successful with this shot, so the building takes some pretty hard licks in the course of a round. That's when I thought of you. There is a pivotal role in the film for you if you want it. Besides fetching sandwiches and doing duty as my stunt-double in some of the more dangerous segments, you would be perfect in a couple of romantic episodes. You only have to disrobe eight or ten times. We can use digital enhancement to get the correct dong size. I'm not sure you'd be right for the rape scene where a disgustingly filthy homeless person is attacked by five lust-crazed supermodels. I may take that one myself, even though you would need no make-up. Maybe you could just stand to one side and hold my pants.

Sawlid is aided in his medical endeavors by Trewley Staktt (Miss Rasch in a heart-tugging role), a cross-eyed and cross-nippled nurse whose proclivity for promiscuity is only exceeded by her nymphomania and her sensational prat. A feeling of mutual attraction develops between them, primarily ignited by her abundant frontal danglers, and they abandon themselves to the pleasures of the flesh, lancing several large boils. She is from Warsaw and he is a Formula One racing fan, so they often use the "pole position," alternating with the Hungarian placement method.

But one of the dangers in Peoria (as you know) is malaria, followed by mail-order diarrhea, athlete's crotch, chronic tight-underwear, short penis, rat's breath and the creeping crud—in that order. Sawlid is exposed to an epidemic involving all of these maladies. It usually befalls everyone who comes in contact with the natives. He also develops agonizing testicle trauma. The good doctor lies for days in a bed (he never tells the truth about sleeping accommodations). His cot is thankfully covered with rat-netting (coincidentally from your condo complex), but Sawlid sinks into a comma, sadly deficient in the art of correct punctuation. He almost succumbs to the spotted fever and an itchy ass. In a display of astonishing courage, he performs surgery on himself with a weed-whacker, a sphincter-stretcher and a cross-cut saw and manages to lengthen his Willie. The fever breaks, the bed breaks and he breaks wind, but his recovery is complete, minus some foreskin.

Upon returning to his mission, the young doctor discovers that Nurse Staktt has run off with a no-account bum who has been passing himself off as the governor of Illinois and getting away with it because he claims he has already served several prison terms. You could be right for this part. Sawlid is understandably crushed, having fallen into a trash compactor. But he carries on with his work and in a ceremony presided over by Statler Moome he is recognized for his achievements and awarded a small certificate, oddly unsuitable for framing. The keynote speaker is Brad Pittsburgh, who is out on bail for the occasion after being arrested for adopting six kids from North Korea. Pittsburgh calls the doctor by the wrong name and erroneously describes his work as "knocker management." At this point, young Dr. Horrsmeet gets word that his surgical skills are needed in Alaska. A bush pilot has crashed while trying to deliver a load of bushes, burying his ten-engine Fokker in a glacier and his ten-inch Fokker in the female co-pilot. She is a former circus acrobat and oragami expert who in the heat of passion (and menopause) somehow twists the guy (played by Slug Ishkohlun) into several complex geometric patterns. The poor man needs an immediate tonsil and appendix transplant, and Sawlid is the only one who has any experience with the operation, because he performed it once on a distant cousin while skydiving.

With spare tonsils and an appendix under his arm, he heads for Badger Snot, Alaska, fifty miles north of Point Barrow. This is a shame, because it puts the town in the Arctic Ocean, whereas the pilot is near Anchorage. Sawlid's progress is slow due to his need to hitchhike, but he is eventually picked up by a ninety-two-year-old ex-bathroom attendant driving a sixteen-wheeler, who is familiar with his evacuation research. The man slows down to forty and lets him off in Indianapolis. From there, he is able to sneak aboard an Arctic Circle Airlines flight disguised as a passenger.

This is not necessarily a good thing. I've flown Arctic Circle Airlines and can safely state that the only thing those dopes are capable of doing is maybe closing a hangar door if they have written instructions. But Sawlid is determined. He learns that Anchorage is the proper destination and takes over the plane's controls, which, typically, goes unnoticed by the crew, along with everything else in their vicinity. Our good doctor makes a belly landing in Juneau (striking a baggage-handler in the belly) and slides up to the gate with minimal damage to the plane, if you don't count a fuselage engulfed in flames and the lack of wings.

Sawlid rents a dogsled and seats himself in the vehicle. After a couple of days he realizes that he has to pull it himself, because the rental agency is out of dogs. But the man never gives up. He traverses the Ural Mountains, passing through Cabo San Lucas, and makes his way to Anchorage just in time to save the pilot from undergoing a funeral with no witnesses. The ground is too cold to dig a grave, so they yank the deceased's trousers down and seat him in an outhouse, hoping that in the spring thaw he will slip through the hole. Sawlid asks around to see if anybody wants new tonsils or an appendix, but everyone claims to possess the proper number of these items. He doesn't want them to go to waste, so he anesthetizes a stray moose and replaces its organs with the ones in his pocket. The animal feels inconvenienced. I'm thinking of calling the movie "The Maltese Moose" We'll see.

"Dr. Horse-Meister," as the people in Anchorage call him, makes preparations to leave. He has dogs this time, but no sled, so he has to ride one of the canines bareback. This chafes his groin, but allows him to brake with his feet. To congenial shouts of "You dumb Ass!" from the townspeople, Sawlid whips his dogs into a rapid departure. They run into each other for a while, then race down the mountain, sadly colliding with a cross-mountain bus. Ten of his dogs are wiped out, leaving him with only twenty-three others. But they are enough to get him on the road. His navigating skills are faultless. Sawlid simply charts a course parallel to the railroad tracks leading to Seattle, watching passenger trains rush by at regular intervals. He stops overnight on two occasions, once at a quaint, rustic inn run by a Bulgarian cactus farmer, where the doc and the dogs are given a room that thankfully contains two beds. The only other guests are Paris Radisson and a guy from Bayonne. Another time, he finds shelter in a moose-mangling plant just outside Caribou Crap, British Columbia, where he sits in on a few moose-mangling procedures. Back on dry land, Sawlid turns the dogs in to the rental agency and visits a high-voltage rock bar to get some well-deserved rest. It's there that he meets the most appealing woman he has ever known, a motorcycle babe with enormous bowsprit handles and a tendency to forget who's burrowing in her caboose area. Can't get any better than that. She sports several tattoos, all of which feature arrows directing the observer to her lower body area, so the doctor is almost certain he's in love. He knows he's in love with her lower body area.

This brings back fond memories of a girl I knew in Holland when I lived there. Marlees van der Bakkyord was a warm-blooded little blonde number who fancied short skirts and long tussles in the sack. We immediately sensed a mutual attraction based on carnal desire and the ability to pay for it. But I was fair and didn't charge her more than my usual fee. She pursued me shamelessly, often getting me out of bed in the middle of the night by calling my neighborhood bordello. Marlees showed me how to tap dance wearing wooden shoes and introduced me to her uncle, Horace Koller, a Calvinist minister and author of smutty children's novels. He took me to a couple of coffeehouse gatherings where he read from some of his latest medication labels. Marlees cooked dinner for me on occasion, using every pot and pan in the kitchen, mostly to kill insects.

I want to take this occasion to mention my loathing of motorcycle gangs here in California. These are guys with small crotch equipment who are trying to convince the universe of their masculinity, but who are actually suffering from massive insecurities because their meat isn't long enough to swing:

"I've got a nine-million cc-Bazooka-Bullet and it'll go 800 miles an
   hour."
"Yeah, but you can't piss past your shoes."
"But my ride makes a lot of noise."
"So does your ass."

I like to pull up beside a bunch of these bikers at my favorite intersection and gun the engine. They take off like a rocket and I turn the corner. They think they've left me in the dust, but I take a shortcut and wait for them at the next traffic light. Their heads swivel around and half of them fall off their bikes when they see me. I lower the window and say, "You should trade that slug in for something with speed." Drives 'em nuts. Now their Willies are really tiny.

"Hey man, what have you got under that hood?"
"A twelve-gage over-and-under nuclear-scamper double-honed torpedo
   blaster."
"Cool, Man! Where did you get it?"
"I put it together myself."
"Wow! Can we see it?"
"Screw you, I'm late for my ballet lesson."

The same to you, Grover,
   Luddy

25

Hey Grover,

This letter reflects some important philosophical musings that occur to me as I sit here in England on the banks of the Argyle and watch the river barges run into each other. Today, we're going to the London museum where they have the heads and arms on exhibit that are missing from all those beat-up statues in other museums. As I change my underwear (changing into what I was wearing three days ago), thoughts of a profound nature dart through my consciousness, and you too will probably be led to consider issues of greater significance as you read and flush.

I have been blessed with the opportunity to see many parts of the world. My work in the fields of pubic research and second-hand sewage reclamation has taken me to numerous exotic places. I've scaled some of the highest peaks in the mountain ranges of Indiana. I've watched the sun come up in the Moroccan desert where those playful Bedouin bastards left me. I've danced the night away to the music of Aye-bin-Sikk and his All-Female (except one) Castanet and Hedge-Clipper Orchestra. I've harpooned guppies off the coast of Mindanao and rescued attractive damsels in the Middle East from a life of horrible virginity.

I've studied to be a painter (beginning with kitchens and bathrooms), eventually commissioned to do a portrait of the Imrah Kahn family in Peshawar, making me sort of a Kahn artist, get it? Ha, ha, ha! I've raced across the Argentine pampas, trying to duck those damn *bolos* the gauchos keep throwing. If you've ever been pasted with one of those things you won't forget the incident, but you do seem to forget a lot of other stuff. My pony that day was an especially feisty mount and tried to throw me several times, but the boy who was leading him around the carnival ring didn't let him go too fast. I've visited the *souk* in Istanbul, that sinister indoor market where astounding bargains are to be had. I was able to pick up a nifty second-hand nine-iron that had just a few scratches on it. Only cost a buck. I'm sending you a catalog. In addition, I was able to purchase, with discount coupons, a full-length Turkish female gown with a full-length Turkish female still in it.

I've visited the former Soviet Union, thanks to Natasha, whom I met in Paris. She was a real looker, with hooters out to here (photo follows) and traveling with the Moscow State Circus in those days. Her lion-taming act was sensational and consisted of the big cats doing acrobatic maneuvers, several of them flying through the air at once. She wore a provocative outfit consisting of a skimpy bikini over an ankle-length fur coat. Natasha's approach to training the beasts was somewhat different from the norm. Some performers reward animals with food, but if the lions didn't do what she wanted, Natasha kicked them in the testicles. A close observer would notice that several of them suffered from a definite limp during any given performance.

I've helped the French Foreign Legion defend a fort in Tunisia from packs of frenzied door-to-door Avon salespersons. I've helped perform drive-by autopsies in Albania, often on deceased individuals. I've dined with members of royalty in Bysikklestan (after they've been deposed and tossed in the clink), and I've almost had my ass shot off in a bedroom in St. Louis.

I've dealt with political leaders in sticky situations everywhere, including my run-in with the mayor of Kyoto. Utterly groundless suspicion on his part, but for some odd reason he got the notion that his lovely Frau-Mayor-San was practicing extra-curricular carnal activity. Some guys really get a porcupine stuffed up their butts over nothing. I don't know who the rat bastard was who tipped him off, but I can swear on a stack of women's underwear that I was simply paying my respects and trying to help her get a chocolate bar out of the pencil-sharpener when my clothing accidentally fell off. Gravity can be a person's worst enemy.

And through it all, I lived by an ethical creed that I developed during a short prison term in Shooshinestan (another case of mistaken identity) when I was locked up for relieving myself in a public place—on the hood of the prime minister's car. You'd be astonished how narrow-minded some foreigners can be when it comes to vehicular urination practices. Anyway, I got out by agreeing to pay a fine of 40,000 Dinhars ($2.75 in actual cash) and take the Prime Minister's daughter dancing. Sheherazit wore a veil (thank god) along with her XXXXXX-Large outfit, and we did the Charleston and the Minneapolis to the strains of Mozart's Requiem, although she wasn't easy to steer. It was sort of like moving a home freezer around that had a grand piano strapped to it. Around midnight, her veil fell off, but I quickly scotch-taped that dude back in place. You've never seen a case of "bad-face" to match this one. Try to picture a football stadium full of armpits struck by a meteor. Her father dropped strong hints about matrimony, but it would have entailed seeing her naked and actually touching her, so I declined by subtly leaping from a third-floor balcony. I landed on two old ladies and a cat, so no harm was done (to me, anyway). If you ever consider tying the knot again, I could set you up with her. The fact that she is relatively undiscriminating would count in your favor. Her sister is also available, but only on weekends, so the marriage would not be endangered.

One of our neighbors, Defford Kayschunn (everybody called him "Deffy"), exited our ranks just before we set out on our trip, called to that celestial corral up yonder. He had suffered from heart problems, high blood pressure, a flapping butt-valve and severe gas spells for years, so it was no surprise to the community to learn of his passing. I should also mention that his departure was accelerated somewhat by being run over by a flatbed truck (delivering a load of flat beds to the local Sleep Emporium). In California, the pedestrian has the right of way on secondary streets, but it's not a good idea to issue challenges to drivers. You never know what frame of mind they're in.

After he retired from his job at the town dump, Deffy spent a good part of his day darting out in front of moving vehicles and when they slammed on the brakes, he'd pop back up on the sidewalk and laugh like a hyena. He picked the wrong guy this time, though, an ex-con who wasn't taking any shit. It seems the fellow's parole officer had reprimanded him for picking his nose and wiping his fingers on parole documents and other report forms, so he was in a downcast frame of mind. He chased Deffy along the sidewalk and down an alley and nailed him in the bread aisle of Ozzie's Open-Air Food Mart, just about where the rye meets the whole wheat. The Deffster might have survived the trauma, but as emergency personnel were wheeling him to the ambulance, a speeding squad car pulled up and collided with the gurney. Tossed poor Deffy up onto the hood, where he entered his final agony. None of the witnesses faulted the truck driver, even though he was observed plumbing his nostrils throughout the entire incident. The driver of the squad car received a commendation for rapid response time and for knocking Deffy off the hood with few well-placed rounds from his sidearm.

Deffy's widow, Forna, was almost inconsolable at the funeral, because she had to miss her shift as an exotic dancer at "Jimmie's Jug Joint," the local hustler bar. She hated to lose out on her substantial earnings by attending the funereal festivities. As she passed by the open casket without glancing inside, the bereaved woman was heard to mutter, "I should be grabbing the pole and sticking my can out right now." When asked about the fact that she ignored the corpse (which was little more than two-dimensional despite the mortician's use of a bicycle pump), she replied, "I just want to remember what's-his-name as he was—never home."

Forna is well into her fifties, but still looks good with her chest blimps hanging out and is very popular with the barroom crowd. She's managed to keep in superb shape all her life by practicing insertional yoga, often in a group environment. Forna rarely uses the pole on the stage during her number, but prefers to pull one out of a customer's pants. This goes a long way toward explaining the large number of cars on the street in front of her abode on any given day. She offers valet parking, in case you were wondering. Forna has a soft spot in her pants for any guy who's not on life support.

A brigade of sanitation workers showed up at the funeral in uniform, green things that needed dry-cleaning. They had sent a large wreath with a ribbon that said, "From Your Pals at the Municipal Waste Collection Site: Rest in Peace in Your Personal Landfill." Very thoughtful. One of Deffy's former colleagues, Poopsen Klumps, gave a stirring eulogy, calling his departed friend a mentor to many and an inspiration to the disposal industry in general, with an encyclopedic knowledge of rubbish. "He was our garbage guru," Poopsen said. "Always ready to talk trash."

Muffolt Bumschotts, in his rich baritone, warbled the scrap sorter's theme song, "I Did It My Way," accompanied by Gassy Skweekerz on the tuba. Forna kept looking at her watch and told the person next to her, "I should be shakin' my ass at the Happy Hour bunch about now." At the cemetery, Earl took it upon himself to sing "Happy Birthday," then promptly fell in the hole on top of Deffy's sports-model coffin (with the spoiler on the back). Two of the neighbors, Bud Stinx and Heathcliff Flooger, hauled him out. Earl wheezed, "Guess I missed that first step." Each member of the sanitation crew dropped a symbolic handful of earth in the grave. When it was Forna's turn, she grabbed a shovel, hiked her mini-skirt up a few more inches and started flinging dirt as fast as she could.

I requested a post-planting interview with her for my column, and Forna invited me to accompany her to Jimmie's in her limo. It was an exciting ride, since she changed into her work clothes on the way. Mighty fine piece of momma-type posterior, I don't mind telling you. I asked her if she would miss her late departed and she said, "Yeah, like I miss the wart I had removed from my ass last winter. Deffy was okay, I guess, but he tended to obsess about his profession. He'd bring discarded objects home to show me, like a dented hubcap from a 1924 Stutz-Bearbutt or a monogrammed pair of soiled panties that he figured Madonna had thrown away. I tried to share his interests, but I couldn't generate any enthusiasm. Besides, I was busy working my ass off. Or at least giving it a workout." I later talked to some of Deffy's neighbors for background, and they all agreed that he was a bit restricted in his thinking. Many comments were similar, like "Whacko Peckerhead." The woman next door, Claire Saylin, summed up most of the neighborhood's feelings with, "He was an asshole."

In the coming election, I don't know whether to vote for the Republigoons or the Democraps. I'm genuinely sorry Rosemary Klump didn't make the cut. She promised me that if she got elected we'd do it in the Oval Office on the Coolidge Couch and the Roosevelt Rug, then wash up in the Kennedy Krapper using the Taft Toilet and the Buchanan Bidet. I guess it's out of the question now. Reminds me of the time I wrote a fan letter to the great Ukrainian actress, Nokya Soggzov, whose popularity was aided by chest adornments out to here (I am holding my hands about a foot from my body). I included a snapshot of my groin area on the occasion of a superior mast unfurlment (if I say so myself), so she invited me to her room at the

Holiday-Schlobnik Inn on the outskirts of Sebastopol. We looked in each other's eyes and began a torrid game of strip poker, and by 7:30 the next morning I had her down to her overcoat. I lost the next hand, which reduced me to knee socks and snowshoes, and Nokya was struck with a prolonged laughing fit. I saw nothing amusing in the situation and ripped her coat off. This revealed masses of traditional Ukrainian garments consisting of several peasant blouses and full skirts over layers of camisoles and petticoats, all closed by dozens of tiny buttons. With my anatomical essentials hanging out, I began feverishly undressing Nokya's theatrical babeness. Forty minutes later I had worked my way down to a massive corset and thick wool stockings. At this point I fell asleep, the victim of disrobing fatigue. When I awoke and reached for her thespian foredeck, Nokya was gone. A note on the pillow explained that her agent had called and told her she had to leave for a hockey game in which she was scheduled to be the starting goalie. The note directed me to come to the theater that evening.

To kill time, I made a Xerox of my prong. It was a hard copy. I got to the theater about nine and entered through the unattended stage door. In the dark, I tried several doors that were locked and opened one to see an old guy taking a dump. Opening the next door, I spied Nokya standing next to a couch in a sheer nightgown. I rushed in and tackled her, visions of the old Dipper lodged in her candy compartment. We landed on the couch and my aim was true. She hissed, "Not now!" But who can stop the runaway train when it's headed for the station? Just as I was about to off-load the cargo (if you catch my hint), I happened to glance to the side and realized that in my enthusiasm I had failed to perceive a theater full of people. Must have been over a thousand of them, all pretty much leaning forward. Man, I've never been so embarrassed in my life! I got out of there fast—after maybe ten or fifteen minutes (if cargo work is left unfinished, you can develop blisters). Anyway, the applause was deafening. What this story has to do with anything I can only guess, but if some rational thread occurs to me, I'll let you know.

While we're here in Great Britain, Madge called. She says Earl has signed up to donate his organs to science (we were disappointed to learn that he intends to die first), but his brain has already been rejected by Waste Management, Inc. If you bat him a good one in the dome with a 2" x 4" you just get sparks and he stares at you.

With all the affection you deserve, Harold.   Er, wait ... it'll come to me,

Ludlow

26

Hey Grover,

Okay, my film projects didn't turn out so well, but I have a sure-fire investment opportunity for you this time. You'll love this one and you can help me make it successful. Mucho dinero will soon be yours. Let me tell you how I came to this insight. I ran into one of our new neighbors the other day when I was out walking around. I like to get up early and crap on a dog owner's lawn. Sometimes I switch "For Sale" signs around and put them on different houses. My neighbor's name is Harry Nudds and he told me he had inherited a successful restaurant from his father, Radklee. It has a Southern French motif and it's called "De Gaulle, Y'all." Harry's wife, Hazel came out of the house at that moment and it would take some real effort to categorize her as remotely appealing. Nice personality, but a complete waste of feminine gender construction. I couldn't help but notice that the woman is totally flat-chested. She's the type who puts her bra on backwards because it fits better. Hazel also suffers from what the medical lexicon calls "an immense butt." That's when the inspiration hit me.

Follow my thinking on this one. What's one of the largest gender segments in this country? Women, right? And what do women want? Don't be disgusting. I mean besides that. They want to be attractive, that's what. They want to look young and shapely and they're willing to pay almost anything for it. Tell a woman you can make her beautiful and you can make her every time. Now, there are a lot of females like Hazel, women who have poorly developed chest accessories or a mountainous keister, or both. And I've developed the perfect way to help them.

You're aware that my scientific skills are almost boundless, so it will come as no surprise to learn of my successful research. In my home laboratory, using quality chemicals I located outside fast-food outlets, and utilizing industrial carpet remnants and some alcoholic products (to help my concentration), I searched for compounds that might enhance inadequate bosoms and eliminate superfluous butt-volume. Some of that time was admittedly spent sweeping up debris from ill-fated experiments, but I was able to do a lot of them in neighborhood basements when no one was home, thus confining most of the resultant damage to areas outside my own dwelling. The neighbors bitched about broken glass and loud explosions for a while, but they've become less critical since I managed to disperse them with random shotgun blasts during two particularly confrontational marches to our place attended by a couple of thousand touchy individuals who have nothing better to do.

Undeterred by threats and violence, I was able to develop a couple of formulas that can be our ticket to untold wealth. I can hear you sucking in your breath. Or is that a beer? No matter. Your investment doesn't have to be too large, but you may want to send me your bank account number to make things easier for us. I want to open a "Butt and Bosom" Salon on Rodeo Drive in Beverly Hills. That's where the cash is. Either there or in Tijuana. Rich ladies will do anything to look good. I can almost feel the increase in your blood pressure. Or it may be gas.

My well-trained, carefully-selected male staff will pamper the living crap out of our clients and apply my wonder ointment, *Booby-Booster®*, to the appropriate female area. The jugs, Grover. Pay attention. This formula contains microscopic spheres of balloon material filled with helium under pressure. Topical application of *Booby-Booster®* causes the treated area to swell to amazing dimensions, and the procedure is pleasurable for the client and the practitioner as well. I have to tinker with the ingredients to achieve the right size and taste for every body type, but I'm working that out with ladies from the local senior center who are convinced they're getting a massage. They don't have the faintest idea what's going on until I undo the restraints. A lot of these women resemble cadavers, and nauseating ones at that, but a few of them aren't that bad, so I'm getting you a season pass to their locker room.

For those unfortunate females whose problem is lower—that is, surplus-bum sufferers, I'm pleased to report that I've come up with a second miracle-working chemistry masterpiece. Sometimes my genius surprises even me. This highly-acidic astringent based on sodium hydroxide, cabbage extract and grapefruit juice is injected directly into the anus with a bicycle pump. Because it's so harshly vile and bitter, the patient's internal tubing recoils about four or five feet up into the colon and sucks the buttocks in with it. Voilà! Instant rump reduction! I call this composition *Awful-Ass-Away*®. Though the treatment is somewhat exhausting, women not only look pounds trimmer, but the procedure is environment-friendly, ridding the area of unsightly blubber. Afterwards, the gals are also able to pick up loose change when their hands are otherwise occupied.

Assembling the proper crew for my salon is not easy. I want to be absolutely certain that I apply the highest standards in staff selection. I tried to train Earl to use his fingers properly, but it's difficult to make him take his hands out of his pants. I also screened some applicants who answered my ads in "Rod and Reel" and "Hustler," but that led nowhere. Virtually all of them had significant experience in the breast-and-butt-squeezing arena, but almost to a man they had very few teeth, wicked-looking tattoos and metal parts in their faces. Sometimes tattoos on the metal parts. I've talked to a few high-school kids, but they want to leave the ointment out and go right for the boobies. The youth of our nation continues to disappoint me.

This is where you come in. Not only will your investment free us from overhead concerns, but you can become our number-one mammary manipulator and can-master. I know you're a hands-on type of guy. I'll have the place up and running by the time you get out here, right after I cash your check. It should only take about six-hundred grand to get started. In the meantime, I've already begun to work out a low-cost ad campaign designed to attract clients. As you realize, it's easy to spot a woman who needs our help. Naturally, there are a lot of good-looking babes in these parts, but the market is also ripe with women that the knocker-fairy shortchanged or who got second helpings of butt-mass dumped in their panties. You can spot these malformed unfortunates wherever there is heavy pedestrian traffic, so I figure we can hang around outside supermarkets and other retail establishments to make contact with them. I realize you do that already, clad in a raincoat. Your training will therefore be minimal.

I intend to carry a sign that says, "You've Got a Big Caboose!" You can hold the one that reads, "You Call Those Jugs?" Both signs will indicate our website, *Boobeez-R-Us & Butt-No-More.com*. I'll need your credit card to develop the web page. Women will be intrigued by our directness, of course, and when they stop to talk to us, we can grab them by the can and the upper torso, thereby causing them to focus on the appropriate problem areas. Fondling their handicapped regions will enable us to keep them stationary so we can make our pitch.

I've tested my wonder-products at a few upper-class neighborhood brawls, wedding receptions and other social events, and although I felt a little foolish holding up the signs during high mass, I can state that I stirred some curiosity. Admittedly, a lot of it was mine, but I see some potential there. The key is that most of the women in this region appreciate interest in their anatomy. And they don't mind revealing a lot of it to gage the reaction. The feeling is mutual, as you will see. Not everyone is positive, though. One woman, Fluffy Buttplugg, told me I was nuts, but she's been condemned to a life of celibacy as a result of her appearance. If she had plastic surgery and physical therapy, her face might some day look like a tub full of kneecaps. Of course, in your neighborhood she could be offered a film contract. Send the money soon.

Naturally, we would offer additional services to our clients, like getting laid. They only problem is that most of the gals are not going to be the hottest lookers in the region, otherwise they wouldn't need our services, so it won't be easy to get into the proper mood. This is another reason why I need your input (if you follow my hint). Since we were kids, I've admired your well-known tolerance for physical deficiencies. That's why we didn't need to have the mirrors in the house removed.

In addition, I've grown to appreciate your lack of discrimination where repugnant sex practices are concerned (particularly after I tried some of them myself). It's admittedly difficult to keep your emotional enthusiasm at a high level when your partner is a real dog, but I'm relying on you to maintain your well-known lack of standards and keep their more interesting parts in the right perspective. I never had any problems. I find that watching "Porking Pig" cartoons during the act helps to preserve a sense of excitement. We can work out a title for you when you arrive and you can bunk in one of the bedrooms at the salon, the one next to the high-pressure ass-peeler.

I've got Earl chalked in for anus-prep duties, so you might have to share a bed with him if he's too tired to drive home some nights. You two would probably get along nicely. You have a lot in common. I realize that Earl's gray matter would fit in a thimble and have room left over for a basketball, and the doctors say he can transmit Alzheimer's Disease just by breathing on you, but I feel you've had the necessary experience for this job. Earl is not a sparkling conversationalist, but he appears to be listening when you talk, so it just might work out. It never seems to bother you when nobody pays attention to what you're saying, and this leads me to believe there's a basis for compatibility there. Make the check out to me.

On another subject, the news from our part of town is mixed. First of all, Buddy Ruppshun came home from work early a couple of weeks ago and heard some noise in the bedroom. He looked in the door and saw his wife, Innta, standing next to the bed with a person of the male gender. Now, Buddy is the jealous type, so he fetched his .457 Magpie from the spare room, came back and blasted that fellow full of holes. Deader than Earl's love stick. Got him with eight of the rounds he fired. Another two went through the wall and killed the cat. That helped him at the trial. When the smoke cleared, Innta informed her impulsive spouse that the guy was just delivering a new mattress. Anybody could make that mistake. I know I've witnessed a similar situation more than once.

It's easy to understand why Buddy reacted as he did. Innta is a real flirt. The lady was outfitted with a massive dose of chest trophies by the heavenly quartermaster. I've been at parties where she managed to push her prow prizes against every male in the house—often all of them at the same time. When she's in the room, it's almost impossible not to accidentally get your hands on those things (or those things on your hands). Dimensionally, she's way ahead of most competition in the nipple-enhanced gland department. Buddy got off with probation and a stern lecture. It helped that the jury was made up of illegal immigrants who didn't want to cause trouble. The judge was also Buddy's brother-in-law. I was a character witness and testified to the fact that Buddy is an otherwise law-abiding citizen with a harmless predilection for animal pornography, serial rape and exposing himself.

There was a big sale at Sorenson's Hardware Saturday. Everyone attended. I wish you could have flown out for it. Mulch was going for five bucks a bag and manure was moving fast, some of it from Earl's shorts. Father Buttblossom gave the invocation at the opening ceremonies in the parking lot, asking the Lord to bless the potting soil. We thought he was done when he launched into a twenty-minute sermon in which he blamed the Los Angeles Lakers for most of society's ills. I couldn't disagree with him. He was very persuasive. Even the Lakers applauded.

There was an exciting moment when a young teenaged girl, Squiggle Floop, won a hair removal kit (pubic variety) and immediately proceeded to try it out. They raffled off a poster showing one of our local news anchors in the shower with her ample jugs exposed. I donated it from my personal collection. It took in $6.27. Chunky Dumper won it and immediately started bitching about nipple size. Members of the fire department put on a cat-mangling demonstration using fire axes and sledge hammers. Check out their website for more information at *hellwithdemkitties.com*. Herda Hormone, the popular so-so-so-prano, sang our national anthem, accompanied on the methane-powered accordion by Gwonnen Tweekdiss. It would have been more effective if he hadn't played an Estonian folk song and gabbed on his cell-phone while she was singing. I guess it worked out for the best, because she forgot the words and substituted part of the text from "Ninety-Nine Bottles of Beer."

I bought a cross-cut saw. I haven't done any cross-cutting in years, but I want to get back into it, maybe enter a few competitions. I plan to start on the one at the church down the street. You would have been impressed with the decorations. Red, white and black banners were flying in front of the store. They all had "YOU'RE A PRICK, FRED!" on them, but they were inexpensive and it was the colors that counted. Earl got a great deal. He bought a John Deere riding mower with tinted windows and lightning racing stripes for two thousand dollars. Too bad he doesn't have a lawn. A gravel truck tipped over on his property ten years ago while chasing a cat, and Earl just left the pebbles where they came to rest.

The Beach Club threw a cocktail party on the dock Sunday. Loads of people showed up just as the last of the garbage was swept into a corner for

Earl to fall into. They invited some Hollywood celebrities to give the evening some much-needed pizzazz. Tommy Lee Jones and Billy Bob Thornton couldn't make it, but Billy Bubba Lee Bob Goldberg showed up. He starred in that film that just came out, "The Female Bar Mitzvah Zombies of Long Island Rise From the Dead and Make Obscene Phone Calls to Everybody in Their Area Code." One film star appeared at the last moment, unencumbered by underwear. It was easy to tell. She didn't have a dress on. The gifted young actress, Lookah Deeze, bent over while trying to tie the laces in her hiking boots and her entire forefront plopped out. I'll remember that sight if I live to be fourteen. Eight volunteers (including me) put them back in for her and it only took fifteen minutes. First we had to dust them off and check for bruising.

Giddy Yupp attended. He's a talented local artist and child molester who teaches at the Kindergarten around the corner. Kind of a rough character with a really grating voice. When he talks it sounds like a can of nails sucked into a garbage disposal. The food consisted mainly of hot dogs and some other junk nobody could identify. Earl tried one of those gut rockets and immediately messed his pants. The cuisine at these functions is usually something called California-Napalm-Albanian fusion, guaranteed to light up your heartburn meter. Madge was in attendance, of course. She's on the board at the animal shelter. Too bad it's not the one that protrudes from the deck of a pirate ship.

A team from the water-ski club gave a demonstration of their prowess. Twenty young participants carrying torches formed a pyramid and whizzed by the dock, pulled by a high-powered motor-craft with Stepford Sludge at the wheel. That was where they went wrong. The boat was supposed to whip them onto the beach in front of us in a grand finale, but the Stepper was going way too fast and he crashed into the dock. The pyramid on water-skis plowed through the crowd, disappearing through the front gate and onto the street, where it was immediately met by dense traffic and brought to a jarring halt. The screams were heart-wrenching.

A few of us were fortunate enough to snag swimsuits from a couple of the young ladies as they flashed past us, revealing some nifty pubic charms and captivating chest furnishings. Earl's run of bad luck remained intact. He ripped Stepford's trunks off. It was a standard gathering for our town. Twenty or thirty people fell in the water and Earl took a leak from the dock. As you would expect, with his sub-standard hose length he didn't get any of it beyond his shoes, which were open-toed. In any other part of the country this would stand out like an erection in a convent, but in California we're used to it.

You never know what you'll experience when you get out on the freeways here. I've given up being surprised. On the way into L.A. Thursday I swerved to miss a kid on a tricycle and ran over a chipmunk. Fortunately, it was screwing a cat at the time. We drove in to the city center (which nobody can actually locate) to attend a concert at the Disney Concert Hall. The South Los Angeles Street-Gang Symphony performed works by Charles Manson and Bruno Hauptmann while exchanging gunfire with members of another gang in the audience. A stimulating evening if you weren't wearing bullet-proof attire. The L.A. Times music critic praised the performance the next day: "This orchestra can't miss," he wrote. Arnold Schwarzenegger was guest conductor for one piece, but he seemed confused about what that entailed, because he punched train tickets the whole time. I think the old Danish proverb is appropriate here: "*Venn yur dunn vidder, rollar ohver.*" (Take two at bedtime).

It brings back memories of your schoolwork. It was apparent to me that it would be impossible to follow in your intellectual footsteps. I was shattered when you were edged out by the school dunce for the title of "Hindered Scholar of the Year." I can tell you now that it was devastating to have my hero (and part-time brother) turn out to be only human after all, or in your case a few chromosomes short. For my own part, I continue to tell everyone of my third-place finish.

Your Something or Other—sometimes (or not).

Ludlow

27

Hey Grover,

Your unexpected silence concerning my request for a trivial capital investment forced me to abandon my plans for the salon in Beverly Hills. You're a hard man to convince. But not to worry. I had a backup plan, as you probably guessed. I've been taking law courses on-line, and after six weeks of intense study I can proudly announce that I have received my law degree from the Swollen Gland, Kansas, School of Drain Research and Jurisprudence. It was an exhausting curriculum, as you can imagine. Here are some of the courses that were required:

Passing the Bar	Choosing a Neighborhood Bar
Wealth Accumulation & Criminality	Criminality, Concealment Thereof
Litigation, Mitigation & Mutilation	Incomprehensible Contracts
Astronomical Fees & Fun Stuff	Effective Double-Billing and Fleecing
False Pretenses & Their Use	Using Pretenses in a False Manner
Chinese Accounting Practices	Advanced Tax Evasion
Divorce or Homicide	Homicide & its Side-Effects
Preventing Reconciliation	Jury Selection & Effective Corruption
Decisions & Appeals	Unappealing Decisions
Contempt of Court	Contempt of Clients
How to Plug a Loophole	How to Plug a Secretary
The Court & Pizza Delivery	The Death Penalty & Zit Removal
The Electric Chair & Bug Zapping	

I passed the bar exam at McNulty's Irish Pub between shots, which were being exchanged by rival gang members. Now I was ready for business. Taking advantage of zoning loopholes and an on-line bribery web-site, I opened my office above a Korean grocery. It's next to the dog pound, and the location allows me to step next door and pound a few dogs every now and then.

Now, you might believe that I would attract mostly mundane clients, but you'd be surprised how abnormal a lot of them are. I'm not sure why that is.

Take Earl for example. In contrast to the conclusion you may draw from my earlier descriptions, he's actually a loon. We attended a gathering at his place the other evening. All the women looked great (except for Madge of course). She wore a paper dress and was later arrested for rustling. This particular evening they had a couple of interesting guests. Wesley Snipes showed up with his sister, Gudder. And Steve Jobs was there with his wife, Odd. Bon Jovi stopped by with his Missus, the lovely Anne Jovi.

One of my first cases was a Latvian immigrant named Stanislaus Volenski. He has a little pushcart that he shoves around L.A., selling cheap jewelry that looks like crap. So does he. Stan wanted me to sue the people who supply him with his merchandise. He gets his goods from some local Italian gentlemen and feels the quality is sub-par. The Mickey Mouse on the watches has his appendage hanging out and most of the emeralds are orange. But it's hard to serve his wholesalers with court documents, because they drop Stan's jewelry off in front of his pushcart from a speeding car on Mondays.

I've had dealings with the Mafia before. I often did favors for Gino Rigatoni and his mob. I hung around with cultivated types like Clemente "Shrivel-Nuts" Bastone, Carlo "Bridgework" Ponte and Luigi "Squeegie" Beejee. The pay was good and the chow was first-class. There were usually a lot of leftovers after Gino's boys had settled the score with some of his associates before they finished dining.

Knowing how lethal the mob can be, I courageously recruited Earl to serve the proper papers. If he gets his ass shot off, who cares? I put him on a sturdy Schwinn bicycle and told him to follow the delivery men. Kept my fingers crossed. Let's face it, the guy's not very bright. He came up to me the other day and asked me if people ever come up to me. He also frequently puts both contact lenses in the same eye. Sure enough, he lost the trail when Stan's next delivery was made. His bicycle clip got caught in the spokes, and that's not easy to do that when it's around your Johnson. Plus, he was seated backwards on the bike. Curses. I was forced to resort to my back-up plan. I mailed the papers to "Local Mafia" in care of the police station. They got the stuff the next day and called to thank me.

Our case is scheduled to go to trial next month, the Hon. Corrupto

Ruffiane presiding. In the meantime, we're trying to locate Stan, who hasn't been around for a while. His pushcart was found, along with half a dozen unidentifiable body parts, under the 405 Freeway, so maybe he changed his place of business. He'll probably call soon.

Another case I have pending is in Divorce Court. Oban Bungvent is trying to unhook himself from his spouse, Gaypin. She's not a bad looker, with everything in the right place except a hotel room I'd like to book with her. Oban was convinced she was screwing around. He got suspicious when he bought a used car and she was in the back seat, naked. I think she only uses underwear to keep her ankles warm. The mister hasn't exactly been sitting around waiting for the marriage to end, though. He's been seen with some of the most eligible young starlets on the Hollywood scene, but they chase him away with mace when he gets too close.

I'm presently sitting here in my office, waiting for my next appointment. Mrs. May-Bea Layte is due any minute. Now, this lady is best referred to as "trouser-swelling buttwork." She would really have everything in the right place if it were on my lap. I'm helping her collect on her late husband's estate following his untimely demise in their swimming pool. Her hubby was an illiterate hillbilly who amassed a fortune by investing in adoptable children for movie stars. At our first meeting, Mrs. Layte parked her world-class fanny in a chair and crossed her legs. I could see all the way up to her thorax, which is joyously located just north of her bovine-type chest decorations. Whenever she's around, I tend to relax in a panicky sort of way.

"My husband drowned and left me twenty million dollars," she explained, "and I need some slow-witted jerk to handle the legal stuff." Ignoring this confidence-builder, I said, "That's a lot of money for a guy who couldn't even read or write." She said, "He couldn't swim either."

The lady reminds me of Yoozda Breaks, a Flemish beauty from Antwerp and the type of woman any man would be after—she was breathing and could stand up for minutes at a time. And she possessed many of the qualities prized by a superficial male—two of which immediately come to mind. Yoozda was sensitive, sophisticated, built like a brick Port-A-Potty and always ready to shake her butt for a good cause. We met in church. She was there to swipe hymnals and I had developed the ability to palm high-denomination bills from the collection plate, so I was making good money. I progressed to an even better income strategy when I started bringing my own plate. The congregation was friendly, but the priest looked at me kind of funny the first time I asked for a doggie bag after communion.

I had recently returned from Africa, where I picked up an exotic disease from the fender of a rickshaw, and the doctor prescribed breast milk. When I explained my problem, Yoozda selflessly offered to let me drink from her ample containers. During the first session she started breathing hard and panted, "Ooh Baby, is there anything else you need?" I looked up and said, "Do you have any chocolate chip cookies?" The job of an ethical, honest and reliable attorney is demanding, but I don't care about those guys. I just keep double-billing Earl.

The two cops on our police force, Everett and Claude, gave out a speeding ticket this month. It was the first citation they wrote this year. A green 1967 Chevy with a Vermont license plate was doing seventy down Rancho Chinga Parkway until it crashed into Rollie Huffsted's manure spreader. The driver was a guy who claimed he was delivering a much-needed drug to our local hospital. Speaking of the hospital, you and I can stop by and have our colons checked one afternoon after my piano recital. Anyway, the Chevy was full of Styrofoam cups and hamburger cartons, and some weeds had started to grow in the back seat. The driver told the cops, "I have to get this stuff to the operating room right away. They need this chemotherapeutic substance to staunch the flow of urine in a patient who just had his testicles repositioned. It's made from the Oklahoma artichoke and replaces the older medication, Getlostalone, that showed some effectiveness against shingles, but there was corresponding pubic hair loss and the inability to maintain an erection." A bunch of concerned citizens had gathered by that time, and they talked about surfing conditions and fishing in Canada for a while, but being thoroughly unimpressed by the story this guy was spreading, they kicked his ass and ran him out of town. That's how we deal with bullshit around here.

Calvin Dworsky's Orchestra was the big attraction at the lake-side concert last Saturday. A lot of the citizenry comes out to hear these ear-drum hostilities. They spread their blankets on the lawn and set up their beach chairs and coolers and tromp on each other's feet, and everybody has a good time except the audience and the performers. The seventy-piece orchestra was on a stage at the water's edge. Except for a dozen of them who didn't fit on the stage and had to stand in the water. Too bad they weren't under it. Calvin bills his group as a "big band." They play all the Glenn Miller stuff like "Stompin' on the Cats" and "Moonlight Violation," except the songs sound more like a cattle stampede through a sheet-metal production facility whose floor has been covered with milk cans full of marbles.

Emmy Lou Stinxx was the homecoming queen this fall. She beat out one other girl for the honor, because nobody else gave a a badger's backside. Emmy Lou rode in a Sherman tank in the parade, in the front hatch just below the cannon. It whacked her in the noggin a couple of times when they went over the speed bumps, but that wouldn't affect her much anyway. They avoided calling her a slow learner in school and decided to use the term "Fast Forgetter" when she received her Grover Smutt Special Hindered Student Award. I got them to name it after you.

As you would expect, I continue to come up with marketable inventions in addition to my legal work. For people trying to avoid the high cost of health care, I've developed a home surgery kit. I call it "Suture Self."

Your fair frère,

Jacques

28

Hey Grover,

We're looking forward to having you visit us. Don't disappoint us again. If I'm tied up I'll arrange for Earl to pick you up. You'll recognize him without any problem. His sideburns are behind his ears and his false teeth have braces on them. I've mentioned that the guy is no beauty. He was arrested for mooning when he was just looking out the window. The accidental shooting at a recent wedding reception down the street was probably a fluke, so you shouldn't worry about it. Things like that don't happen more than two or three times a week, so I wouldn't call it a chronic problem yet. In this case, the bride's family took issue with the decorative piece on the wedding cake, and .38 caliber confetti started flying. The groom meant it only as a joke when he had the bakery affix figures of a wedding couple to the top of the pastry, but it might have leaned a little toward tastelessness, seeing as how the figures were copulating. I think it would have gotten past the critical eyes of the in-laws if the decorations hadn't been battery-driven. You get the picture. No one in either family is a decent shot, so the damage was fortunately confined to the hall furnishings and, thankfully, a stray cat.

You can think of the daily protest marches through our streets as just healthy ways for the sanitation workers to let off steam. We're hoping they'll be back to work in six months or so. In the meantime, I dump our trash in Earl's driveway after dark. There's no limit to the things you can do here, so I'm putting together a full schedule of sight-seeing. If you arrive before Christmas, we can catch the knitting tournament at the Senior Center. It's an exciting day and the casualty count is normally low. Stella Stroganoff copped first prize last year with a bright red body bag that featured yarn handles and a zipper from a pair of Earl's jeans, so it was still partially covered with some dried secretions. She donated it to the city morgue. The sign over the entrance there reads "Remains to be Seen." Ethyl Soffstool was thoroughly enraged that her knitted ovenware didn't win and claimed that Stella was bonking a couple of the judges. She tried to kick one of them in the ass, but she fell down. I know you'll want to attend religious services on Sunday because you always get irritable when you can't witness for the Lord. We'll go to Midnight Mass while you're here. We alternate between two churches. One is Our Lady of Perpetual Intermittence, where they have a communion-wafer dispensing machine. You could call it an immaculate contraption. Last Sunday a guy came into the church on crutches, dashed some holy water on his legs and threw his crutches away. The altar boy ran over to the priest and told him what had happened. The priest said, "You've witnessed a miracle, my son. Where is he now?" The kid said, "Flat on his ass over by the holy water." The sermons can be pretty boring, though. Something about doing good and a lot of other inconsequential crap I don't pay any attention to. The other church is Bob's Chapel of Limited Infinity. The head clergy-person is a born-again former Buddhist Catholic Atheist who isn't technically a priest, so we call him Uncle Morty. His faith outlaws prayer and the Bible. The service normally consists of shuffle-board and arm-wrestling, and then they take up a collection.

On the other hand, you may want to rush and get here for Thanksgiving. Madge and Earl say you have a standing invitation to their annual gout-fest. Earl can't wait to meet you. We could use someone halfway normal to sort of spread the pain, and that's how I often think of you. It's hard to come up with an excuse to miss their spread, so we have to endure their friends too. Stepford Sludge was in attendance last year. It was good to see the old boy again, even though he makes this terrible sound when he clears his throat, like a sheet of plywood being ripped off a wall.

There's a new tile floor at the bus depot I'd like you to see, and I could get tickets to a football game if you want. USC and UCLA are sold out, of course, but I can get us in to the annual battle between Fleebster Tech and Skrue U. Both teams wear exactly the same uniforms, so the game can get a little confusing. A lot of times all twenty-two players line up on the same side of the ball. The Rose Bowl is sold out, so they play at the Thistle Bowl in Puddle Junction, two doors down from the body shop and the tattoo parlor in the swamp area. The field has a big sinkhole in it that may be connected to the one downtown, but they play around it. The opening extends from one goal line out to the thirty-yard marker, but neither of the teams ever gets into that area, so it shouldn't affect the outcome of the game.

It's always a grudge match when the "Powerful Pansies" from Fleebster and the "Screwing Mules" get together. The current feud started in 1912 when firearms were discharged on the field to prevent a potential long gainer and a linebacker stopped a delayed half-a-buck up the middle with an axe handle. The penalties offset each other. The "Mules" had a great hidden-ball trick until the officials stopped them from bringing shovels on the field. And the "Pansies" used an end-around play that required a player to cut through the locker room, circle the stadium and come back in again behind the opponent's bench, at which time he goosed an assistant coach and kicked one of the cheerleaders in the ass.

I don't know if you admire asphalt as much as I do, but it's become one of my passions since we moved here. They should be laying new stuff down on the municipal parking lot during your stay, so we can watch that for a while. They were doing a couple of the side streets just a while ago when the steam roller jumped the curb and ran over a couple of gang members who were stealing a car. There's still a lump in the concrete where this particular event took place. The car's in there too. I'll take you to see it. You can probably get some nice pictures. It's near the plastic surgeon's office, the one with the sign out front that says, "Come In and Pick Your Nose." Our Madam-Mayor, Reelie O'Beese, announced plans to take some time off to get her fanny fixed. You can look into it while you're here too. It's a big project. An outraged citizen booted her in the tailpipe over a zoning regulation that prevented him from raising poisonous mammals in his car. He pretty much messed up her whole backside, although we have to take the doctor's word for it. I don't see too much difference myself.

We should stop by the orphanage and visit the kids too, before the actors in Hollywood adopt them all. Then you might like to attend an auction at the town hall. I was there a couple of weeks ago and got a photo of Houdini going ballistic because he locked his keys in the car. We can head for the factory where they make bathroom-theme devices, which I know you will like, being an authority on pooper goods. You can pick up personalized toilet accessories in their souvenir shop. For instance, you might get a urinal with the image of your favorite member of Congress situated where the piddle hits the porcelain. I recently had a toilet installed that features a remarkable likeness of my senators in the target area. Earl wants you to come over to see his butt-cork collection. It'll be a good photo opportunity with the two of you together. The pictures will most likely be in the paper, so I'll try to make sure they get the names right under the photos, seeing how you guys look so much alike. And I want to take you by the feed store while you're here. Harold Snitt has put up a bunch of marketing posters for his seed packets and I think you'll be impressed by the excitement they generate. Harold knows how to make a visual appeal to the potential seed consumer, I can tell you. Save some seed room in your suitcase for the return trip.

We have a big electronic sign outside the library in the City Center Complex, and I've arranged to have them display some welcoming words for you. It normally has the motto "IF YOU LIVED HERE, WE'D CHASE YOUR SORRY ASS OUT OF TOWN." And below that there are community reminders flashing on and off, like "PICK UP YOUR DOG SHIT!" or "DON'T SCREW WITH THE RAILROAD BARRIER!" But the news of your visit has the whole town in a frenzy, and there's been a contest to determine what kind of greeting should be flashed in your honor. There are already two entries. One is "Who gives a rat's ass?" and the other, a little more personal, is "I personally don't give a rat's ass!" I don't want you to think that this comes from a lack of receptivity around here. It's just that the people in our town don't work up a lot of enthusiasm for every visitor. If the Angel Gabriel marched down the main drag with George Washington, the Dallas Cowboy Cheerleaders, four porn stars and a thousand men from Valley Forge, nobody would shut off the barbeque to acknowledge them unless they brought potato salad.

Gretchen asked me to find out how you like your steak cooked. This is a purely intellectual inquiry, because you won't get anything resembling a steak at our house. I can honestly say that there is only one problem with her cooking. Unfortunately, it centers around the food. Her cuisine could give Superman the galloping runs. She's been perpetrating the same German recipes on me for decades, and if the package doesn't have a picture of

Kaiser Wilhelm or Otto von Bismarck on it, it doesn't get into the kitchen. My Frau is the only person I know who can make leftovers from scratch. I enjoy some heavy brown gravy sometimes, but it just didn't seem appropriate on my birthday cake, although I thought the Iron Cross was a nice touch. Sometimes I call 911 and dedicate a crime to her. You might want to bring some canned goods with you.

There's a Ford Dealer's dinner at the VFW that we could attend on the last Saturday in November. Last year, Chunky Dumper got a plaque for ruining the fewest sales opportunities for his company. It didn't hurt that the staff locks him in the can whenever a prospective customer shows up. The plaque looks like a concrete block if you hold it a certain way—just before you chuck it in a dumpster. The grub is followed by a dance, and I think this year the shindig will be a lot more entertaining. I attend every year with Earl. People invite him everywhere to make the other guests look attractive. I don't know why they always want me to come along. A year ago, Carmela Whistlebox did a modern dance number that didn't work out too well. At one point she slipped on a condom that somebody had discarded and plunged headfirst onto one of the tables, where she struck a metal serving dish with her face and knocked out four of her teeth. Carmela is a trouper, though. She spit out her bicuspids and finished her number by doing the splits. Lamentably, she was wearing no undergarments, so she couldn't get back up off the floor because of the suction. It took half an hour to locate a shoehorn.

We've got to take the tour at the Kruddy-Vatt Brewery. It's an old brick building that resembles a Bavarian castle and then morphs into a tractor shed. The beer is called Golden Dreck and tastes like hell, but I doubt that you'll notice. They show a nice historic film of the old horse-drawn wagons on their runs. The exceptional steeds were so familiar with their routes that they were often sent out alone to make deliveries and collect the money. Apparently there were very few complaints about their confusion when giving customers change. The bar at the end of the tour is authentically historical, with period furniture right from the antique factory.

Did you hear that? Never mind, it's gone now.

If you need me I'll be in the bathroom. **Bye for now.**

29

Hey Grover,

Earl and Madge got into it again, and it was really bad this time. I told them how concerned you are about them. I had hoped they would postpone their annual exchange of attempted manslaughter until after the New Year, but the rockiest marriage west of the Rockies continues to live up to its billing. The union was actually shaky from the beginning, though that may come as a surprise to you. At the wedding when Earl said, "I do," Madge said, "Don't use that tone with me!" Then she pasted him with her bouquet, in which she had concealed a pipe wrench.

The latest fisticuffs started when Madge put on some new perfume in an effort to enhance her appeal. Earl took a sniff and said, "What's that smell?" Madge smiled seductively and said, "Guess." And Earl tromped on the detonator with, "Isn't that the crap you use to clean the hamster cage?" Because of your sensitive nature I hesitate to describe the carnage that followed, but very little of the furniture (that had been brought in after the last massacre) survived this massacre. The house suffered extensive destruction and the crapper was in shambles. No wait, that was before the fight.

Anyway, Earl got in a bunch of licks this time, with his face on one of Madge's frying pans, and managed to land a single genuine punch. It was purely by accident and occurred when the missus turned to pick up a potted plant as Earl bounced off a wall. He kicked his bride in the beam while he was in mid-air, before he hit the parquet. It wasn't exactly a Herculean task to connect with her can. If you're in the same room with Madge and you take a random kick in space, you'll hit her ass nine times out of ten.

As law enforcement and emergency personnel attempted to restore some order to the devastation, Madge was seen tearing off a table leg and trying to climb into the ambulance to finish her dear hubby off. They intervened in the nick of time, whatever a nick is. In the emergency room, Old

Hollow-Skull was diagnosed with several cracked ribs, a cruelly flattened kisser, a busted ass and a miserably low IQ. The rectal examination revealed a normal thyroid. Madge was at his side, but was barred from future visits when she pulled a blackjack out of her purse and jumped up on the bed. Madge rarely leaves a beating unfinished. She led the security people a merry chase around the room and through the halls until they cornered her at a vending machine, trying to extract a cheeseburger on the run. Earl was oblivious to the whole thing, lying there with a splint on his rod and his balls in a cast and watching a cat-crushing contest on TV (one of my favorites). There oughta be a law. Oh, I guess there is.

Speaking of laws, you may already know that many of our modern laws come from the reign of Gluteus Maximus, the most famous of the Roman emperors. The old saying that Rome was not built in a day is true. The Romans actually took a week and a half to do it (without union help) by working thousands of slaves to death. I know you would have done the same.

I happen to be an expert on Roman Imperial history, having studied Latin with Señorita Wanna Peesadiss in Starto, a suburb of Quito (do I have to explain that one?). The superb language skills I developed during our friendship enabled me to decipher ancient languages, such as when I was fortunate enough to visit the pyramids, even though the clowns in those days wrote exclusively in Egyptian Hydraulics. Be that as it may (or maybe it be that way), Gluteus Maximus was acclaimed as he returned with his victorious armies to Rome after defeating two old guys who had tipped over the senate outhouse. Their actions were considered repulsive, since half a dozen senators were in the facilities at the time. The entire population turned out in the Coliseum to proclaim the emperor's heroism with cries of "Yo, peanuts over here, buddy!" The celebration was short, since the place had to be prepared for a hockey game that evening. Later scroll inscriptions inform us that the home team put the puck in the net four times and in the opposing goalie's keister twice.

Gluteus, also known to the citizenry as Yukon Pete, had a manly physique, handsome features and superb oratory skills, though these traits were offset by a stunningly short pubic member. His ass was a little saggy, as well. Gluteus was responsible for a number of improvements in the empire, though, including more numerous and efficient executions, public dog disemboweling and "Vestal Virgins Strip Nite" at all the popular watering holes in the empire's capital, where by senate decree it was not necessary to wear a tie with your toga.

You doubtlessly learned from your third-grade history lessons that being the emperor was not the safest job in the world. Intrigues, plots, murders, assassinations and people sticking their tongues out were rife in the empire. In fact, the most dangerous professions in those days were emperor, gladiator and tax collector, followed closely by drive-by genital inspector and anyone who was bare-handed and confronting five people with swords. The good monarch, though immensely popular with eight or ten of his subjects, surprisingly had a few enemies. He subsequently met an untimely end, hastened by the insertion of a spear about four feet up his colon. This discomforting event occurred during a get-together for chow and serious debauchery with some of his buddies and a bevy of warm-blooded, unvested virgins. These things still take place in your neighborhood, in case you didn't know. I'll send you a list of venues.

The Emperor immediately took to his bed and the next day he ceased to breathe, which led everyone to believe that he might be dead. To make sure, they held a pillow over his face. He was put to rest at the mortuary run by Equationum Quadratus, whose motto was "Funerals For All Occasions." They later exhumed him and he was cremated, his ashes spread over home-plate at the Roman Dodgers ballpark, where he had spent many happy hours cheering his favorite team to victory or executing them at the end of a poor season.

Gluteus was succeeded by Protractud Sillinus, who was elected by a standing-room-only senate that had been properly oiled and bribed for the occasion. Before the fourteenth ballot, Marcus O'Reallyus spoke in favor of a fornication break, so the vote was postponed for forty-eight hours. Sillinus finally won unanimous approval (52% of the vote), helped along by the judicious use of assassinations and torture. The new top doggie (or "canino superiore") was credited with banning public urination without a license and the use of javelins in the washroom. Chariot drivers were required to wear jockstraps with shoulder harnesses and to refrain from bowel movements while the vehicle was in motion. Sillinus also introduced the bicycle to Rome. This transportation marvel had been brought from Carthage by Marco Polo (or maybe an Albanian) and was not an immediate success. The prototype had square wheels, which made acceleration difficult, although it could stop on a dime. The bicycle clip had not yet been invented, and that omission contributed to the high mortality rate of riders who kept getting their togas (and their dongs) caught in the spokes—sometimes of other bikes—and, in many cases, of passing chariots and horse-drawn sewage tankers.

As the new emperor, Sillinus gained a certain amount of prestige and respect, sometimes by the generally popular qualities of affability and moderation, but more often by drunkenness and sexual perversion, which were among the most admired attributes of the day. I myself am still receptive to these innocent undertakings, as I know you are. Brutus Scrootus, his top military commander, expanded the empire significantly by overpowering hordes of women and children and sacking defenseless cities and quarterbacks who couldn't get rid of the ball. His commanders encouraged their men and urged them to be unafraid and optimistic even when they carried no weapons, offering them selected stimulants and free sex following the battle.

Brutus himself inspired his troops by his cruelty, a natural leader. The ferocity of the combatants was also intensified by the threat of having their testicles chopped off if they lost. The army was in the habit of charging with their manhood hanging out, but my investigation of statuary from that period reveals a laughable deficiency in Johnson power on their part. Thus, though they subsequently inflicted widespread savagery and debauchery on the humblest of subject territories, killing, pillaging, kicking much ass and tearing down Burger King signs wherever they found them, I can be reasonably certain that the "Whopper" does not date from that period.

"Silli with the Soft Willie," as the opposition party called the chief executive, attempted to be merciful and just—virtues all the more welcome to the populace because of their unfamiliarity. De-nutting was outlawed except in the case of a third traffic violation (the chariot was burned) or failure to yield the right-of-way to a honey with big melons. Severe dick-twisting went a long way to discourage double-parking. In addition, crucifixions were instituted for major crimes, like public flatulence, in which spikes were driven through the perpetrator's belly and sometimes lower. This served to curb repeat criminal behavior (and respiration).

But Sillinus was only at the controls of state for a short time. His loudest critics were Fittabi Titus and Letsava Peppsee, two wealthy citizens whose immoral, disreputable and violent characters made them keen candidates for high office and two of my most revered role models. History shows that they were investigated but never convicted for a number of attempts on the emperor's life when he was in the act of relieving himself. But everyone knew they were behind the scheme to drop a piano on his head from a triumphal arch. Some plotters also tried to poison their ruler at a hot dog stand outside the Coliseum with a foot-longer laced with serpent snot, but he was saved by a propitious evacuation, preceded by a momentous toga whistler incited by the mustard.

The fate of the good Protractud Sillinus was later sealed on a military campaign to wrest the region of Lower Intestines from the barbarians, led by Herb the Terrible. The kid got his hindquarters sliced off (in the act of taking a leak) while camped with his troops before the battle against the fearful Nordic Kitty-Cats, where he coined the immortal words, "Vasto fecum! Directum nel Poopamus! (Aw crap! Right in the stern!). He was buried just outside the senate bowling alley, next to a dumpster, where his interment was attended by a crowd of mourners (two) and some dope from Naples who was looking for a place to get a brewsky.

Encyclopedius Britannicus followed Sillinus to the throne, bringing his A-Game Momma, Curvaceous Rumpus, with him. She was one saliva-producing piece of patootie. The lady was admired throughout the empire for her good works, literary interests and sensational can. Little is known of her bra size. The scrolls that describe her focused on her popular lack of morals and her stamina in the sack. These graphically detailed writings fill one entire wing in the Museum of Imperial Slut-Tactics located outside of Cincinnati.

As head of state, Britannicus retained the religious custom of murdering his entire family and sacrificing a chamber pot to the god Zoos on school holidays. Lavish gifts were distributed to his cronies, mainly consisting of young girls and supple senior citizens. Some of the latter were female. Men of ethical pretensions (who were in fact scoundrels) demonstrated the corruption of their natures by shamelessly accepting bribes of property and broads of all ages. They stand as examples for our elected officials today. But beneath it all, the emperor was as contemptible for his stupidity as for his absurd appearance, able to win only some small amount of popularity for his distinguished record of exposing his gigantic member in the streets from a moving chariot (known as the Rod-Mobile). It was considered an impressive sight. The Latin texts often refer to Encyclopedius as "Jeezus Whoppun Harpoon-Man!" presumably for his ability to hit the urinal from an adjoining room.

I can identify with his situation. I know what it's like to be ridiculed for having an exceptionally ample love-nozzle, but the inconvenience is easily offset by the welcome one receives at group violations and other orgiastic gatherings. The Whoppster's policy was to direct his normal deviations from virtue into more perverse channels of indulgence. His training in carnal abomination was admirable and quite thorough, and the strong attraction of fleshly pleasures often interrupted state gatherings. Coincidentally, so did mine. No sexual novelty seemed excessive for this pervert, and his methods set an example for me throughout my trench-busting career. I think I mailed you an outline once.

The "Britt-Meister," as he was known in secret, rivaled the greatest orators of his day, speaking with imperial fluency and spontaneity and sprinkling his speeches with a liberal mention of the most appealing areas of female anatomy. His finest talent was the ability to be obscure in great detail. However when he began to speak in the senate (and a few corner bars) of his foresight and wisdom, nobody could keep from laughing. Many gave him the finger.

It was at this time that Washrum Publikus was convicted of urinating in a corner of the Senate (and on a couple of senators) and screwing around in general. He was sentenced to allow two military commanders to violate his wife and to commit suicide at least three times. "Washer" was unaware that his little woman had already served her sentence several times long before his conviction, and was amenable to continuing the practice. He obeyed the directive and fell on his sword—the handle—and so was unharmed. The unfortunate man was then executed by having his dick clamped shut, and so he died of unrelieved urination and perforated eardrums. There were three methods of execution in those days. I've already mentioned forced suicide. In addition, a person might be strangled with a chain-mail jockstrap (used) or have his heinie beaten with a cricket bat until the fatal requirement was satisfied.

The Romans of that time bequeathed us many learned maxims—words that can still guide us as we shuffle along on this "mortal coil," as Shakespeare or some jerk once said. By the way, Shakespeare's works include the line, "O flatter me, for love delights in praises." In other words, say something nice about my butt. And he had Hamlet utter the famous directions to his actors, "It should fall trippingly from the tongue, like Earl when he drools." A large volume of priceless quotations was unearthed during the excavation of a group outhouse on Rome's south side in 1899, mostly attributed to Sevenfootus Dribblus, a member of the senate and a hell of a wicker-ball player, but kind of a ball hog. Other maxims are probably from the chisel of Aurorum Borealus, a gravestone artist who was lit every night.

In examining these artifacts, one finds many surviving examples of profound thinking, such as "Quantum digestum posterium fatigus" (Some crap makes my ass tired) or "Succum heini, hippo phallus!" (Kiss my ass, you big prick). We also tend to find these attitudes reflected in writings on ancient Roman tablets from the Peekskill, New York, diggings, inscribed with sayings like "Scissors exitus deficatum" (Cut out the crap) and "Non yoosum draypus vennya gedd offer" (Don't wipe your Johnson on the curtains). A person with your grasp of ancient history is certainly aware that Rome was eventually invaded and conquered by the Visigoths and the Osteopaths.

You'll be interested to know that my venture capital efforts are proceeding nicely. A few weeks ago, I started a company called Arigami, Inc. But it folded. It folded!! Ha-ha-ha! Boy, that's a good one!! The city council met in special session yesterday in order to give themselves a raise in salary. Many citizens expressed their opposition by group mooning during the session and calling the mayor, Reelie O'Beese worthless. I'm thinking of running for mayor against her next term. I hope I can count on your absentee vote, which I can send you. I'm pretty sure I can get the swing vote. Most of the voters have trouble finding the polling station anyway. They drive around looking for a place to put their X's and then say, "The hell with it. Let's go have a beer." Their collective brains wouldn't be enough to grease a small pan. If they had one less chromosome we'd have to water them a couple of times a week.

Yours in greater Groundhog reverence.

Whoever

30

Hey Grover,

Here are some more items from my column in the local paper. It gives you great insight into my journalistic acumin.... akumen.... aw shit, talent.

1. Business News. One of the most successful companies in the health industry is located right here in our midst. Not everyone has been blessed, as my brother and I have, with superb physical construction, especially of the penile variety. There are many males who suffer from severe geometric defects in this bodily region without the possibility of correction until now. One real problem in the relationship area is a bend in the boner, an affliction that is widely known as "Cudgel-Curvature." In the respected medical reference compiled by Poope & Whypit, this sadly misshapen male member is also called "Wavy Willie," "Crooked Crank," and "Dong With A Detour." It's not so bad when you're screwing at somebody from around a corner, but for those who prefer a more straight-forward form of violation, it represents a serious impediment. The company in today's spotlight, **Right-On, Brother, Inc.**, has developed a low-cost rod-straightening kit for home use. By using this product, gentlemen, you can eliminate the curl in your camshaft in the privacy of your own home. In trials to date, the procedure has been successful in over ninety percent of the tests (both of them). It is relatively painless and has no after-effects other than ringing in the ears, swollen testicles, a tendency to walk with a lisp and, in extreme instances, eternal rest. The method is too complicated to explain in this article, but requires only clamps, a ball-peen hammer, blacksmith's tongs, a canoe paddle, a short length of logging chain, an anvil and a string of Malibu lights—available in any hardware outlet.

2. Science at Work. I am sure most of my readers have been at social gatherings where a person in attendance is sadly deficient in personal exhaust pipe discretion. Those around him (or her) are unfortunate enough to hear an impressive but unwelcome hindquarter eruption, sometimes known as a "big-time butt-burp." In fact, guests often fear that they are about to witness a full voiding of the entrails. This repugnant event is a vile, mean, base and wanton perversity, though except for the overpowering odor, relatively inoffensive if one is invulnerable to ear-drum perforation. Nevertheless, I can state from first-hand experience (involving a poorly-sealed sibling) that reckless and inconsiderate behavior of this sort is embarrassing for onlookers if the person in question proceeds to soil his pants. Well, much-needed help is on the way. Working out of his garage since his parole became effective, our own Retcher Lunge of Weejuss Terrasse has developed a solution to this potent challenge of our times. The medication he has produced is called *Gas-Stop®* and is available in liquid or pill form. The powerful liquid is fired into the offending anus with a high-pressure fire hose prior to the soirée, or in the case of a tablet, which is over a foot in diameter, hammered into the guilty orifice with a .45 caliber industrial staple gun. One of the dozen or so side-effects, other than a fatal episode and total nut loss, is the urge to vomit incessantly for the first thirty days, but the almost lethal constriction of the esophagus helps to minimize the range, if not the quantity, of flingable material. Our hats and our nose clamps go off to Retcher.

3. Serial Rapist at Large. The 911 lines have been flooded with calls for the past several weeks, reporting a series of sexual assaults in our community. At least ten occurrences have been described by terrified housewives and young ladies who found themselves in the clutches of this perverse trespasser on precious feminine goodies. Descriptions provided by the victims point to the same criminal, apparently a handsome young man with dark wavy hair, a fine physique and crotch equipment in the stud category. Those who were assaulted report a monster lady whacker. It seems the molester in each case also took the girl's panties when he was finished, thus reducing the range of my potential collectibles. Most of the women who were attacked declined to report the incident until forced by their husbands or male friends to do so. This was because the men were tired of hearing the poor things recount the smallest details of the assault with great enthusiasm on every possible occasion. Your reporter was able to obtain an interview with one of the unfortunate violated individuals, Mrs. Love-Lee Figyer of Wannabee Road, who was kind enough to speak on condition of anonymity:

"I left the bar around midnight," she explained, "and this, like, big animal-type person grabbed me from behind. He was, gee, like, very strong, you know? I couldn't get away from him, even though he put me down when he went back inside to get his keys and then had to use both hands to unlock his pickup. Before I knew it, I had folded my clothes and put them in a pile and I was in the back of the truck and he was on top of me. He must have gone at me for almost an hour. It was, like, really fantas.... I mean, awful, you know?"

"Would you recognize your attacker again?" I asked Mrs. Figyer.

"I'm not sure. It was so dark. But I think I could identify the scratches on his butt that I put there while I was hanging on."

"Have you ever been raped prior to this?"

"Just once before, when the check bounced."

I spoke with several other traumatized victims and they told virtually the same story. Sally Sillikone is a dental technician in possession of a formidable bundle of frontline breastwork who confirmed that her rapist grabbed her from behind and forced her to accede to his wishes. She was accosted outside her building and made to open her apartment door. The attack then took place immediately after she had changed into a casual garter-belt and stocking ensemble. I thought it was a good opportunity to pursue my investigation of sexual behavior in young (hot) females, so I asked Ms. Sillikone what her reaction had been as a young girl to her first sexual experience. She said it was, "Gee, are all you guys from the same bowling league?"

I plan to elaborate on this theme in a future column.

Mrs. Belle Bottoms was another victim of the dreaded pervert:

"My husband was downstairs watching the Dodgers on television, but I was tired so I went to bed early. I'm a heavy sleeper and I woke up with something pounding in my head. Then I realized that it was a lot lower. This man was on top of me, kissing and fondling me, and forcing me to have sex with him. Ooooh, I get shivers just thinking about it."

"It must have been terrible for you."

"Oh, right, and then he had sex with my sister."

"Your sister lives with you?"

"No, but while the guy was taking a shower, I called my sister to tell her what happened, and she came right over."

My questions concerning what the victims were wearing at the time of the attacks went unanswered. Citizens are up in arms concerning this rash of assaults on our fair womanhood. The ladies at the Senior Center have vowed to keep their doors wide open in a concerted effort to lure the culprit inside where he can be captured. Mavis Pendelbust spoke for all of the women at the center:

"Many of us will be staying up all night until we catch this long-gifted stu... er, criminal. We will be wearing very little clothing for extra mobility and we built a spring-loaded trap made out of our lacy underwear to ensnarl him. We can't wait to get him in our pants."

4. Mayoral Debate. The mayoral debate between Ms. Reelie O'Beese and this reporter-candidate took place on Friday evening at Clyde's Hamburger Heaven (in the parking lot). I would like to take this opportunity to apologize for my outburst, when I referred to my opponent as a "Fat-Assed Whore." The words were poorly chosen in the heat of the moment and were due to my frustration at her steady trickle of bullshit. I also regret my decision to punctuate my remark with a gesture involving my crotch. As tasteless as this behavior may seem on the surface, in my defense I can say that those who know the incumbent will probably feel that the label was not far from the mark. Madame Mayor has the body of a roll-top desk and the brains of a duck. I would also like to disagree with the polls concluding that 97% of the respondents said Ms. O'Beese won the debate and that I'm a prick. I'm in this race to the end.

5. Harassment Prosecutions. Several businessmen have been forced to answer sexual harassment charges brought against them. The most recent occurrence was at the hubcap factory, when the office manager, Harlow Bollz, grabbed Ernestine Peggpuller's mammaries and wouldn't let go. In my own defense, I can say that when it was my turn I let go after a while. The District Attorney, Musbee Stukk, held a news conference in which he warned the business community that he would take no shit from men who use their managerial positions to "hit on the broads in their employ." We condemn this reprehensible behavior as well and promise to give it up very soon. Here is a portion of the memo Mr. Stukk sent to every company in the county: "As a manager you are hereby required to keep Sexual Harassment Complaint Forms in the bottom drawer of your file cabinet. Then when your secretary retrieves the documents, you can get a great look at her tail."

6. Election Results Announced. This reporter plans to call for a re-count of the election results that declared Reelie O'Beese the winner of the mayoral contest in a squeaker—45,206 votes to 8. Several of my supporters were accused of voting twice, but they can't be prosecuted because they're not citizens.

7. Local Golfer Wins Tournament. Chester "Digger" Divitt posted the low score after fourteen rounds of the Microsoft Sprint Coca-Cola Canon Budweiser Pepto-Bismol Gassheimer's Baked-Bean Classic held at (and across) the 73 Toll-Road and the Skeet Shooting Facility in San Kakoffee. The "Digger" won on the last hole, sinking a three-inch, uphill, left-to-right roller that broke four feet. His judicious placement of one shoe prevented the ball from going off the green and into a nearby swamp. Digger would never have been able to get it away from the alligators if that had happened. After shooting several poor rounds to begin, the new champion and real horse's ass (reporter's opinion) said in the post-tournament interview that he felt great after a 69.

8. Passings, etc. Mrs. Maude Traschbagg was laid to rest this morning in the burial plot that her husband, Clarence, arranged for her in the backyard of their palatial home behind the town slag heap. Maude's funeral was lovely and the corpse revealed little of the deep cuts, numerous fractures and ugly bruises that preceded her passing. For the two-minute service, the church was decorated with old tires and a wreath of nice second-hand hubcaps from the widower's junkyard and salvage establishment. In her memory, Clarence had his wife buried with her prat sticking up out of the ground so he would have a place to park his bike.

9. Corrections: Due to a typographical error in yesterday's column, a picture of the Dalai Lama was incorrectly identified as Mike Tyson.

Letters to the Editor

Dear Sir, I think the authorities should look into the quality of the food being served in our correctional facilities. The filet mignon is often medium, in contrast to specific requests for medium-rare, and the wine list is woefully lacking in dry whites. *From Thermos Boddel, currently serving a term in the county jail (a gated community) for exposing himself to a nudist group.*

Dear Sir, A little-known, but exciting sport today is backyard love-making. It ought to be included in the Olympics. *From Niftee Clitt, current gold-medal winner of the Heavyweight Competition in the Hammock Fornication Finals.*

Dear Sir, Steptonshaft College should fire its football coach. This horse's ass has his head buried in his urethra and doesn't have the faintest idea what he's doing. How can he justify punting on first down on the opponent's eight yard-line? They ought to run him out of town with a rail stuck up his clipboard! *From Opun Hostiliteeze, President of Steptonshaft College.*

<u>Editor's note</u>: "Coach Razzleass says you're a donkey's dick who doesn't understand the intricacies of gridiron strategy. He adds that his son is the punter and needs experience. The coach also maintains that he can count the team's ten losses this year on the fingers of one hand."

Dear Sir, When are you jackasses at city hall going to do something about dogs crapping on my lawn? I'm going to beat the next one I see anywhere near my property with an ax handle until his brains run downhill, and I include you mindless dolts at city hall in that statement. Respectfully yours. *From the Rev. Cedric Neissguy, St. Irving's Parish.*

All of this sort of reminds me of this girl I knew in Latvia a long time ago. As you can surmise, I had to be constantly careful that I wasn't overwhelmed with sexual opportunities. But I still don't know why some women refuse to dress up in a Nazi uniform with a short skirt and a swastika on their panties. I say sex is nobody's business except yours—and the other dozen or so people involved.

You know,

Me

31

Hey Grover,

I'm trying to fit my writing career into my duties as an ace journalist. I was assigned by our local television station, KRAP, to cover the Short-Circuit Court of Raccoon County the past couple of weeks, and I had a chance to report on several interesting cases.

The Honorable Cumming Geddess presided over a courtroom filled with felons, perverts, deviants and miscreants of all types, and there were many from outside the legal profession, as well. The docket began with two large policemen who brought in a man from the home for deaf mutes. "Your Honor," one of them said, "we arrested this guy, but we didn't know if we should tell him he has the right to be silent." The judge looked at them scornfully for a moment over his fashionable aviator glasses (he wore an aviator cap too), threw the case out of court, the defendant down the stairs, and had the bailiff kick the cops in the ass. He also called them mouse-brains.

The next item on the docket involved a riot in our local funeral home, right next to the toilet-bowl reclamation plant. The disturbance had apparently become very serious, with people fighting to get a look at the deceased, a popular young male movie star who had expired while visiting our fair city. His corpse was found in a dumpster behind the courthouse motel annex with his scrotum badly mauled and little hope of reviving him because his head was missing. He was identified by dental records found in his pocket. The judge fined the rioters two hundred dollars plus court costs after he fired two shots in their direction and missed. He also missed a cat that was lying on a window sill, so he picked up another cat that he keeps behind the bench for such occasions and blew its brains out. I gave him a standing ovation.

A third instance involved an Eastern European immigrant woman, Peddlee Nass, who was arrested for soliciting. She must have been at least seventy, and that was just her bust measurement. She said, "I don't feel for pretty good, Mr. Judge. I find lump under breast" The courtroom fell silent. She continued, "But fortunately was only belt buckle." The judge asked her, "Have you had a check-up recently?" She said, "Naw, just couple Romanians."

The town scuzz-ball, Boozun Bukketts, was sentenced to thirty days for public drunkenness and exposing himself in the hardware store. He explained that he was only trying to measure some wood for bookshelves. It was clearly a case of *déjà poopée*. In other words, we had all heard this crap before. The judge reminded him that there were few places in town where his unsheathed cudgel did not figure prominently. The lawyer was put in the same cell with his client and the key was mailed to Pakistan. I had appeared before Judge Geddes a couple of times myself. The first time was on a misdemeanor charge of giving enemas without a license. I explained, "I'm sorry, but I have a terrible burden. I'm so smart, I'm not only a genius, I'm a super genius. I can't be held to normal standards. You can't imagine the pain I endure because I'm surrounded by idiots." The judge said, "Your pants are on backwards." The next time was when my neighbor's dog dumped on my begonias and I shot the little beast with a BB gun. I wound up in a pellet court. A pellet court! Get it?

Another time, a complainant told the court he had come home to find his wife in bed with Phlebitis, the delivery boy from the Greek market. The judge sentenced his wife to meet him in his chambers. Next, an Amish farmer was fined for polluting. It was determined that the horse that was pulling his buggy had a faulty exhaust system and the emissions were piling up on the roadway.

A complicated affair was one in which a teenager named William Jones was accused of raping his date, Janie Warmdrowerz. A witness, her friend Marybelle McShidder, was on the stand. She told the court, "Janie was in the car with William. I looked in and observed Janie on her back and I think I saw a writer too." The judge said, "A writer? Why do you say that?" She said, "I saw William Faulkner."

Miss Awfle Bustee testified in a sexual assault case that she had been attacked by Terry Mupp, a bad customer if there ever was one, and a person who was reported to have a wickedly substantial wand. The lady possesses a pleasing frontal display of Grade-A low-hanging fruit. "Did he actually penetrate you?" the prosecutor inquired. "Not too much," Miss Tryle admitted. "How did you keep him from raping you?" he asked. She said, "I was able to beat him off."

She reminded me of a girl from Hong Kong I met when I was stationed in Iceland some years ago. Her name was May-Bea Soon. The first time I saw her was in this sleazy place I would ordinarily not frequent, but entered merely to make an adjustment to my shorts. In the course of our friendship, I picked up a few useful Chinese phrases. For instance:

Wat Yu Chu Wing?   (Off your diet already?)
Tin Kyoo Wong   (I believe you're mistaken)
Yoo Shee Den Mee   (You're full of it, buster!)

Fortunately, she agreed to join me in an out-of-pants experience. But that's not important now. What's important is that her old man didn't find me in the refrigerator. Back in the courtroom, the judge fined Marvin Nawstrooldriller two hundred dollars for nauseating public behavior. This guy is always picking his beak, which looks like a potato. He roots around in that thing until the third joint on his finger disappears. Marvin often shouts **Paydirt**! when he digs out a piece that's so big it's hard to carry with two hands. If he can lift it, he flicks it on a store window or dumps it in a mailbox. Then he laughs like a hyena. He looks like a hyena too. The judge shot him.

At that moment, the bailiff came up to me and whispered, "There's a hole in the ladies washroom and I'm going to look into it." This is a guy who wanted to be a professional baseball player, but he had to quit when he caught a line drive on the fly. On the fly!

A monk from the local monastery, The Holy Brothers of Eternal Peace, appeared before the bar, accused of refusing to answer a policeman's questions about the lack of noise in the neighborhood. Then a young woman was brought before the judge. This was a floozie if I ever saw one (and I've seen more than one). The prosecutor said, "Isn't it true that on January 14th you were having sex with a one-legged dwarf and a donkey on the roof of a car while going 100 miles an hour in a blizzard—in reverse?" She said, "What was that date again?"

It's clear from your parole record that you appreciate the complexities of the legal system and our local contribution to truth, justice and all that crap. As for me, I try to relax after a hard day at the courthouse. We ate out at a seafood restaurant the other night, and I fell down as we were leaving. I think I pulled a mussel.

We must have this time together less often.

Ludlow

32

Hey Grover,

The city council had an open-house and open-air New Year's party, and the weather was beautiful. All the free-loaders and advanced cases of brain-leakage attended, which accounted for just about the entire population. Masses of people crowded the buffet tables that were set up in the parking lot at the city hall complex. I wish they had kept the cars out. The ground was covered with a blanket of white (a heroin-smuggler crashed his car in front of the library). The people were like a swarm of demented locusts, only uglier. You should have seen them fight for a chance at the grub, catered by the firm of Uppchuck & Heeve. Among the goodies were barbequed swine and rhino tongue in a Lysol gravy. The rutabaga casserole was popular too, as were mashed turnips on toast, collard greens in chocolate sauce, kidney on a stick and other delicacies. I saw a large platter of brains on the table, but I think they were from a few unfortunates who were trampled in the race for the armadillo stew. Many of those in attendance were later seen bending over potted plants and engaging in involuntary vegetal eruptions. I can describe my reaction to the whole thing with just one word: Pretty bad!

I go to this travesty each year to observe retardation in action. Unfortunately, the celebration was in full swing when the street commissioner decided to put a final layer of asphalt on the parking lot, and I'm afraid the noise distracted a bit from the festivities, but it was fine for those who cherish the smoke and the smell of tar. A couple of people from out of town tried to crash the party, but we chased them out. A few warning shots usually suffice.

We had just gotten back from a trip to Vancouver to visit a lawyer we met while in England in September. He invited us to come to his place for a change of pace. Actually, he didn't really invite us, but in England he said he hoped to see us again and we made him pay for that remark. At the party we were cornered by the usual lobotomized individuals and newly-released hopeless mental patients. "Snotty" Wafflepants caught us and wouldn't shut up. To give you an idea of how much he drinks, when he gives blood, the hospital uses it to sterilize their instruments. He brought his girlfriend, Busty Nowt, and she's no poster girl for anorexia. I think she took the gold medal at the last Olympics for accumulated fat molecules. Busty has enormously flabby thighs, but her belly covers them pretty well. She once went to a biker party looking for a little action and took off all her clothes. They gang-dressed her. She thinks she's incredibly clever, but she doesn't know which way to sit on a toilet. She stood under the mistletoe at Christmas last year and she was still there at Easter.

Tex Reebait was hired to provide the main entertainment at the party in case we got tired of watching people wallow in the egg salad. Tex is a country singer with a two-man back-up band (cello and bass drum). He started twanging on his guitar and yowling about some redneck crap. As he moved around on the stage, Tex got the power cord from his electric guitar caught between his legs and somehow wrapped around his scrotum. He ended his first song with a high-tension riff that shot several thousand volts through him, concentrated on the genitals. Lit up like a religious parade in Guatemala. Everybody thought it was part of the act. He flew off the stage in flames and into the center of the buffet offering and the applause was deafening. Even drowned out the asphalt spreader for a moment. Tex was mostly charred black and he set fire to the vinaigrette in the porcupine salad. Stepford Sludge managed to save a little when he went for a second helping, but he had to pick out some carbonized pieces of Tex's tail-section.

Tex suffered serious burns to his testicles, his caboose and the soles of his feet—and his Johnson is no good anymore either. If he pulls through, he'll need an ass replacement and new toenails. If you're interested in becoming a donor, send me your rear-end dimensions and pertinent trauma history (kicking, mauling, goosing, etc.) and I'll forward the information to the local Butt Unit. There was some talk in the emergency room of just shooting the poor bastard (we don't attract high-quality health care practitioners here). The last I heard, Tex was propped up and strapped to a board and they were feeding him with a garden hose from about ten feet away. I went to visit him and still can't figure out how they knew which end to squirt the chow into. The hospital staff predicts a slow and painful recovery and even then he won't be much more use than he ever was. Fortunately, the crematorium announced that they were prepared to give him a discount.

The act that followed Tex was a bagpipe quartet playing some Lawrence Welk songs, a Beethoven overture, and something by Fats Domino. I've been spending a lot more time in the field of music lately and I found that the best way to tune a bagpipe is with a pitchfork. Ballzer Growss wasn't at the gout-fest. He usually enlivens our get-togethers by exposing himself. He has a nice appendage, so we missed him a lot. Ballzer has spent his whole life defying authority. Somebody told me U.S. Marshals are after him for transporting cocker spaniels across state lines and dumping in an un-flushed federal toilet. I think his antisocial behavior stems from the fact that his mother refused to breast-feed him. She only offered to shake hands.

Kermit Littledong attended with his wife, Lyka. You may have heard of him. He invented a pooper-scooper that can be converted into a soup spoon and soda straw. His wife could be subtly described as "heavy with accessories." This babe is a real goddess. If I know she's going to be at a gathering, I dip my Johnson in a bowl of *Pleeze-Go-Soft®* before leaving home. It's a little concoction I put together using one part vinegar and two parts sulfuric acid, with a few rubber bands dissolved in lemon extract. A pinch of nutmeg improves the taste. Wherever Lyka appears, drool secretion and erectional mass increase at an explosive rate. She wore a low-cut, clingy outfit that emphasized every square inch of her jock-tightening anatomy, which is thankfully crowned by an award-winning set of majestic suckables.

Eyefull Tower, a tall blonde beauty from our neighborhood, arrived with her boyfriend, Lumpy Gigglechunks. Lumpy was booted out of college for urinating in restricted areas, like the Dean's desk drawer. From the hallway. He tried out for several sports and played drawback on the football team, as well as third-string substitute base-runner on the baseball nine. They dropped him when he tried to steal third base by cutting across the pitcher's mound from first. He was such a lousy athlete he even missed when he was trying to shake hands with the other team. The only reason Eyefull hangs out with Lumpy is because he is said to posses a monstrous cavern whomper. She is one big Momma! She played basketball in college because she's six-five, but she had to quit. Her knockers were bigger than the balls and she couldn't see to dribble. But the guys in the stands dribbled. Anybody who climbs up on her will need one of those alpine tools, but it'll be worth it. She's managed to make jogging a spectator sport. Because she's so tall, it's hard to look down her blouse, but that much easier to peek up her skirt, which is why you find me tying my shoelaces whenever she's around.

She reminds me of a gal I knew years ago in Sweden, a real smorgas-broad. When I think of the past it brings back a lot of memories. Poo-Lynne Punchiss was a babe who couldn't keep her hands out of a guy's pants, and those are the best kind. They don't need to complete a training program. Contrary to popular belief, not all Swedish girls are nymphomaniacs—only about ninety percent or so, thank the good Lord. Poo-Lynne was big in two places—her chest and her generosity with her can. Her idea of safe sex was with shin guards on. She was attracted to me because of my Middle-East reputation as a defiler of virgins. My love for her did not go especially deep, though, or my Johnson either. The doctor traced it to a case of shrinkle-pox. He figured I had picked it up from a toilet seat that was lying around outside a bordello junkyard somewhere in Mongolia. I'm determined not to go there again, and you may decide to curtail your visits too.

But I digress. At the party, Ron Denron, who is always going around in circles, came up to us and started talking about something incoherent. He must be over a hundred. He just got out of the hospital, where they took out his liver and put in a whoopee cushion so they'd be able to tell if it was working. As you would expect, our favorite couple arrived at the party in time for Earl to attack the grub like a starving weasel with rabies. I suspect that he actually has rabies. Nogga Toff, a female parolee who was serving at the buffet, told him to quit horsing around and clocked him in the noggin four or five times with a soup ladle (full of soup). Didn't slow him down. Madge and Earl had just returned from a bus tour to Fresno. They checked into a hotel there and found towels that had been stolen from their house. I may have already alluded to the lack of molecular movement in Earl's gourd, but sometimes his cranial devastation surprises even me. He figures he'll improve as a lover if he practices alone.

Crewell Joake is the owner of the local racing stables. He's a scabby little runt who only outweighs his jockey (Caesar Boobeeze) by about two pounds. No bones, all skin, and sharp as a beach ball. The guy has a collection of nags that's been rejected by every glue factory west of Long Island. They should all be pulling a plow, which is what they look like during a race. The horses he runs them against aren't much different. If you go to the track, you can watch these emaciated Clydesdale look-alikes spring from the starting gate with the alacrity of a crucified slug and then have lunch, a shoe-shine and a healthy dump for yourself before they come down the stretch. In one race, his horse collapsed a few yards before the wire and Caesar had to roll it across the finish line. It still won by fifteen lengths, because the rest of the donkeys were back at the turn leaning against the rail, wheezing and trying to catch their breath. Horses tend to tire quickly here. I guess it's human nature.

The next part of the afternoon's entertainment featured a demonstration by the high school cheerleading squad. The school has a singularly unattractive student body, and most of the ugliness seems to reside in the cheerleading corps. Note that I use the future derogatory tense for this description. Their ugliness is nicely accented by the sheer enormity of their cans. You should see these teenage pachyderms try to build a pyramid. You've never witnessed so much sweating and grunting in your life. Several of the parents shouted encouragement to their "little" (used in a literary sense only) behemoths and urged them on with promises of burgers and fries after the struggle. You can already guess what mom and pop looked like—layers of cellulite spread on monster cans with a grease trowel. Some couples shouldn't be allowed to breed. The kids screwed around for twenty minutes and finally got one lard-ass to stand on the shoulders of two other heavyweights. At that point the bottom layer sank almost a foot into the asphalt. And that was the part that had already hardened. The rest of the estudiantes (Latin for "monstrosities") just stood around and tried to keep their underpants from riding up in the crack of their butts.

Chunky Dumper circulated through the crowd, groping fannies and bellyaching when somebody pasted him. He has never been successful in the area of intimate relationships—or any other, for that matter. Chunky was in a bar a few weeks ago where I went to ask for directions. He was trying to latch onto a nice-looking Momma. He tried his pick-up line, "My father is dying and I stand to inherit his fortune." She's now his step-mother. Chunky has been sighted around town recently with binoculars in his hand and his pants around his knees, so he appears to have developed another interest.

The New Year's party broke up about midnight when the council had had enough. They turned the lights out and chased everybody away with a bulldozer. A couple of people who were still trying to sneak in got crushed, but they'll blend into the asphalt. Stepford Sludge was a little slow and got run over, but almost everybody else took the hint and got out of the way. The Stepper was lucky, though. The treads on the bulldozer pulled his pants down and he just wound up with a flattened Johnson. No big deal. He hardly uses it anyway.

Our life here is rich in culture, augmented by the many edifying programs we have on TV. I tape them all the time. With duct tape. I put it over the screen. Instead of watching that ____, I've immersed myself in great literature, reading everything written by Ernest Anyway and the biographies of great figures in history. I've traced the lives of great men to cull their secrets of success—men like our more notable presidents, Reesearch Grant, Calvin Coolwun and Warren G. Hardon. But no person inspired me more than that famous historical figure who was born during a kitchen explosion in France. His name was Linoleum Blownapart.

Under separate cover I'm sending you a gift certificate granting you luxury toilet privileges at many service stations in your area.

Tu hermano con el guano,

Ludlow

Ludlow Smutt

THE BUZZARD CROTCH LEPERS
A MAJOR-LEAGUE BASEBALL FRANCHISE
69 AVENIDA PROCTOLOGICA
BUZZARD CROTCH, NV 86224

January 15, 20--

Dear Mr. Smutt,

As a fervent sports fan and former stellar athlete, you have almost certainly heard that the National Baseball League has granted a team franchise to the people of Buzzard Crotch. The Lepers Organization is devoted to representing all of the citizens of Southern Nevada, eager to compete with those turkeys who currently defile base paths in a neighboring state which we shall refrain from naming. We chose the name "Lepers" to reflect the possibility that attendance, among other things, could fall off in the future. With financing put together by the Wall Street firm of Sokum Downdah Dare-Soxx, our organization boasts the most talented ball-brains in the country. We are now proceeding to develop our player roster, looking for proven skills on the diamond. Your brother, a marvelous individual and an outstanding athlete in his own right, has suggested that you could be an asset in this area if you are amenable to entering competition at the highest level once again. We greatly respect his opinion and are eager to pursue negotiations with you, prepared to spend whatever is reasonable to get you into our clubhouse. Our organization will need to begin slowly and work our way up to world-class competitive ability over a period of several years. For that reason, the initial team will consist of players like yourself, those who are not yet household names (depending on the vocabulary employed), but are in your general age group and able to function at a level commensurate with the superb athletic talents your brother assures us you possess. There are definite advantages to being your age. For instance, kidnappers are not interested in you and your uniform will not have the chance to wear out. We have already signed some fine players who are in your category. Judd Shanker, formerly with the Omaha Oafs, is coming on board. Judd hasn't quite retained his past pitching brilliance, but nevertheless fits our

222

requirements. For instance, when conversing with him no one would suspect that he doesn't have any underwear on. But he can still throw a mean bean-ball at your pubic section. "Blister" Pfister, the scourge of the old Negro League, although not black himself, will lead off for us. He overcame a difficult childhood to make a name for himself at our national pastime. "Blister" lived in a neighborhood that was so dangerous the local police force shot everyone on sight. His current physical condition can best be described as "alarming," but he has promised to undertake a regimen of diet and exercise as soon as he is able to walk again after the sawmill mishap. Trevor "The Trapper" Flemburger is reporting early in order to work on his fielding, trying to recapture the wide-ranging talent he displayed with the Fairfield Felines. This Hall-of-Fumer has a nose like a bloodhound. The rest of his face looks like one too. He was involved in an interesting ruling during a close game many years ago. When he was in the field, a line drive smacked him in the head and the ball split in half. Part of it went over the fence and the right fielder caught the other part. The umpires gathered at home plate for twenty minutes trying to figure out what to do. They finally awarded him second base, so he took it and left the ballpark. "The Trapper" has been plagued with problems of a sexual nature for most of his life, not always limited to the ballpark. He went to one meeting for premature ejaculators, but had to leave early. Manuel "Ciego" Ortiz will very likely roam center field for us. He was at one time the greatest outfielder in Lago Putrido, Guatemala—or one of its suburbs. His eyesight has dimmed a little since then, and we understand that he relies on the sound of the ball coming off the bat to locate fly balls now, but we have every confidence that he can snag them almost as well as ever. He plans to join us as soon as he gets out of the hospital, where he is being treated for extreme bruising over most of his body and multiple fractures of the skull. Our equipment manager is working on a padded vest for him that will cover most of his body and he will be issued a football helmet to protect his squash. We thought that you could room with Manuel and be his interpreter at the same time. I would caution you, despite your probable fluency in Spanish, to avoid certain phrases when speaking with Manuel. Please don't use expressions like, "Dios mio, Chico, que eres muy feo" ((Holy shit, buddy, you're an ugly number!) or "Has recibido muchos bolos en la cabeza?" (Have you speared a lot of liners with your turnip?). And we leave it to you to avoid mentioning his stunted male member (unless you're interested in establishing an intimate relationship). We have a few other suggestions to keep in mind. Your brother (we cannot emphasize enough the respect we have for him and his accomplishments on the athletic field) has described some of your early activities, and it is our hope that you have abandoned certain practices (concentrated in the pelvic region) which could bring adverse publicity and downright shame to our organization if you were to continue their use. We know, for instance, that when you reached first base (a rarity in itself), you often changed into clown shoes in order to touch the next base faster. We would like you to concentrate less on footwear and more on getting your ass on the base paths. You should be aware that the rules of our club prohibit lying on the dugout roof during a game and checking out female groin areas in the stands. We know that you also used a fungo bat to push some skirts higher in order to expand your field of view. This habit is particularly unwelcome, since you often did it when you should have been at the plate or in the field with the rest of the team. The umpires will for this reason be checking bats for foreign substances, including body fluids, and we suggest that there are other ways to satisfy your animals urges. It was brought to our attention that you sometimes threw your bat in fits of anger after striking out ten or twenty times in a row. Fortunately, we hear that most of these incidents occurred in the shower, but it would be a good idea to keep a lid on that type of reaction. Referring to the paragraph above, we feel that the shower is a good place to satisfy your animal urges. This is a fine opportunity to assume your place once again alongside some of the most admired players of the past. Please take the time to provide us with the information requested on the attached forms. Your past ballpark exploits are of particular interest to us and will guide us in coming to terms with a person of your skill set.

Sincerely,

Grafton Fatt   President

EVALUATION SHEET

Batting Average _____(No fractions please)

(Lifetime average—including pickup games, Little League, high school, minor leagues, town teams, company teams, dicking around by yourself)

Number of Balls actually hit out of the Infield (Indicate Type)

____ Dart   ____ Rope   ____ String   ____ Hard Shot

____ Bunt   ____ Dribbler   ____ Chopper   ____ Squeaker

____ Roller   ____ Laugher   ____ Used Rubber

____ Dead Buzzard   ____ Infielder fell down

Choice of Bat

____ Louisville Slugger   ____ Boston Basher   ____ Florida Flailer

____ Memphis Mallet   ____ Tree branch   ____ Hockey stick

____ Oar   ____ Axe handle   ____ Length of pipe   ____ Rake Handle

____ Ten-pounder   ____ Nothing too heavy

____ Whatever they call that Cricket Paddle

Swing Characteristics

____ Right-handed   ____ Left-handed   ____ Stand on the plate

____ Step in the Bucket   ____ Step in theDugout   ____ Step in Excrement

____ Like to bunt   ____ Will bunt on any count   ____ Full swing is bunt

____ Tend to crown catcher   ____ Haven't hit anything yet

Favorite Pitches to Hit

____ Flamer   ____ Smoker   ____ Creamer   ____ With Hop on it

____ Slow Curve   ____ Knuckler   ____ Thumber   ____ Drop Kick

____ Underhand Toss

Vision

____ A Hawk ; A Mole   ____ Can distinguish beach balls

____ Difficulty with moving objects   ____ Can see rough outlines

____ Night-vision goggles necessary (also in daylight)

____ Is anybody there?

Estimated Speed

____ At my best going downhill   ____ Stakes must be driven

____ Need a push   ____ Frequently overtaken by turtles

____ Normally timed with calendar

Quickness

____ A panther ____ A ferret ____ A weasel (also describes integrity)

____ Hurts when I get up ____ Snot on a tree ____

____ An ox (expecting?__ Yes__ No)

Retention of Signals

____ Good memory ____ Study notes on base-paths ____ Could use GPS

____ Confused by hand signals ____ Confused by crotch signals

____ Admire crotch signals ____ Shouting more effective

____ What's the sign for beer?

Sliding Technique

____Need directions to target base ____ Feet first ____ Head first

____ Elbows first ____ Ass first ____ Feet in the air ____ Crotch exposed

____ Slide starts 30 feet out ____ Pick up loose change on the way

____ Help drag infield during slide ____ Spike infielders (and umpires)

____ Keep bat handy ____ Sometimes resort to firearms

____ Frequently reported missing between sacks

Desired Fielding Position

____ Standing straight up ____ Bent over a little

____ In the shade ____Like to lean against something ____Camp stool ?

Most Experience at Position

____Pitcher ____Catcher ____ First base ____Second base ____ Third base

____ Other base ____ Outfield ____ Outhouse ____ Bleacher seating

Fielding Ability

____ Like a cat ____ Like a vacuum cleaner ____ Able to get some

____ Don't get many ____ Where are they? ____ What do they look like?

Locker Preference

____ In vicinity of ball park ____ Near bus lines ____ On the bus

____Corner of parking lot ____Next to buffet table ____ Adjacent to restroom ____ In owner's box ____ Near ladies room ____ In ladies room

How Salary Is Paid

____ Cash (Albanian Currency) ____ Check ____ Offshore Account

____Mailed home to Momma ____ Supermarket coupons

____ Cathouse passes

Awards & Recognition

____ Batting Title ____ Golden Glove ____ Most Valuable Player

____ Least Valuable Player ____ Shitty Player of the Year ____ Cursed

____ Stoned ____ Cursed and Stoned ____ Mauled and Pummeled

____ Thrown out of Clubhouse ____ Attacked by angry mob

____ Ass regularly kicked ____ Drive-by castration attempt

Chewing Preferences

____ Tobacco ____ Bubble gum ;Club sandwich ____ Boobies

Physical Handicaps

____ Extremities accounted for ____ Some fingers missing

____ Feet smell ____ Scabs ____ All ten toes on one foot

____ One or more lost nuts ____ Pigeon-toed ____ Duck-assed

____ Squirrel-peckered ____ Balls coming loose

____ Plugged nostril ____ Plugged ass ____ No hole in dick

We'll call you.

33

Hey Grover,

You're oddly quiet about my appeal for financial support for the many worthwhile projects I described to you, so I assume you're giving it a lot of thought. Because you didn't respond right away, however, I'm unable to publish my coffee-table book with pictures of books abut coffee tables and I'm saddened that you can allow a few thousand dollars to come between us and millions in revenue. You undoubtedly have a good reason to reject my request, and I respect your reasons. After all, you are one of my favorite brothers (next to me). I was only trying to appeal to the fact that you and I are twins. Both of us.

But nothing holds me back, as you know, not even your disregard for my desperate condition. No, the hopeless straits in which you have placed me simply illustrate the importance of my determination to succeed. This time, my project has success chiseled all over it, and you know I can identify with that description. It's a cultural masterpiece and a chance for you to realize profits beyond your wildest dreams (if they ever deviate from young ladies in deficient states of vesture).

In this specific case, I have composed a modern opera which I call "Un Ballo in Maschera." This can be translated as either "A Masked Ball" or "One Nut Wrapped in Masking Tape." It is therefore designed to appeal to a wide audience, from cultured art lovers to anatomically aroused perverts and you. The music reflects many influences of the Baroque and Ice-Age periods, along with contrapuntal marching band effects and faint echoes of the Daffy Duck theme. There are two reasons for this. The first is that these music forms were the easiest to copy. That's also the second reason. At times the emotional impact of the work can be overwhelming unless you don't care. I expect it to open at the Met in Lincoln Center very soon, although I have not heard back from anyone there since I submitted it.

My opera is set in the small Italian village of Garibaldi Heights in the eighteenth century and celebrates the miraculous power of deep passion, profound affection and disgusting sexual practices, with a sub-plot involving a nasty case of short-shaftedness, all of which unite to bind the central lovers together until one of them can get loose and call the cops. The overture opens with several well-known strains, including the one suffered by the tuba player while lifting his instrument. A series of adagio themes are introduced by the violins, thankfully drowned out by the trombones and the collapse of the brass section, as the bassoon player leans over to clock the oboist with a spare clarinet (everybody hammers those clowns when they get a chance). It works out well, since I didn't write anything for the oboe. All of this is accompanied by a twenty-minute timpani passage played in a soft fortissimo from offstage (two blocks away). The principal motif (from a Viagra commercial) is taken up by the cellos at this point (because it fell off the music stand), with an underlying pissimo response in the background from a duck decoy. As the curtain goes up, the musicians break for lunch, taking advantage of a hotdog stand that is wheeled through the orchestra pit.

The villain of the piece is Count Disgusto Vomitari, a rich but ugly number whose wand is regrettably only eight centimeters in length (divide by 2.54 for inches) when fully erect, which is all the time (and is incidentally responsible for calluses on both his hands). There are few words to adequately describe his genital shortcomings. They begin with a woefully shriveled scrotum that resembles a sun-baked prune, on top of which fate has contrived to award him a dismally meager skewer. Besides that, his member has the physiological characteristics of a cheap shoelace, brown and limp. For many years, the count (also called "Butt-Hole Extraordinario") has been the object of hate mail, assassination attempts, rock-throwing, extreme ridicule, and kids avoiding his house on Halloween for disappointing many a hot Mamma because of his stunted condition, but you know what that's like. He has undergone several treatments with a waterwheel-operated hose-stretcher, but the process gave him a stomach ache.

Vomitari's only redeeming quality is his admirable habit of exterminating cats, often by beating them to death with another cat. The count laments his penile inadequacy in the poignant "Coupla centimetri woodabee benvenuto" (An inch or two more would be welcome). His wife,

Nauseata, is every bit as appealing as he is, which is zero. Her face would stop rabbits from mating (even with other rabbits). I know it stopped me. This broad is really fat. She has what's known as a ballpark figure. Secretly, Count Vomitari has the wild screaming hots for Dolce-Keester, the daughter of Piccolo Brainsi, a simple woodcutter who has lost his job because he couldn't hack it. Ha-ha-ha. Sometimes I crack me up. Piccolo, a name that coincidentally describes his IQ as well as the length of his hammer, has managed to find temporary work cleaning sewer residue from septic tanks, although it makes his tongue sore. But despite his low condition, which includes abject ignorance and the direction in which his Willie points, he has vowed that the count will never touch his little girl unless he gets cash up front and describes his resolve in the touching aria, "Se non gotta dollari, è tu baddo" (No money, no honey).

Without her father's knowledge, which is pretty easy to arrange, Dolce-Keester develops a relationship with another admirer, Lungo Pecceroni, a simple but dumb farm hand. The first time she sees him, he is picking cucumbers and his fly is open. She takes one in her hand (the cucumber) and says, "This reminds me of my ex-boyfriend." The young man is puzzled by her remark and assumes that she means the guy had dirty hands. Lungo has the mental alacrity of a geranium, but he makes up for it with the length of his mule basher and is therefore immensely popular with the local ladies (as well as various females outside the district and in certain parts of Chillicothe, Ohio).

Determined to get him some Roman butt, Count Vomitari consults a local physician, Tayktoo Aspirini (who couldn't diagnose a case of hammer-induced flatness), and finds hope in an operation developed by Dottore Gonna Slyssaway that promises to add some lumber to his woefully undersized crank. The count undergoes a surgical intervention whereby the end of his rod is threaded so he can screw on an extension. This accessory comes in various lengths and colors, starting with the modest "Ho-Hummer____" proceeding to the six-inch "Whaler" and thence to the "Nifty-Knockin' One-Footer," which is the product most in demand among those handicapped by limited plunger capacity.

Once firmly locked in place, a wire is run from the hose extension to the scrotum, thus enabling the fornicator to experience a high-voltage electric impulse at the height of the struggle that loosens the teeth and often results in hair loss and colossally loose bowels. One disadvantage is that the recipient must carry a twelve-volt battery with him at all times, but this apparatus is readily available from Voltaire, for whom the volt was named. As we all know, the volt is a measure of square footage of an electrified fence. But back to the medical theme. Few men who survive the operation avoid crapping their drawers during their first use of the newly-mounted device, and that's even before they actually engage in a pelvic waltz with a native of Slutsville.

The count's procedure is done on an out-patient basis, where he is run past a drive-through window on a hay rack, and side effects are confined to an inconsequential six-month period of searing agony and the inability to urinate without passing his wiener through a wringer. He is actually fortunate, since in many cases, the nuts are lost forever. Of course, the agony of the recovery period is minimal when compared to the pain endured during the operation itself. Since there is no anesthesia, the count is rendered unconscious by clubbing him several times with a two-by-four (Italian: *due* by *quattro*). One good bash would be sufficient, but the surgeon takes an instant dislike to Vomitari and uses the occasion to get in some extra licks. This naturally results in intolerable neuropathic spasms, along with agonizing somatic nerve-destruction, some of which I have experienced when leaping from second-story windows, but that's another stack of bovine exhaust. When he regains consciousness, Disgusto considers it odd that a hog-extension procedure has produced multiple internal fractures, a dented skull, lacerated testes, and a sore ass, compounded by a desire for cantaloupe slices.

To complicate the situation, the mayor of the town, Buttoxo Monstruoso, has discovered that Lungo Pecceroni is wanted in Milano for wanton wiener practices with several women who believe they were assaulted, but want to re-enact the process in order to be certain. Monstruoso confides his discovery to Count Vomitari, who pays him handsomely and pats his fanny. The mayor sings the haunting "I mani sono clammi onna butt" (Thy Clammy Fingers are Cold upon my Rudder) which only elicits a firmer, calming grip and an exchange of fifty bucks (seventy million lire). Monstruoso conspires with Vomitari to notify the local polizia, urging these hick cops to pick Pecceroni up (preferably by the genitals) and whisk him away to Milanese justice, basically consisting of ass-whacking and stone removal.

The two conspirators engage in a dark and sinister duet, caused by a power failure, entitled "Il phalloso deve disappearre" (Let's get the prick out of here) which I composed in the key of C, because the black keys fell off my piano. Many people fail to realize that the first piano consisted of only one long white key. It wasn't until the cracks were invented that piano music really got off the ground. But that's not important right now. In the opera, the gendarmes are actually fit only to issue fines for double-parked horses (the villagers often work their way around the statutes by stacking the nags two deep), but they promise to search for the fugitive. All-points bulletins are nailed to prominent trees in the village and the surrounding forest—and to a couple of dimwits who don't get out of the way in time.

In Peccorini's defense, what happened in Milano is that some members of the feminine gender had heard rumors of his super-sized tool and simply asked him to bring it in for substantiation purposes. In the course of the examination, which quickly grew in enthusiasm, several ladies lost the battle of their garments to the force of gravity and Lungo's instrument happened to fall into a couple of their sugar-bowls (if you understand where I'm going). So it was difficult to call off the scuffle once it started. To do so would have required ropes, nets and tranquilizer darts. Pecceroni recalls this dicey situation in a sweet soliloquy, accompanied by snare drum and alarm clock, called "Non posso retrievare la carne!" (I can't get the meat out!). Unbeknownst to her father and the count, Dolce-Keester pursues a platonic friendship with Lungo and meets him behind the village pharmacy, which specializes in bat wings and chicken poultices, along with lottery tickets. Their first meeting results in ardent, frenzied and savage intercourse of the fiercest sexual variety, soon leading to kissing, a dreadful taboo in the village.

I have written a beautiful duet for the humping couple that they perform while naked and grinding against a dumpster, underscored by an atmospheric chant from the chorus which has gathered to witness their sweaty gymnastics. The duet, "Più profundo, Bambino! (Deeper, Baby!) and "Non è ancora al fine!" (It's not all the way in!), is panted in the foreground by the frantic couple to the choral exclamation of "Regardi la scatola sulla Bimbo!" (Look at the can on that Broad!) perpetrated by the male members of the chorus. The women supply the overarching remainder of the fugue with "Dovè possiamo ordinare un dipstick come questo?" (Where can we lay our hands on a bazooka like that?).

In the second act, a further complication is brought about by the arrival of Guacamola Insalata, Dolce-Keester's half-sister by a second-cousin twice removed, or perhaps by her mother's financial advisor, Inclemente Weathero. This super-assembled fox has been absent for years, practicing high-speed streetwalking in Venice. For a long time, she has been working both sides of the Grand Canal, so she is an excellent swimmer. Guacamola has posed for the Victoria's Secret catalogue on several occasions and has also married and divorced three of her cousins—or maybe her brothers. In short, nobody knows who the hell is related to anybody else, which draws the audience into the plot and sickens them at the same time, deftly deflecting their attention from the music, which is so much horseshit.

Guacamola has intermittently abandoned her prostitution-heavy activities and is currently a trapeze artist in Barnum & Bayleaf's Three-Ring Circo. She manages to display her nicely-carved butt throughout her high-flying act by relying on the use of loose knickers and cooperative gravity. On this occasion, she is wearing a dress so thin you could read an insurance policy through it at midnight while lying in a sealed coffin. Watching her hang upside-down by her toes is a spectacle few males want to miss and produces a high number of shredded codpieces. Once in the village, she has her eyes set on Lungo's wiener, which she has noticed during the annual long-timber contest held in the village every six months. He wins first prize each time without cranking out enough to divulge the true dimension of his dong, harvesting murderous stares from the lesser-hung males of the region, but collecting wild applause from the girls and a dog named Lowell.

Guacamola also finds enormous appeal in Count Vomitari's classic features, his aristocratic bearing and his currency collection. Little does she realize at the beginning that she is dealing with a guy who is poorly gifted in the dick area. This soon becomes apparent, however, when she happens to spy him relieving himself at the theater in a potted plant (located in the box seats below).

Gucamola sets out to seduce both men, hoping to reap the double satisfaction of Vomitari's untold wealth and Peccorino's impressive tail-tamer. The count falls for her feminine sultriness and her indifference to underwear, but Pecceroni remains true to Dolce-Keester. That is, until Guacamola corners him in one of the rings during a circus performance, inviting him to join her on the back of a dancing bear. Well, I don't have to tell you what the combination of a trapeze artist and a bear does to male hormones, especially if the animal is unequaled in performing the Charleston. I'm sure you've experienced the calamity many times. Therefore you will understand that Lungo succumbs to the thrill of the moment and enters into fervent pubic-focused activity with the cursed seductress (once she succeeds in directing his interest away from the grizzly). Pecceroni sings his principal aria, "O fornicazioni celestiali!" (I like it!), highlighted by an F over high-C when the bear nips at his stones.

The role of Guacamola was inspired by a girl I knew back in Transylpoopia in the good old days. Ewe Reeka was perhaps the most vicious piece of pure animal lust I have ever known, except perhaps for her mother. Come to think of it, her sister didn't veer too far from that description herself. We met at a sheep-shearing convention outside of Viagratestamonia, which is in the deep south of the country, not far from the Spanish border. You may not be acquainted with the profound sophistication and peerless hospitality of the average illiterate and putrid citizen of that Antarctic country, but Ewe and her female family members knew how to make a guy feel at home in a pile of wool.

I happened to be engaged in traveling sales efforts in the area back then, working for Dung-Rite Products Corporation, trying to drum up interest in our electronic outhouses, a truly cutting-edge apparatus designed to make evacuation efforts more pleasurable and infinitely more efficient. The deluxe model came with a TV screen, picture window, ceiling mirror and stirrups. The lack of electricity in the country presented a challenge for me, I admit, so I had to rig up a sheep-driven device. It made the structure somewhat crowded, but even without power the Electro-Dung was a fine improvement over the popular evacuation systems of that period. It remains so today.

But to return to my masterpiece, through a fateful coincidence, Dolce-Keester happens to enter the main tent at that moment, dressed in a skimpy uniform consisting of coveralls and a bearskin overcoat, and selling popcorn. As she makes change for a drunken bum who fondles her anatomy, giving him a couple of nickels, a sharp rap in the gonads and her phone number, she spies her lover and her (maybe) sister engaged in third-gear sexual intensity and she nearly faints. Guacamola has already fainted a couple of times herself. The dancing bear has now drifted into a spirited foxtrot, and the fox is not amused. At this point another coincidence brings Count Vomitari and his retinue to the circus. He is accompanied by his footman, his elbowman, his buttman, a bagpipe repairman, the guy in charge of wheeling his battery around, and an old guy with toilet paper.

As fate would have it, a young nobleman, Prince Yoofah Mizzum, and his hunting party pass through the region looking for maidens and their heads (get it?) and are attracted to the tent by loud cries sung by the circus audience in the choral torture entitled "Questa merda non è possibile!' (Who thought up this crap?). Upon entering the tent, the prince spies Guacamola and falls immediately in heat, smitten by her sensuous movements and monumental bust measurements. He catches her eye, which falls out during one of the bear's more energetic pirouettes, and tosses it back to her. She smiles and mouths the words, "Get lost!" The woman has a built-in shit detector. Dejected, Yoofah kicks a retainer in the ass and tells him to pass it down the line.

A hush falls over the crowd, which is a welcome relief from the music. Pecceroni looks at Dolce-Keester. Dolce-Keester looks at Gucamola. Guacamola looks at Vomitari and the count looks at the bear. A gleam comes into everyone's eye and the opera audience hasn't got the faintest idea what's going on, but doesn't give a raccoon's rectalia by this time anyway. The music grows louder to drown out the snoring. The four main characters now join hands and sing a rousing sextet called "Non è da shits, l'amore?" (Ain't Love Grand?) with Guacamola and Lungo descending slowly from the bear. As the curtain falls (by popular demand) accompanied by a gasp from the woodwinds (the rest of the orchestra has given up by this time) and a loud groan from the injured oboe-player, Dolce-Keester and Guacamola rush off together with their arms around each other. Count Vomitari moves toward the wings in a tight embrace with the bear, who is lugging the twelve-volt battery. Pecceroni has his cell phone out and is trying to raise the Women's Auxiliary of the Johnson Research Society of Milan. The circus audience erupts in loud cheers of "Vogliamo Partire Subito!" (Let me the hell out of here!).

Magical, isn't it? I only need about twenty grand from you for rehearsal costs. I'll let you know how much more to send as the actual performance draws near. Better still, a blank check will make things easier. You will be mentioned in all the publicity announcements as a major benefactor and in the program notes—with a slight modification on nights that the bear is not performing and you replace him.

I asked Earl if he wanted me to include a greeting to you from him. He said, "What?"

I think they're gaining on us.

Ludlow

To: California Election Commission   February 15, 20--
From: Ludlow Smutt
Subject: Candidacy for Governor
cc: Grover Smutt

This is to formally announce my candidacy for the high office of Governor at the next election. I would like to take this occasion to elaborate on my exemplary background, my years of unparalleled experience and my proposed platform, in order to assure the electorate of this great state that a vote for me is a vote for progress and lots of other good stuff that I plan to think up pretty soon.

To begin with, I overcame difficult origins and two twin brothers (one of which was me and each with an advanced case of the mange). I am a man of the earth, brought up in a log cabin on the plains of Illinois, the same as Lincoln (who drove one of the first Continentals—though it was left off the five-dollar bill). Our home was a ranch-style structure with a picture window (that looked out onto a picture of another window) and nearby excrement facilities, constructed by my paternal grandfather on my mother's side with help from funds provided by a stage coach robbery. My courageous ancestor (and grunge-factory) braved wilderness, snow, hail, alcoholism, penile warts, a sadly deformed ass, and the need for a face transplant to carve out a rudimentary existence for his family out on the prairie over four blocks from the nearest supermarket. I inherited his sturdy genes, and they have imbued me with the desire to render service and establish a legacy for posterity, in spite of the fact that posterity has never done anything for me, the bastards.

I hold a degree from a major Hungarian university, majoring in squirrel farming and Buddha pest control. Get it? These two disciplines came in handy when dealing with my relatives, because it's often difficult to control those squirrels. Speaking of squirrels, I can safely state that I am a lover of animals, merely in a platonic sense of course. For years I had a dog named Crawford. I loved that dog, and though he was slow and never learned to play dead, he was quite proficient at calling in sick. When he was only a couple of years old, the poor thing developed a small twitch in one eye, so I shot him.

I was an avid sportsman, frequently competing in water-ski pinochle tournaments and ice-skating shuffleboard contests with an obscure twin brother, whatever his name was. He frequently disappointed me, but then he was never sensitive to my feelings. As an example, during a friendly game of golf, he repeatedly expressed annoyance when I tuned my banjo during his backswing, which was so slow he started it in the locker room or in the car on the way to the site of his botanical debauchery. Although I myself was blessed with almost incredible athleticism, excelling in many other sporting events such as canoe and prostitute paddling, I found time to care for my brother, who suffered from a severe impairment. According to the mental health professionals, he was born with a defective sibling. In his defense, however, he was instrumental in providing significant financial assistance to our family. He took trumpet lessons for years, with the result that we were eventually able to buy all the surrounding property at low prices (but continued to suffer hearing and stomach problems).

After being driven from my home state and, subsequently, from the country by slanderous accusations involving a small group of teenage girls (well, okay, a large group), I arrived in Stockholm, which was in Sweden at the time, but just barely. I had only the clothes on my back and a bear trap on my foot. At first I found casual employment in a brickyard. The yard was mine, and the bricks were thrown into it by smart-aleck revelers during the night. Success was slow in coming. In fact, it never arrived. But I remained undaunted and took correspondence courses to learn how to eek. This allowed me to eek out a meager living by cleaning the stables at the reindeer race track. The reindeer always won because they raced in snow against guys on bicycles. My work was difficult and not without danger. The reindeer were okay, but I was gored several times by Swedes. They occasionally tie antlers to their heads (or have them surgically implanted) and then run through residential areas trying to mount females, many of them human. The danger comes when you get between them and their target babes. The best localities for this activity are described in great detail in the Swedish tourist brochures under the heading "Air bie tunnsa grate butt rownd heer" (Don't miss the clambake). After several months, I gave up my position because of the commute. The racetrack was in Copenhagen. It was at this difficult time in my life that I was forced to subsist on donations left lying around by careless homeowners in unlocked houses. But providence intervened. By a stroke of fate, I met a woman who initiated a string of circumstances that provided me with the capital I desperately needed. I was leaning against a car parked near the stables, trying to clean reindeer dung off my shoes, when a blond beauty approached. She was gorgeous, with just the right combination of serene good looks and a prominent bust. She jumped in the car and drove off, causing me to fall into that portion of excrement that I had thus far removed. As she disappeared in the distance, I looked up and saw a set of long, unbelievably attractive legs. There were four of them and they belonged to a reindeer, but by glancing past them I could make out the nifty butt of another girl walking into the crapper.

The situation took my breath away. Reindeer poop will do that. I hurried to the restroom and waited for the young lady to reappear. When she emerged, accompanied by two guys and a moose, I knew I was in love. But I suppressed that feeling and tried to concentrate on the girl, who was buttoning her trapdoor. She was towering and slender for a person four feet tall and fifty pounds overweight, dressed in a casual, sequined snowsuit ensemble with high-heeled ski boots. This young lady was a knockout. I say that because she was carrying skies over her shoulder and when she turned, she pasted me in the gourd with them. I fell to the ground, stunned, and she inadvertently stepped on my scrotum. She bent down, looked at me with big blue eyes and said, "Uw oor een azzhole!" (my fault). Then she kicked me in the tail and walked away. Attempting to rise, I reached out to a passing gentleman for support and tore his pants down. His shorts came away in my hand, leaving me to my surprise with a fat wallet in my mitts. He chased me through the streets for more than twenty minutes, but due to my incredible quickness I was able to elude him, because his wheelchair was one of the slower models. With that impressive amount of money, I returned to the States on a steamer (they broiled lobsters during the entire trip) and built a solid off-shore ass-busting business in partnership with some gentlemen from New Jersey whose noses were slightly twisted. Our company served the needs of people who required the removal of animals, friends, neighbors or difficult family members. I'm sure you have had occasion to use similar services. In order to avoid unnecessary suffering, primarily mine, we eliminated most of the unfortunates by administering a massive dose of sleeping pills and then clocking them with a sturdy fencepost. Those who hesitated to take the pills were given an efficient pre-expiration funeral. This approach saved pharmaceutical and labor costs and was offered at a steep discount. An important plank of my platform is to abolish poverty. I assure you that I have nothing against poor people, but when I pursue them with my car and run them over they mess up the undercarriage. They make my ass ache. I took a survey of our citizenry in the washroom at the Shell Station concerning the most important issues of our times, and the results indicate that nobody gives a shit one way or the other, so I doubt that there will be any resistance to my programs.

I would like to say a few words about my prospective opponents, whom I admire greatly, especially that large-rumped Reelie O'Beese, the current mayor of my fair city. I don't know what she ever accomplished in office aside from keeping the town cesspool in operation around the clock by spreading so much crap. If she ever gets an intelligent thought, the scorekeepers will probably miss it. This woman thinks germinating means becoming a German citizen. O'Beese never shuts up. She's been known to talk on the phone for twenty minutes after she dials a wrong number. This so-called woman has constantly ridiculed my plan allowing guys to use women's restrooms, a clear case of gender discrimination. There's nothing wrong with females being treated to the sight of an unsheathed male member when they walk into the can. The occasional glimpse of a nicely-formed Willie would do them good and loosen up some of the sourpuss broads around here.

Also on the list of clowns who think they're better than I am is the assemblyman, Ezra Kilogram, a prime donkey from out in the desert near Lake Drybed. He's so phony. His constituency probably consists of half a dozen homeless people with one tooth (among them) and suffering from bad breath. Nobody else would vote for him. I don't say his last election was rigged, but the polling place was in his bathroom. On the positive side, he has a pimp for a brother, so at least he has someone he can look up to. Lake Drybed falls into the category of towns you would most want to see sucked into a mine shaft or used for nuclear testing. I've always felt it should be moved to the epicenter at the first sign of an earthquake. I plan to give it to Mexico. If they don't want it, I'll offer it to Washington, D.C. They can use it as a landfill if they figure out how to distinguish it from the downtown area.

My exceptionally tolerant nature is well-documented, but there's going to be some serious sack-slitting when I take office. The purges will be enforced in government offices, the business community and the public sector, especially aimed at that bastard down the street whose dog always craps on my hydrangeas. The folks in the state capitol better hang onto their asses, is all I can say. I plan to clear out the over-staffed government agencies whose bloated payrolls are bankrupting the state. They'll be out on their fat asses in the first twenty-four hours. The Department of Motor Vehicles is in for a big shake-up. There is no reason for the long lines of degenerates you see there every day. And I'm referring to the employees. We will stop issuing drivers licenses. Anybody who wants to drive a car, a truck, a motorcycle or any other apparatus that can get up to thirty-five is welcome to it. Just hop in and rev it up, Charlie. Why do we need licenses? Have you ever seen a driver in any state who seems to have a license? They all drive like mental cases. Let's not waste our money on things that obviously have no reward.

And no more reality shows. I'm sick of watching things like "Diving for Excrement." Families without television sets are already able to generate their own sex and violence. I will get rid of TV evangelists and there will be no cooking programs unless the hostess is topless. And she better be a killer Mamma. No more fat-assed chefs with their fly open either. News broadcasts will be modified to feature female journalists with most of their upper torsos bared. And there will be close-ups of what's under the desk. The viewers want to check out the bottom half of these babes while they read the stories. I especially like Bubbles Grossboozum, who in my opinion deserves to be the number one anchor on the air after I nationalize the networks—or whatever the state equivalent is. And I'm going to shut down TV wrestling programs faster than you can look at a picture of Wall Street executives and puke in a dumpster. Broadcasting that crap makes as much sense as appointing Roman Polanski the lifeguard at a girls school.

After only one term as governor and owing partly to my vibrant personality, I will undoubtedly be asked to run for president. As Adlai Stevenson once said, "Anyone can grow up to be president and that's just one of the risks you take." I already have some good ideas about how to improve our great country. But we shouldn't eliminate our dependence on oil. How else would Dolly Parton get her clothes on? With my knowledge of history and my many travels, I am keenly qualified in the field of foreign policy. I am well-traveled in this country too, and it was a pleasant experience, when I recently visited a large number of states, to have so many people wave at me—some with all five fingers. I have attended church services in Beaver Balls, Minnesota, where the night club is in the YMCA and the church choir is responsible for many conversions to atheism. I have traveled as far as New York, where the first thing that strikes you when you visit there is a taxi. One of my first acts as governor will be to appoint Mr. Grover Smutt (no relation) to be Chairman of the Fondling & Fornication Commission, a new but sorely-needed agency. I have known Mr. Smoot for most of the past century. He is an upright citizen and an ardent patriot, and though of limited knowledge concerning legal reproduction methods, I would nevertheless entrust him with my entire Linda Lovelace library. His bureau will oversee and regulate carnal activity within the state and perhaps many outlying jurisdictions. Working with legislators here and across the country, Mr. Snottt will supervise important sexual events such as the Self-Abuse Conference, the National Dildo Show and the annual Hand Job Festival, to name only a few. Some of his personal artifacts will nicely augment the products in the Rape Tool Exhibit. He brings a wealth of experience to this assignment, attested to by convictions in numerous localities, mainly Crudball County, but not limited to that perverse and filth-infested region. I am convinced that with Mr. Smutt on the job the genital organs of our great state will be in good hands.

Your candidate for spare change,

Ludlow Smutt

34

Hey Grover,

My newspaper assigned me to travel with two local policemen for a week in order to report on the situations they encounter in the course of their duties. It also gave me the opportunity to beat the ambulance to the scene and thereby build up my legal business. I was privileged to accompany Sergeant Stanley Steenkole and his partner, rookie Patrolman Jethro Slopsack on their beat. Steenkole is a hardened veteran (mainly in the pants) of over twenty years with the city's finest, after serving as town dogcatcher for a short time with the Sum Beach Canine Control and Castration Squad. Slopsack is a relative newcomer to crime fighting, having received a degree in Law Enforcement and Live Animal Interment from the Fresno School of Applied Fisticuffs. Here are some notes I took while observing the crime-busting activities of our gendarmerie, reported from up close (and sometimes through heavy lenses from behind the black-and-white).

Our first call was to an apartment complex on Noah Fogging Way, where a domestic disturbance was reported. There were loud cries and screams of terror outside the dwelling, but they subsided when the cops told me I didn't have to go in first. We entered the domicile and found a runty little male, Octavio Hernandez, whipping the snot out of his rather large wife, Grossella, with a ball bat. He was taking some nice cuts, but tended to dip his shoulder a little.

Man, this woman was a hulking, rotund and gargantuan monstrosity, an offense to optometric focusing. "Take that, you fat puta!" the little guy hollered as he bashed his elephantine partner on the turnip. The officers pulled him away and he shouted at her, "You lousy lard-ass! You put on two hundred pounds since we got married! I can't stand to look at your greasy *culo* any longer!" Steenkole quickly rose to the occasion. He pushed the little twerp out of the way and smashed the wife across the nose with his nightstick. I kicked her in the ass, using a three-step drop. Slopsack took notes. The hubby thanked us and we left, our duty done.

The next stop was at the scene where a body had been discovered under the Route 12 underpass. The corpse had been decapitated, his fingers had been cut off, his pants were pulled down, tire tracks were all over his ass and his testicles were missing. An eyeball was rolling around in the gutter. Jethro squealed, "My god, he's dead! What are we going to do!?" Steenkole said, "Well, we haven't undergone resurrection training yet, so I guess we'll allow him to be dead." Based on the evidence, we concluded that death had occurred from a traffic accident until a by-stander pointed out the eighteen-inch knife protruding from his chest. Some nosy people just can't mind their own business. We began to interview the people at the scene (many of whom had run over the corpse a few times as it lay on the road) and also tried to hit on phone numbers from the babes.

The Crime Scene Investigation Unit arrived, but their van was going way too fast and they skidded into the corpse, tossing it about thirty yards, pinning it against a dumpster and mangling it some more. They also knocked down about a dozen people who were tramping on the body, obviously trying to take a shortcut along the shoulder of the road on the way home. A lot of blood splashed on us. Ooh, icky! But the good news is that we could now safely declare the cause of death a traffic accident. Officer Slopsack took notes. The eyeball was later used to identify the deceased based on optical records. He was a Vietnamese member of an Hispanic gang that was under the control of the Italian mafia and run by a bunch of Russian mobsters on loan from Albania. We turned the case over to the precinct truancy officer.

A few minutes later, we were directed to a building where a young man was threatening to hang himself. When we arrived, we looked up and saw an inconsequential little male standing on a ledge on the twentieth floor with a rope around his neck, the end tied to a metal strut on the roof. He appeared to be in his twenties (maybe sixty) and had a scruffy beard. He held a curling iron to his throat (not my choice of a life-termination device) and wore torn jeans with half his ass hanging out. I notice things like that. Nobody was paying attention to him, so we decided to do the same and grab some grub. We were about to leave, but the dispatcher told us to get our rears in gear and we rushed into the building after catching a cheeseburger and a soup sandwich at the fast-food place on the corner, "Cholesterol R You."

We took the elevator to the twentieth floor, playing with the buttons and goosing each other, then made our way to the window where we could see the mouse-brain who wanted to hang himself. We pleaded with him to come back inside, using proven suicide-prevention tactics. Following police procedure, Steenkole called out, "Get your silly ass back in here, or we'll kick your scrawny ass around the block." The guy shouted, "Don't try to stop me! I'm going to end it all! My girlfriend left me, my parents threw me out of the house, I ran out of toilet paper, my dick hurts and there's no more lunchmeat in the fridge! I have nothing to live for!" He began to cry. I told him, "Don't give up. Your dick might get better. Mine did." He pulled his Johnson out. It was covered with scabs—shriveled and gangrenous. "It's already a lot better," he said. "You should have seen it Thursday."

The good sergeant pulled his pistol and warned him, "If you jump, I'll shoot! You'll never make it down alive!" Something seemed wrong with that approach, but I couldn't put my finger on the problem. At that moment the culprit stepped off the ledge. I thought we were too late, but the sergeant lunged, quick as a cat, and heroically cut the rope. "Scruffy-ass" plunged twenty stories, struck a guy on a twelfth floor terrace who was watering his daffodils, bounced off a ledge, tearing a nut loose, and landed on a little old Italian lady who was walking her dog. It was a popular breed, a stick retriever. As Isaac Newton once said, "Ouch!" Steenkole said, "Oops."

"Scruffy" ricocheted off the old biddy and was struck in mid-air by a squad car that was arriving to help us. He was killed instantly, landing in the middle of the street, his pants torn off by the impact. One of the officers wrote the departed a ticket for jaywalking and inserted it in the crack of his butt, which was sticking up in the air. The old broad pulled through, but her hound bought it, struck by a large TV set. It was an admirable shot, considering we had to drop it twenty floors to hit the little mongrel. At least we could point to some measure of success. Jethro's notes read, "Suicide prevented. Manslaughter investigation opened involving reckless dog-walker."

Some time later, the car radio woke us and blared out that a kidnapping was in progress right around the corner. We hurried to the scene after stopping to ask directions from a screaming girl who was being pulled into a car by two bad-asses in the process of yanking her jeans down. She was a good-looking little Mamma. I noticed a nice set of munchies in her shirt and suggested Slopsack add that observation to his notes. One of the suspects had his hand over her mouth and the other one on her can. We recognized the Bump brothers, Speed and Goose. These two depraved individuals had done time in Sing Sing for genital exposure—standing on a street corner and pulling people's pants down. The filthy ruffians were currently wanted by the authorities in Brooklyn for stealing those little scented cubes in public urinals and were known to traffic in stolen arms. Many of the people whose arms they had taken were unaware of the fact until they sat down to a meal and realized they were unable to hold a knife and fork.

Taking up pursuit, we followed them to a deserted warehouse filled with people. The crowd was in formal attire, dancing to the music of Phil Spitvalve's string orchestra that exclusively featured brass instruments. We observed the two suspects, giggling uncontrollably, hauling the unfortunate babe into an upstairs room. Carefully mounting the stairs, we burst in with guns drawn. That is to say Sergeant Steenkole had his gun out. Slopsack took notes. I hung back to give them a chance to draw fire. The good sergeant threw a bucket of ice water on the two kidnappers and shouted "Freeze!" The brigands were quickly subdued, and as soon as the constables read them their rights they shot them in the ass.

We called for backup and another orchestra arrived. I took the occasion to cut in on a couple and began a mambo, but the guy couldn't follow my intricate steps. "Whom are you?" he asked (he had been to night school). He didn't like the fact that I was staring at his girlfriend's breasts (I had removed her clothes to do so). He called me a vile, polysyllabic name, a word borrowed from the Phoenicians that I feel we should return to them as quickly as possible. His date was a hot little redhead wearing see-through glasses, and I led her around the room in a waltz, which was not easy, since the band was playing the Star Spangled Banner. I didn't realize at first that she had a glass eye until it came out in the conversation. Steenkole and Slopsack danced with each other.

After a few more numbers (one of them was 15), we decided to look for the kidnap victim, because drinks were only available from a cash bar and I didn't want to break a one. A thorough search of the upstairs room revealed that the girl was slumped in a corner, completely naked and pretty nice, man! After ten or fifteen minutes, the cops covered her with a blanket to avoid embarrassment, then asked me to get out from under the blanket. I was just looking for background for my story.

It turned out that the girl, Pepper, is the daughter of one of our town's wealthiest industrialists. His name is Saul Schayker and his holdings include a casino on Rikers Island, a Lenox furnace dealership in Death Valley and sand-manufacturing factories in several North African countries. He's well-known for his philanthropy, providing hookers with the opportunity to make a living, but I think he's a no-good bum. Several people have urged him to consider stowing away on a kamikaze plane. His wife is also active in charitable works. She hires a woman to do her cleaning so she can volunteer at the school where her cleaning woman leaves her kids. She's so skinny she wears her wristwatch around her neck. The family has a house on the next street from us. The psychiatric clinic is also on that street, so we call it a mental block. The frantic parents were overjoyed to get their daughter back after three days, because they were headed to Vegas and wanted to know where to leave messages for her to stop screwing around.

The dispatcher later sent us to a barrio home on Tennuss Court to deal with a hostage situation. Hector Rodriguez-Gonzales-Cassidy, an Eskimo from Tokyo, was standing on the front porch holding a cat hostage. He brandished a machete and threatened to slit its throat if his wife didn't quit screwing around with all the other undesirables in the neighborhood and come home to cook his dinner. His *mujer*, Mathilde. was on the front lawn, screaming for him to release the cat and trying to negotiate part of his demands. When we approached, she told us, "Please don't let him carry out his threat! I think I got him to drop the dinner part!" Slopsack took up a position with a sniper's rifle in a nearby tree and drew a bead on the porch. "Do you have a target in your sights?" the sergeant asked him by radio. Jethro said, "Say again." Steenkole said, "Again."

Jethro said, "I think I have a clear shot." He fired and blew out a tire on our squad car. It was now a squat car. But no matter. "Correct for windage,"

Steenkole told his partner, "and also for stupidity." Slopsack fired again and plugged the cat right between the eyes. The bullet went through cleanly and struck Hector in the nuts (he was scratching his crotch with the animal at that precise moment). Mathilde let out a loud cry and rushed forward. Jethro fired at her and missed. Steenkole shot his partner out of the tree. Fortunately, it was only a flesh wound—right in the ass. The frantic wife jumped up on the porch and retrieved the machete. "If he damaged my best kitchen implement, I'll shoot him myself," she said. I took notes for my column and wrote, "Savage beast eliminated in residential area while holding pet. Cat suffers .45 caliber coronary."

Slopsack couldn't sit down for a while, so he was assigned to sweep the floor at police headquarters. With physical therapy he may be able to assume his former duties, but the doctors say he'll probably always have a hitch in his lower intestines and may have to carry a bucket around with him. This is on top of a history of health problems. For some time, he has had to contend with the lumpy dumps, an ascending colon, and a descending Willie. His replacement was Mitzi Gaynor's son, Haff. This policeman had eight years of experience in the narcotics division, so he was pretty well wasted when he joined us. His speech was slow and his eyes were out of focus. Sort of like you get when I'm trying to explain something.

That evening, the three of us were observing the activity in a rough neighborhood, parked in the drive-through lane of a KFC, when a BMW sped past. "That's a stolen car!" Gaynor shouted. "How do you know?" Steenkole asked. Gaynor said, "It's my car, man!" We took off after the vehicle, burning rubber and knocking over the KFC order apparatus. Our squad car gained on the suspect, but we lost some ground when we bounced over a corner and sent a taco trolley flying, along with the Chinese guy who was selling them. I grabbed a chicken burrito as we whizzed by, but had to eat it without soy sauce.

At the next intersection, we were forced to swerve and miss some people from the sign-painters union who were on strike. They were marching in front of the Sign Language Institute and carrying blank placards. We struck a couple of them a glancing blow. One guy's pants fell down and a young lady wound up on her back on our hood. Her legs were spread open on the windshield and she was wearing very appealing undergarments. We were doing ninety, both the siren and the female on the hood screaming, swerving all over the street and flying across lawns and sidewalks.

The squad car ricocheted off other cars and we crushed a number of dogs and cats. That part was quite rewarding. Gaynor shouted, "Can you see, man?" Steenkole said, "Yeah, she looks good from here." We flew over a series of speed bumps and sent two teenagers flying. I looked back to watch other vehicles run them over. It was pretty neat. Steenkole nudged me. "See if you can get the chickie off the hood, but try to save her for later!"

I leaned far out the window as the sergeant attempted to hold the car steady, but he was weaving in and out of lanes, trying to avoid groups of gang members who were assaulting people. I reached our passenger on the hood and checked her body parts for injuries, then tried to pull her into the car. She smiled and applied some lipstick. I grabbed her by an ankle (aiming for her higher protrusions) and pulled her toward me, but lost my grip and watched her bounce off the canvas roof of a convertible that was going in the other direction. She flew in a high arc, landing unharmed in the reflecting pool in front of the library. She plowed through the water, soaking several passers-by who started screaming at her and bitching about surfers in general. Gaynor fired a few shots at them and that shut them up. "At least I got her underwear," I reported. "Better than nothing." Steenkole muttered.

Cars shot through intersections from all directions, just missing us. Steenkole careened into another row of parked cars and left a string of doors and other automotive accessories in our wake. Gaynor's BMW turned a corner on two wheels (the rear ones) and sped down a side street, headed for the freeway. We zig-zagged wildly and made the turn about fifty yards behind him. "Don't let my car get away, man!" Gaynor cried. I said, "Get closer and maybe we can get a shot off at him!" Gaynor punched me in the back of the head. "Don't scratch my car, man!" he shouted. "My lunch is in it! It's a baloney, peanut butter and marijuana sandwich—my favorite, man!"

The Beemer sped onto the entrance ramp and joined the traffic on the highway, headed north toward whatever is north of there. The driver exhibited great courtesy in using his turn signals, even though he was going the wrong way. At that point, the situation became intense. Both our cars were weaving in and out of high-speed oncoming traffic, our velocity at nearly one hundred miles an hour. Nobody paid attention, though, since this is nothing out of the ordinary on our highways. We do slow down to eighty when going the wrong way on side streets.

We came to a bridge that's always jammed. The congestion is so bad you can change a tire and not lose the place in your lane. And no driver will let anybody in front of him. The only way to get into another lane is to buy the car next to you. We pulled alongside Gaynor's wagon and the driver smiled at us and finger-saluted as he exited the freeway at the next ramp. He gunned the vehicle down the street of a residential community with us spinning around and following in hot pursuit. We almost had him, but we spotted a local politician and chased him around the block a few times with the siren still wailing. We almost ran him down, but lost him in an alley. Gaynor got off a couple of shots, but I think he missed. Sergeant Steenkole returned to the chase, but the BMW was nowhere in sight.

The next day, I was standing in line at the bank, when two grubby-looking guys in old army jackets pulled guns. They fired a couple of shots into the ceiling and one of them shouted, "This is a stick-up! Everybody down on the floor!" His companion started to comply. "Not you!" he said and slapped the guy a couple of times. After they collected a couple of money bags, the leader started to leave, but his buddy stopped him. "As long as we're here, I'd like to open an account," he said. The first guy told him. "Okay, but hurry up," What a couple of dopes! With my keen talent for observation, I was able to supply the police with a perfect description of the robbers. They arrested the mayor of Los Angeles, two U.S. Senators, Paris Hilton, Earl, and four Koreans who were getting off a plane from Seattle. Truth, justice and the American way prevailed. I take my duties as a citizen seriously.

Our next intervention involved still another would-be suicide. What's wrong with these people? When we got to the edge of a tall cliff above the ocean, a middle-aged guy was standing with a rope around his neck tied to a large rock, with a gun in his hand. He had obviously decided to take a Kevorkian header into the briny to close his earthly accounts with a leap and a splash. This clown wasn't taking any chances. He gulped down a big slug of poison, set fire to his clothes and jumped. At the same time, he put the gun to his head and pulled the trigger. The bullet missed and severed the rope, the water extinguished the flames, and he swallowed a lot of seawater which made him throw up the poison. We hurried down and dragged him out of the waves, then whisked him to the hospital, where he died from hypothermia. I had never whisked before.

Stay tuned to this mailbox,

Ludlow

Ludlow Smutt

California Electoral Commission
One Fordamunny Square
Reno, Nevada   69069

March 15, 20—

Mr. Grover Smutt
1422 South Institutional Lane
Mental Health Springs, Virginia 18118

Dear Mr. Smutt,

A person of interest has petitioned the Commission for permission to stand as a candidate for Governor of the great state of California. Ludlow Smutt, whose last name is curiously similar to yours (though hopefully his appearance is not), referred to you in a list of personal references that includes Donald Trump, who seems to delight in wearing a faded golf course divot on his head. We know that the name Smutt is quite common, right after Smith, Jones and Wafflcczniewski, and therefore deem it acceptable to request information from you regarding the background and moral standing of the candidate before we decide to enter his name on the ballot or kiss the clown off.

Our mandate is to go through these motions until we can arrange for an accident, and therefore your assistance in this matter is greatly appreciated. For that reason, we have enclosed a form to fill out—or you can have someone help you to do so. Some of the questions may seem quite personal, but we ask you to be entirely candid in registering your opinions, in order to aid us in filtering unwanted individuals out of the political process. The potential candidate speaks highly of you (overlooking the use of some unseemly language accompanying his appraisal), and we urge you to refrain from responding in kind in the margins of the attached document. Thank you for your help and we trust you can find a qualified person to read this letter to you.

Sincerely,

Oswald Snotshovel Commission Chairman

Electoral Commission Questionnaire
Candidate: Ludlow Smutt, 22 Bilge Road, Sewage Springs, California.

How long have you known the candidate ? _____(in Roman Numerals)

Relationship
; Coincidental _____ Pleasant _____ Unintended _____ Impossible to avoid
_____Forced on me _____ Strained _____ Ugly ___ Crappy _____ Sexual
Candidate's Character
_____ Honest _____ Occasionally honest ____Honest whe forced
_____ Scum _____Untrustworthy with valuables _____ Untrustworthy with
non-valuables _____ Notorious Bullshitter _____ Cheater and adulterer
_____ Underwear dirty
_____ Steals from small children _____ Steals small children from parents
_____ Steals hot coals with bare hands _____ Steals jockstraps in a huddle
_____ Would hit on your wife if you aren't careful _____ So would I
Social Circle (Associates with):
_____ Judges _____ Senators _____ Executives _____ Upper classes
_____ Average citizens _____ Lower classes ____ Pimps _____ Jockeys
_____ Con men _____ Bunco artists _____ Loose women
_____ Sewer workers _____ Lawyers ____ Crooks (same thing) _____ Me
Political Experience (Offices held): _____ Dog catcher _____ Alderman
_____ Councilman _____ Mayor _____ State legislator _____ Bagman
_____ Fixer _____ High-roller _____ Pimp _____ Tavern-keeper
_____ Ass inspector _____ Brothel certification _____ Used-car salesman
_____ Wal-Mart greeter _____ Racetrack tout _____ Sewage removal
_____ Outhouse maintenance _____ Breast-enlargement counselor
Personal Impact of Candidate
_____Entertaining ____Empathetic _____ Not outgoing ____ Noy personable
_____ Makes you puke _____ Overly friendly with livestock
_____ Shifty Eyes _____ Shifty Ass _____ Flatulence problems
_____ Breaks wind _____ Breaks glass _____ Breaks sound barrier

Hotel Habits on the Campaign Trail
____ Eats breakfast in bed ____ Eats ice cream in bed
____ Barbecues in bed ____Entertains farm animals in bed
____ Farm animals refuse to join in

Hygiene
____ Extremely sanitary ____ Lax in this area ____ Kind of cruddy
____ Averse to water ____ Smelly ____ Insect-infested ____ Dirt-bag
___ Covered in dung ____ Needs to be hosed down
____ Pollutes area ____ Smells ____ Wire brush recommended
____ Poor wiping habits ____Doesn't wipe ____ Wipes others
____ Butt especially grimy ____ Mangy ____ Crotch dandruff

Popularity
____ Loved and admired ____ Respected and supported ____ Liked a little
____ Considerate—can play the accordion but doesn't ____
____ Not well known ____ Hard to reconize ____ Ignored
____ Disliked ____ Hated ____ Vilified ____ Attacked in public
____ Risks being shot ____ Has been shot ____ Shot mostly in the ass
____ Contract out on him ____ Willing to take the contract
____ Urinates in flowerbeds ____ Needs kick in the ass
____ Have given him kick in the ass ____ Enjoys kick in the ass
____ So do I

Campaigning Ability
____ A Born campaigner ____ Good speaker ____ Charms crowd
____ A Gabber ____ Bullshits well ____ Real Blabbermouth
____ Can't shut up ____ Promises the moon ____ Wets pants during speech
____ Soils pants during speech

Police Record (Known arrests, indictments and convictions for):
____ Vagrancy ____ Theft ____ Graffiti ____ Littering ____ Flatulence
____ Gambling ____ Goosing statues ____ Exposing himself
____ Exposing others ____ Pecker fraud ____ Computer hacking
____ Coughing and hacking ____ Safe cracking ____ Boot blacking
____ Waffle stacking ____Between-meal snacking ____ Hot-dogging
____ Leap-frogging ____Toilet-clogging ____ Should enter monastery
____ Embarrassment

Other Personal References
____ Some may exist ____ Will try to locate ____ List attached
____ Not likely ____ Who's got the time? ____ You must be nuts
____ Forget it ____ Check police files
____ No one dumb enough to consider writing one
____ No further contact please

35

Hey Grover,

I'm writing to tell you I can't write to you today. This is from tomorrow. I forgot to mention we had dinner with Earl and Madge again. Couldn't avoid it and nobody else wants us. The grub is great if you can stomach the two of them. Jimmy was there too. He cracked some corn, but I didn't care. During the evening, Earl told Madge he wanted one of those large-screen TV's, so she moved his chair closer to the one they have. To give you an idea of the size of Madge's can, we were at their place to watch the last Olympics, and when she walked in front of the TV we missed four events.

On a more important subject, you remember of course that I have ever searched for universal enlightenment and true religious understanding, often sacrificing the pleasures of the flesh and the crap tables to gain insight into that age-old question: "Why is there no federal accordion subsidy?" In my religious fervor, I devoted myself some years ago to theological study and devout good works, which resulted in a position with The First Church of Discount Forgiveness and Low-Cost Novelty Items (Gift Shop on Premises) as its "Assistant Bishop, Chief Circumcision Advisor, and Stone Spiritual Dude."

The Managing Cleric was Randall Weaselringer, an eloquent speaker, convicted vending-machine molester and nude harp-tuner, who chose the straight path after serving a sentence in upstate New York for counterfeiting cocktail napkins. Most of his incarceration was spent in solitary confinement with two other guys. After his release (by the authorities and the two other guys), he found his true calling, despite an arrest for calling call girls by the wrong name and being caught having intimate relations with a storm drain. Randall claimed that he was lying in the snow on his parole officer's front lawn early one morning (with his appendage hanging out and a female friend attached) when he received a vision from Saint Roxie (she of the instantly removable undies), directing him to establish a house of worship. Finally, some direction in his life, similar to your experience.

A higher power had pointed the way to redemption and reward, so he's now the head hog in the trough. I joined his movement (non-bowel) and we rented space in a urinal warehouse in Moose Mucous, Massachusetts (we used these items on occasion as baptismal fonts). Our original edifice was next to a combination billiard parlor and adult sex-aids store. The pool hall and the sex store often used the same balls. To prepare for the ministry I took up meditation, because I didn't want to sit around and do nothing. Our intention was to build a massive devotional complex replete with modern restrooms (some inside) paid for by the faithful after a relatively brisk fleecing. Attendance soon blossomed and our services were sold-out, mainly because we advertised lap dancing and an open bar. As the old saying goes, fools rush in where they have often been before.

We were on our way to spreading the story of pious hope and financial sacrifice to the weary and heavy-laden. Besides messages of solace and junk like that, we counseled losers in need. I developed the ability to speak with great religious conviction, and the congregation was often riveted by my sermons, many of them inspired to colon looseness. My message was one of purity and reverence, interspersed with tips on rectal hygiene and the proper way to mix alcoholic beverages (the two procedures often pursued simultaneously), as well as directions to the best places to buy a flute.

I also revealed some tasty bits of gossip about members of our flock who had fallen into sinful ways and were screwing around in general. Take Martha Bawlstomper, for example. What a body! Her figure would cause cardiac arrest in an otherwise healthy yak. Martha had spiked hair and wore leather clothing decorated with barbed wire, a tough-looking sexpot if I ever saw one. She reminded me of a young lady I met some years later in Morocco when I stopped in a Bedouin tent outside of Marrakesh for a scotch and sand. Her name was Oogle Beeps, and she was the daughter of a camel driver, downhill skier, and part-time urine analyst (his taste buds were amazingly talented). I asked her if I could see her home and she showed me a picture of a two-story ranch dwelling. Her sultry eyes scanned my face as she drank wine from a goat skin (the goat appeared uncomfortable) and took off her roller skates. Oogle agreed to have dinner with me as long as we were accompanied by her mother, four aunts, six male cousins, her nine brothers, and the goat.

We dined at a fast-food outlet, the gourmet meal consisting of camel burgers and French flies. Later, we went to a square dance (the dancers were tourists from Omaha). Get it? **Square** Dance! Nuts. Then we went back at her tent when her relatives left to play Arabic Bingo. These people were wild about the game. They play it seated on camels. The Bingo cards are huge, so the players need transportation to fill in a line. I tried it once, but it was the wrong type of humping, so I gave it up. I was about to embark on the serious part of the evening's project, softening Oogle up for the finals. Her robe was open and the meat bus was about to pull into Snugville, so I asked her if she had any protection. She showed me a switch-blade knife. I tell you, that gal was great, or as the Chinese say, "Blah Dee Soo Pah." When we had completed the deed, I asked her, "Were you a virgin before this?" She said, "I'm not sure. Most of the guys are undecided." That was the year I entered the International Free-Style Coital Competition in Romania, but only got a 9.4 from the judges. It must have been the dismount.

Anyway, back to my ecclesiastical endeavors. Martha was but one of several misguided persons whom I attempted to help. Owda Bounce was another. She was a horribly unattractive female in our congregation who was frustrated at her lack of success in finding a mate. I admit that she had large dairy cartons in front, but that didn't make up for the wanton crime she perpetrated on your peepers. Revulsion to the fourth power. Owda had one of the most irritating voices you can imagine. She sounded like a tiger suffering from a hernia being goosed with a chainsaw while sliding down a blackboard.

Dingle Shortwand was another parishioner who came to me for guidance. If you think Owda was devoid of any redeeming quality, this guy's kisser would cause a slug to leap ten feet straight up. Real barf-bag overload. I didn't like the guy. He was always spouting some kind of political nonsense, like how Benedict Arnold was his hero and women should have the right to vote. I told him to consider self-immolation. Chaos, panic and disorder—my work was done for the day. As I was driving home, I stopped to moon a bunch of guys who were exposing themselves and a female cop arrested me. She told me anything I said would be held against me. I said, "I love what's in the front of your uniform.."

Our denomination soon grew geometrically (mostly squares and parabolas) and we were able to construct our modern worship center. We could even flush some of the crappers. Threw sand over the rest. It didn't hurt that we had devoted space to an off-track betting room where wagers were made in great volume. The money poured in, mainly because we didn't show actual races on the screen. Instead, we ran films of old races, so we knew who the winners were and never had to pay off. There was also a large casino, with slot machines and crap tables (although we encouraged people to use the washrooms). Our church bulletin kept the faithful informed. Here is an excerpt from one of our publications:

- *LOW SELF-ESTEEM SUPPORT GROUP MEETS FRIDAYS AT 8:00 P.M. USE THE BACK DOOR AND TRY TO BE INCONSPICUOUS.*
- *WANT TO QUIT SMOKING? BRING YOUR UNUSED CIGARETTES TO THE CHURCH AND WE WILL BURY YOUR BUTTS.*
- *WE ENCOURAGE THOSE ATTENDING THE ERECTILE DYSFUNCTION SEMINAR TO KEEP IT UP! IT WON'T BE HARD.*
- *THE CLOTHING DRIVE IS ON AND WE NEED UNDERWEAR. DROP YOUR PANTIES IN THE BASEMENT OR LET US TAKE THEM DOWN.*
- *MARGE HOTTBLOOD WOULD LIKE TO THANK THOSE WHO HELPED HER EAT WHILE SHE WAS PARTIALLY PARALYZED. JED SLIMEY FED HER THE PORK ON SEVERAL OCCASIONS WHEN SHE WAS UNABLE TO MOVE.*
- *RONDA KORNER'S VETERINARIAN REPORTS THAT SHE HAS A REALLY NICE SCHNAUZER.*

The complex of buildings was devoted to our saintly activities, with plenty of slot machines in the pews and a blackjack dealer at the end of each row. We arranged to have a couple of dozen cheerleaders in skimpy outfits in the sanctuary during services, urging the worshipers on and handing out discount coupons for five-gallon bottles of communion wine and pizza. Brawls often erupted over opposing interpretations of the sacred writings. I remember one particularly confrontational episode when two factions came to blows because they couldn't agree on the meaning of the verse, "Let him who is without sin stop trying to get to the head of the line." It seems so petty now. The gift shop was expanded to include full-body jock straps and cleavage-revealing T-Shirts with clever Biblical sayings. I don't know if you got the ones I sent you.   Some of our best-selling phrases were:

> Take up thy bed and walk (And get the hell out of here!)
> Love thy neighbor (Her old man's out of town)
> Give ten percent to the church (Finish up in the bathroom first)
> Turn the other cheek (Your sack is dangling in the soup)

In Sunday School we provided contraceptive devices to teenage girls and cautioned them against sexual activity with unattractive males and animals. If I had known Earl in those days, we could have put his picture on the wall to represent both categories. Our parish was engaged in good works throughout the world. We poured loads of money into Africa, sponsoring a bunch of natives so they would stay there. And a large contingent of missionaries was sent to the far corners of the globe, dispensing the word of virtuous behavior and armed with the appropriate antibiotics. Also trained in penile amputation.

I accompanied many such groups to little-known areas of the Third World, including Zimbabwe, Rimshottistan, Slambanger and Grand Rapids, but everyone agreed that your town was lost to Satan for all practical purposes. Upon hearing that news, many of our members decided to move there. You may have noticed them lying around in your parking lot.

I almost forgot. Linda Dorksoffner was another chickie I fell into sin with a couple of years later, during my sojourn in Argentina. But we didn't hit it off right away. I merely bring this up because I like to recall her copious upper-deck architecture, known locally as "Gaucho's Pouchos." If this gal ever burned her bra, it would take the fire department four days to put it out. I met her on the patio of a bar in Buenos Aires one evening and bought her a drink. She eventually warmed up (after I set her skirt on fire) and came back to my place. I was numb from my toes down. Linda looked at my collection of primitive African wood carvings and said, "What's that long thing on the mantelpiece?" I explained that it was a phallic symbol. She laughed and said, "I'll be darned. It looks just like a pecker."

I often think back to our childhood together. You were so easy to get along with, even though we kidded you, taunted you and insulted you. But we could do those things to a great guy like you because you had no idea what the hell was going on. On the other hand, I remember nobody liked me because I was so popular. You'll be relieved to hear that Earl is recovering nicely. He's now able to sit up and blow the foam off his medicine. Listen, I don't know if this is a national phenomenon, but I've noticed a lot of sheaves in this area recently. If you see any around your place, you should probably bring them in.

I hope you're continuing to devote your energy to the ultimate social achievement of not being indicted for the string of sex crimes I described to the authorities.

Your Secret Sibling,

Ludlow

36

Hey Grover,

I'm now writing an advice column for the local newspaper. The younger generation, especially, can use my counseling. Let's face it, they don't know which part of a baseball cap goes in front, or that jeans should only go down past your butt when you're safely in the bathroom. I say to the younger generation, don't listen to the critics. Listen to me. People will try to discourage you. You may stumble. You may fall. But remember, Edison was a failure too—until he won the lottery. I'm talking about Steve Edison, Thomas Edison's cousin. Here are a couple of my columns from last month, entitled "Ask Noah Kownt."

From Dr. Maude Lynne—Portsfootandmouth, Massachusetts.

Dear Noah. I'm a successful neurosurgeon at a large metropolitan hospital, one of the first of my gender to reach such a position. But although I enjoy to some extent the excitement of sawing people's heads open and hacking big pieces out of their brains, I don't feel completely fulfilled. My dream, ever since I was a child, was to be successful in the world of baton-twirling. Should I give up a lucrative career in the medical field and follow my dream?

Doc, my advice is to get away from that dead-end career of yours and into the baton business. Follow your bliss, as some donkey once said. Lots of gals are making big bucks doing the twirling crap, so don't miss out on it any longer. And stop practicing surgery on yourself.

From Chloe Sklozzit—Stringbean, Pennsylvania.

Dear Noah. My husband just got back from a year in Afghanistan as a civilian advisor. It can be kind of dangerous at times, especially when guys start snapping towels at each other in the locker room. He told me that's how he wound up with a hammer that doesn't work every well. Darryl stepped on a land mine and almost lost a foot, but managed to escape with no serious effects other than the fact that he kind of lists to one side when he walks and veers into the wall a lot. Our sex life has been reduced to a shambles. Darryl is only interested in doing the "lance lunge" if I dress up like an Arab woman and do a belly dance to get him in the mood. My question is: Do you know any good places to buy belly-dancing goatskins that come in triple-large sizes?

Chloe, my dear, I'm sorry about Darryl's tussle with a land mine, but glad to hear he wasn't seriously hurt. Probably only picked up a bad case of "missile-toe," right? Ha, ha, ha. I'm going to come clean, darling. Despite everything I do to block it from my mind, I can't erase the image of your obviously voluminous can in belly-dancer duds, causing the bile to rise in my throat. Even if I knew where to buy the vestments you require, I wouldn't commit the federal crime of helping you get triple-size hooker rags off the rack. Why don't you sew them yourself? Just get an infield tarp and let it out.

From Lee Meelone—Anchorage, Wyoming.

Dear Noah. My in-laws came to visit us two years ago and brought their four dogs, seven cats and nine other children with them, none of whom are housebroken. They're still here. I've dropped subtle hints that I would like them to leave, such as "I would like you to leave" and "Get the hell out of here!" but they ignore me. It wouldn't be so bad, but we have a small house with only one bedroom and one bath, and they lie around everywhere. I haven't been in the can since they arrived, reduced to urinating in the bushes behind the house. I have to go to the YMCA to take a shower before I go to work at the asylum every morning and then I dress in the car.

The animals have scratched up every stick of furniture in the place and contaminate our abode wherever the mood moves them. These people are driving me nuts. My wife tends to take her parents' side, especially when I complain that her dad usually sits around in his skivvies and sometimes forgets to put them on. He has this tiny, shrunken member, an infirmity he shares with virtually all the male residents of our community, and it's pretty embarrassing when the minister and his wife come to Sunday dinner or my wife's bridge club meets. Any suggestions?

Lee, my man, my first impulse would be to shoot the bastards, especially the pets and children, but there's an outside chance that it could lead to trouble with the authorities unless you have extensive experience in disposing of bodies. There's nothing wrong with pitching your in-laws out on their butts. I've done it many times myself. And if your wife objects, pitch her damnable ass out with them. In-laws everywhere have a history of ignoring the most courteous comments. Get a ball bat, or as I call it, an "in-law extractor" and chase those feeble-minded sickos down the highway.

From Mona Lott—East Northside, South Carolina.

Dear Noah. My boyfriend and I have been together for fourteen years and we have eleven kids. "Slug" has yet to find the type of employment that would lend dignity to his sensitive nature, so he hasn't worked since he moved in with me. Slug is too fragile to help with any of the housework and spends his days lying on the couch watching TV and doing dope or shooting pool and playing cards with his friends. In addition to my main position as a federal employee at the re-cycling center, I hold down three cleaning jobs so we can make ends meet. Every so often I bring up the subject of marriage, but Slug says he has to think about it a little more because he's not sure he's ready to make a commitment yet. Should I quit pestering him?

Mona, I have some bad news for you. You have got your sorry ass into a scenario from which there is only one chance of escape, and the reason you are in this fix is that you are obviously thicker than a rock. It would be hard for me to envision anyone above the level of a stone who could get into the psychotic relationship you share with the sub-species you call your boyfriend. Here's what you must do: Get a hammer and lace Slug in the face with it about five or six times. No jury on earth would convict you after hearing your story and presumably getting a good look at you, but you may have to spend some time in a brain shop to get your cranium adjusted.

From Pete Pantz—Sing Sing, California (Chemical Delivery Section).

Dear Noah. Hey man, I'm sitting here on death row awaiting execution for a crime I didn't commit. The D.A. cooked up a scenario based on shaky evidence that included thirty-seven corpses in my basement, positive DNA and fingerprint results, incriminating gunshot residue testing, and a Chicago

Cubs jockstrap. At the trial they also described some of my petty failings from the past, like multiple convictions for manslaughter, assault, burglary, kidnapping and rape, along with a charge for sodomy that my lawyer got reduced to "following too closely." I don't think any of that was fair. My current lawyer says another appeal is a waste of time and calls me an "animal." But I'd like to try again, even though the last fourteen were turned down. You're my last hope. Do you think I have a case?

Pete, old buddy, don't take this too personally, but I'm delighted to serve as your last hope. You definitely have a case—a case of taking up too much space on the planet. After receiving your letter, I volunteered to do the final injection myself, using a javelin dipped in curare from about ten paces, after your sack has been separated from your rotten carcass with dull sheep shears. So long, Sucker.

From Conrad Spunt—Macon-da-Bacon, Georgia.

Dear Noah. I want to get my wife something special for our twenty-fifth wedding anniversary, but she's kind of hard to satisfy. She hated the set of wrenches I got her last year. I'm desperate.

Conrad, Conrad, you haven't got a clue, you silly ass. How little you understand the complex set of internal reflective impulses that constitute the female psyche. You're obviously not tuned in to the critical emotional make-up of your feeling-oriented partner. Women need caring and receptivity on the part of their spouses. They want genuine consideration and a comprehension of the soft and sweet forces that comprise their beings. Your gift choices, if I may quote Sigmund Freud, are horseshit. You have to reach down to the depths of your own soul and discover an intimate present that will excite this woman as never before. Give her cash, you damn dummy, and tell her to quit griping.

From Lucy Goossie—Skunktown, Indiana.

Dear Noah. I'm completely devastated. My husband came home from an office party last night with lipstick all over his shirt and the front of his pants. His clothes were in disarray and he smelled like a whorehouse. He claims he was merely the victim of a couple of flirtatious women in his department, but he couldn't explain the naked blond who was passed out in the back seat of our car. I also caught him trying to wash a thick layer of cosmetics off the hood.

Lucy, Darlin,' I'll tell you, boys will be boys. You don't want to hold it against your hubby if he lets loose once in a while to have a little innocent fun. The situation you describe doesn't sound too bad to me. I can think of a dozen scenarios that would explain the gal in the car, although I might not believe any of them myself. Cut the guy a little slack and get yourself a boyfriend.

From Arkady Senko—Rockslide, Maine.

Dubcêk Noahski. I am just arrive couple months ago your country from Vladivostok and admitting I have real problem adjust it to new culture. Is many thing I not be understanding, such as how to making new friends or getting pretty good piece sex for what he got it. Up to here only working in cafe sweep it up and wash it for plates and shit. My English be almost perfect so wanting become job in bank or something close. Having two questions: What best way to find such job? Also how meeting young female type womans who go church and agree screwing guy like me with pretty nice erection?

Ochistrastenya Arkady. Can give pretty good piece advice at you and any Russki-type Slavic persons who having difficult fit it into new culture for what he got it. Is most important go to bank and tell them you want job and insist it they don't be messing around with you. You say them, "I don't take no crap from you clowns." Is attracting positive attention and earning you pretty good respect right away or can be sooner. Second, if you wanting attract female woman of gender that is opposite from whatever you are being (and is not male person), is best show her what you got in you pants for what he shake it. Is making swell impression when taking out "Bazoopka" early in conversation and giving nifty preview what for bopping they can expect from serious Vladivostok guy. As be saying you countryman, Vassily Kropotbelly, "Yanyavo dobritchoss! Ha, ha, ha." Then you got it knocked.

From Chuck Alugg—Idaho City, Oklahoma.

Dear Noah. Were any handicapped people prominent in the history of our country?

Hey Chuck, there weren't many, but who can forget that physically hindered traitor of Revolutionary times, Bentdick Arnold?

From Kay Kineedit, Old Jersey, Maine.

Dear Noah. I met a guy in a bar about a week ago and we started talking. He had Slav features and his English was very bad. After a couple of minutes, he took his wiener out of his pants and waved it at me. Then he told me that he would like to have a "pretty good piece sex." Well, I slapped his face and ran out of the bar. Now, however, I find myself thinking abut him and obsessing about his rod, which was quite impressive, I have to admit. I can't get it out of my mind. Do you think I was too hasty in terminating the conversation?

Oh Kay, I can tell you from personal physiology that a well-formed crotch log can be a pleasant tool (Ha, ha, ha) for breaking the ice in a social situation. Perhaps your acquaintance was only engaging in behavior that is considered polite in the country or institution he comes from. You should try to refrain from forming opinions based on limited experience with international genital display. I'm going to help you out here. Send me an Email at *noahhookups.com* and I'll forward the guy's address to you. It's an opportunity for you to give the young man another chance, get one more look at his crank, and take it from there. I will also send you a picture of my own log to download in the event you care to spread a little "pretty good piece sex" around.

From Randy Myle—Rectalbreath, Tennessee.

Dear Noah. I want to know if you think this is fair. My girlfriend has recently taken out a restraining order that prohibits me from approaching within five hundred yards of her or her residence. I can't even say hello to her on the street. And I thought we were pretty close. I don't believe there is any fairness in her behavior at all. Well, she's not exactly my "girlfriend." She's an acquaintance I saw coming out of a movie and I was attracted to her, so I've been hanging out with her for a couple of months. She obviously didn't consider my feelings when she went to the cops. Okay, she's not really an acquaintance. I used to hide, and when I saw her on the street I'd sneak up on her and grab her by the jugs. But is that any reason to shun me like a common criminal? Yeah, yeah, I admit I've shoved her against a building a few times and rubbed my wand against her, and fondled her butt and tried to pull her pants down, but ....   Aw shit, never mind!

Okay.

Well, Grover, in the hope that you will soon recover from some of this, I remain

Ludlow

Dr. Phil T. Butt
May 1, 20--
The Palomar International Scientific Society
1423 Lobotomy Corner
Springfield, Illinois   66600

Dear Dr. Butt,

This is in response to your inquiry concerning Grover Smutt, whom you are considering for the prestigious 2009 "P.I.S.S. Award" for outstanding contributions to the well-being of mankind and selected large animals. I will try to give you as much background as I can. Grover Smutt, or as many of his acquaintances call him, "The Squirrel," has not had an easy life, as will become abundantly clear. Let me start at the beginning. The person in question was left as a child with my parents and me (over our vehement protests) by a band of gypsies who were making their way across our vast family estate, pursued by the county sheriff and diverse groups of concerned citizens brandishing implements capable of inflicting considerable bodily damage. These nomads insisted for some reason (which became abundantly clear only later) on abandoning the charming little tyke, although he seemed a delightful, baby-faced bundle in his diaper and baby clothes, lying in a primitive crib and sucking his thumb. He was fourteen at the time.

Upon questioning, we were told that his mother had expired while giving birth to his older brother and his father was killed at a Sunday School picnic when he slipped on a buffalo chip and the gun he was carrying went off, detaching his scrotum from the rest of his torso. For many years, the youngster was afflicted with a deep but understandable fear of scroti. His real name was Molenbutt Gooblechefsky, but we took him in and named him Grover, after the well-known and revered "Father of His Country," Grover Futtzmeyer of Estonia. The new addition to our family grew up amid all the luxuries our family could bestow on him, including a weekly change of underwear (he changed with a neighbor across the street), dry straw in his mattress each month, an engraved butt brush and his own toilet paper, although it took a long time for him to use the last two items properly. My folks did everything they could to make his existence pleasant and presented him on his next birthday with a slop bucket boasting his personal monogram. He never let it out of his sight. Nor did he empty it very often.

Grover (as I shall henceforth refer to him through clenched teeth) almost immediately began to think he was my twin brother, which is laughable, but understandable when one considers the respect he had for my spirited intellect, though he never achieved in his own right the full spectrum of manly attractiveness that I displayed from the start. Not only that, he was unable to profit from the sadly unequal distribution of crotch-meat at birth, although this turned out to be unimportant, since he never learned to use it properly anyway. Cracking walnuts with your love-log hardly seems an appropriate application.

My new sibling was poorly educated when he joined us. Somehow, his mental equipment was not tuned to the proper channel. His working vocabulary was limited to "Hello," "Good-bye" and "I like shock absorbers." It was with no little difficulty that we were able to teach him the rudimentary procedures of putting socks on the proper feet and eating with utensils. You can imagine the disgusting image he generated when devouring spaghetti with his hands while naked. I hesitate to paint a picture of him in the same room with soup. It wasn't until much later that we succeeded in getting clothes on him (he preferred Bermuda shorts and a derby). We also had to break him of the habit of voiding in the bushes behind the house. This preference may have been caused by the fact that he had been kept in a dark room for years and, consequently, displayed the characteristics of a mushroom.

To break him of his outdoor growling activities, I eventually came up with the idea of paying a small child to creep up behind him in the grass during the skirmish and whack him in the nuts with a ping-pong paddle. Prior to this approach, I tried it on myself to test its effectiveness, and I can say with certainty that there is virtually no pleasure equal to that of terminating the experiment. The method proved exceedingly efficient, though, and Grover stopped his outdoor evacuations after only four and a half months. From that time on, he crapped in the house. That is, on the living room rug. But through a dozen or so judicious applications of a cattle prod (set to "full zap"), we finally got him on the hopper. He fell off a lot in the first few days, but the installation of a safety belt resolved that problem once he learned to buckle it, (though he preferred to put it around his feet).

I tutored the young chap in his studies, and thus improved his grasp of a few numbers below ten, although he had the intellectual velocity of a kumquat and never got any of them in the correct order. In elementary school, which he failed to comprehend in any way, including how to get there, he showed little interest in anything that was not female in gender and located below the waist.

My adopted brother unfortunately brought a lot of violence on himself, pulling pranks on his comrades, like smearing peanut butter in their shorts so they would think they had messed their pants. As a result, many considered themselves to be part of the Poopsie Generation. He liked to corner a girl on the playground and remove her underthings, promising to wash them and have them back to her the following Tuesday, but he was invariably several days late. On other occasions, he insisted on exposing himaelf (or someone else), which sickened entire classrooms (except for a couple of brazen little hussies). In addition, Grover suffered from the propensity to scratch his ass in public. Though this was a fairly innocent practice, it was nevertheless unhealthy because it soon led to the habit of scratching the asses of people around him, provoking angry remonstrations, not necessarily from those whose keisters he raked.

Grover was easily led astray, and when my much-needed supervision was diverted elsewhere, such as in the girls' washroom, he often fell in with the wrong crowd, leaving secretions in some very intriguing locations. I warned him to stay away from a young temptress named Charlene Rufflebutt, but he succumbed to her seductive magnetism. Charlene was not the prettiest girl in the world, but she did have an encyclopedic knowledge of things to do with a pecker. This relationship led Grover to many acts of lewd, revolting and unsavory behavior, many of which I wrote down for further reference. The federal government once considered declaring his pants a disaster area. He was for a time involved with a group that went around mutilating weasels. I'll never forget the time I saw him at a formal reception with his face in the punch bowl, blowing bubbles. On the positive side, his collection of vintage toilet seats continues to intrigue intestines experts to this day. But I always felt that he was a great loss to the blacksmith trade.

Influenced by a nauseating scene in a public washroom (which he initiated with my encouragement), Grover abandoned the use of underwear, and I think that was a critical point in fashioning his philosophy of life. He ultimately expressed the desire to play a musical instrument and chose the cymbals, despite the fact that we urged him to concentrate on the hydraulic jackhammer. He practiced for hours, able after many months to master the C-major scale. The noise was deafening and led me to insert a layer of heavy felt between the two pieces, held firmly in place with Velcro and a strap attached to his crank. When he opened the cymbals to bang them together, the apparatus yanked on his hammer. He seemed happiest in this activity.

Grover soon became discouraged by the fact that so little was written for the cymbals as a solo instrument and decided to give them up, turning his efforts to the kazoo. His repertoire quickly grew to two pieces, the second of which was exactly like the first, both of them based on Eastern European national anthems and the sounds of foundry activity. His perseverance was impressive, and Grover subsequently appeared in concert with renowned classical groups, including the Memphis Homeless Symphony Orchestra, the Sing Sing Death-Row String Ensemble, and the Cleveland Gay Men's Banjo Sextet—a group seventeen strong. Most of his appearances took place outdoors and went a long way toward enlivening lynchings, cattle branding, spelling bees, wood-chopping contests and yodeling tournaments.

After devoting himself to this difficult instrument for several years, he was finally accepted into Julliard—as a janitor. The position didn't last long, though, because he repeatedly got his dong caught in the wringer on the mop bucket. Some suspect still today that it was intentional. I did my best to guide Grover in the right direction and was able with some difficulty to obtain work for him in sewage treatment, but he couldn't do shit. The poor boy went from one job to another. The problem was his habit of shouting his sales pitch during church services, funerals, and once during a coed proctology tournament at the State Hospital for the Criminally Impolite.

His disrespect for decent behavior led to sex with amputees and other handicapped individuals, though he thankfully avoided a risky relationship with a dog named Lowell. Succumbing to the dark side of his personality, Grover eventually served a six-month sentence (he was out in two years) for collecting underwear from groups of unsuspecting damsels by luring them into a game of strip horseshoes. These innocent members of the fair sex had their panties snatched by a deft flick of his fingers, which he perfected by plucking live chickens and playing the harp while riding in the sidecar in cross-country motorcycle races. I never understood how he could steer the vehicle at the same time, but such was the enigma he presented to us. The lad was so adroit that he could divest horses of their metallic hoof-wear at full gallop. My sticky-fingered quasi-sibling's fame spread rapidly, and he was once challenged by a member of the Chicago Bears to remove that player's shoes during a post-season football game. The first half ended with no cleats missing and my "brother" was soundly ridiculed, jeered and spat upon. However the surprise was deafening when midway through the third quarter, and in full view of the fans, the members of both teams realized that their jockstraps were gone, along with one set of goalposts. Grover was fortunate that the authorities recognized his immaturity, and he was the only person in history that I know of who was tried as a juvenile when he was forty-two.

It was at this time, however, that a remarkable transformation took place. One day, while attending a Child-Pummeling Seminar, Grover carelessly stepped into the path of a freight train. Since he was never fleet of foot, the speeding cars nailed him before he could react, all sixty-three of them. The cumulative effect seemed to unlock something extraordinary deep in his psyche and he soiled his pants. From that day on, he was something of an adult child prodigy. He was suddenly able to compute complex mathematical derivations in his head, give the casualty counts of all the battles in the Punic Wars (sorted by asses and dicks), conjugate irregular Norwegian verbs in the subjunctive, and recite the Latvian Constitution backwards, although the latter two abilities prompted little interest on the part of civic organizations looking for luncheon entertainment. He was one of the first to notice that there are two different ways to spell "bob." In addition, he could reproduce from memory the pelvic measurements of practically every female in the county, information he got from a list I kept.

It caused a large number of females from out of state to establish residence in his neighborhood.

The news of Grover's superior intellect raced through the academic community, and he submitted to a battery of tests that used highly sensitive instrumentation in an attempt to establish his IQ. Masses of wires, polar diodes and electronic devices were attached to his body, running between his toes but focused mainly on his testicles. The resulting number worked out to be either 287 or 14, depending on how tight the cables were stretched or if an erection was involved. In a major breakthrough, he shocked the scientific world when he came up with a solution to Pudd's Puzzle, a problem that had stymied mathematicians for centuries. With a brilliant stroke of insight, Grover filled a blackboard with exotic formulas and was able to prove beyond a doubt that the quantity $(\Sigma \ \mu + \prod - \Phi)$ is a positive integer unless you screw around with it too much. In an unequalled display of superior mental adroitness, at the end of his proofs he added "Marjorie Shacklebutt puts out."

This achievement sealed his fame and he became sought after by learned institutions everywhere, invited by prestigious universities and intellectual groups around the world to lecture on arcane subjects that only he understood completely and nobody else gave a shit about. To name just a few, he made a presentation to the American Chemical Society explaining the use of a gas chromatograph to determine the level of impurities in Bud Lite and mule urine (similar in chemical composition). In Cairo, he shocked the archeological world with a new translation of the Rosetta Stone and certified that the inscription actually read, "Yo, King Tut. How they hanging, Buddy?" At MIT he showed computer technology scientists how to use a downloaded Microsoft program to print out liverwurst sandwiches.

Visiting Harvard, he demonstrated that Avogadro's Number was off by thirteen molecules and called him a horse's ass. At a meeting of top European scientists in Brussels, Grover proved that carbon dating was worthless and that you should take the broad to a bar and buy her a beer. He catalogued and diagrammed all of the amino acids, laying the groundwork for a polypropylene waffle. He defined the most efficient exit trajectories for ground-fired propulsion devices, easing garbage removal. And he shook the academic sector when he wrote the key to the universal field theory on a passing Chevie. The Nobel Committee in Stockholm never quite named him a prize recipient, but they did slip him a couple of bucks and got him laid.

But then another transformation took place. Up until now, I have intentionally avoided mentioning the most personal aspect of Grover's life, but at this time the baser side of his nature began to re-assert itself. It was subtle, but one that a person with my keen instincts was able to perceive. Things began to slip for Grover. His massive intellect began to exhibit a few flaws, chinks in the armor of his outstanding brainpower. On infrequent occasions he put his clothes on backwards, walking in the wrong direction for hours before the error occurred to him. At other times he was unable to recite the square root of thirteen to more than two hundred places after the decimal. And most disturbing of all were the tastes he developed, such as an intermittent desire to urinate in a fishbowl.

He began leaving notes written in women's washroom stalls, suggesting disgusting acts of the lewdest sort involving pie dough and a bicycle pump. To my surprise, women responded positively to these messages, which only increased the imaginativeness of his twisted mind. I feared for his sanity, which had never been too firmly rooted to begin with, and so I abandoned my own career, that of elephant-washing manager in a traveling circus, to devote myself to preventing him from destructive behavior. It was difficult to ignore his poignant gaze, directed at a fishbowl or, less frequently, a bag of groceries.

As his intelligence quotient plunged, his lowest desires soared in the same proportion. He accosted women on the street and made the most lascivious proposals involving their butts, even entering their residences in an effort to indulge his wanton practices. Unfortunately, most of them acceded to his requests to use their bathrooms, where he left their toilets in abominable condition. Grover was headed back in the direction from whence he had come, sinking gradually into a chasm of deplorable, ground-floor intelligence. I tried to reason with him, but he ignored me and took to kicking me in the buttocks, many times pedaling his tricycle several blocks to do so. He was still able to function somewhat in his dwindling genius capacity, but it became ever more difficult for me to cover for him, and I was forced to carry a scrub bucket and cleaning supplies with me wherever we went.

The force of his excellent mind did not leave Grover completely, though, and this enabled him to make an acceptable living as a school-crossing guard. He is currently just a shell of the person he once was. His prior fame has faded and he is forced to content himself with watching the Jewelry Channel and subsisting on partially-cooked pancakes. One satisfying aspect can be seen in this unfortunate situation, however. There is probably no obstacle in the path of his evolution to complete mental deterioration. I hope you will see fit to make Grover Smutt the recipient of your award, if only to recognize his outstanding achievements in the fields of toilet-tissue friction and manure delivery.

Respectfully,

Ludlow Smutt

37

Hey Grover,

This is an outline of my dissertation from back in grad school, for which I was awarded an advanced degree and a five-minute head start. I run the risk of providing you with something that could be boring because it lacks prurient interest, but I wanted you to know that my academic efforts were generously rewarded by an agreement not to prosecute, which should make you proud and give you some hope concerning similar transgressions. The dissertation is entitled "People: The Early Years," and provides the public with a better understanding of dog bludgeoners. In this essay I compare primordial generations with the modern era, and my fact-free document was the result of serious investigation into the anthropological origins and early history of our species (in this regard little of it concerns you). It also contains insightful references to corresponding modern social trends. I will gloss over the part where our early ancestors were descended from dreadfully ugly sub-marsupial life-forms, because in your case that might hit too close to home. Anyway, I'm glad that you progressed to activities beyond athletics. I admired your decision to begin a physical exercise program that was not based on eluding law enforcement. And it made me proud when you found more meaningful work in the field of international laundry sorting and vandalism.

But to continue, it took early man many years to invent civilization, and when he did, it exhibited characteristics that are still prevalent today. In other words, it wasn't worth a turkey's stern valve. The human condition was pathetically unenlightened and there is little evolutionary evidence to contradict that opinion when evaluating our society today. One only has to observe the inhabitants of your neighborhood to see that this is so.

It took primitive man a long time to figure out what was important in life, and after a lot of thought he finally settled on the correct answer—primitive woman. The first such revelation occurred to one horny cave-clown when he spied somebody's girlfriend washing out a few under-things. She had ditched her animal skins to include them in the laundry, and this Ooga took a good look at her topography, grabbed a buddy by the arm and said, "Look at the can on that tomato!" The exact wording may have been distorted by tectonic plate pressure around the fossils, but it's what I would have said.

Popular myth has it that courting practices at the dawn of time involved clubbing a nice piece of female stern and dragging her off to the cave. This is patently ridiculous. And bullshit too. No healthy male would use this kind of persuasion and risk mutilating nifty bodily areas he might want to use again. I refer to my own pertinent experience in this area. I will admit I have resorted to using the club approach on a few occasions, but it was under extreme circumstances and in the face of unreasonable resistance when the young lady in question was regaining consciousness. In almost every instance I was released with only a warning. My heart still beats faster when I pass a night-spot that advertises "Live Girls." It gets me thinking about the alternative and how often I had to resort to them.

Anyway, our hairy forefathers from the earliest periods didn't go around bopping sugar-mommas with clubs to break the ice. They brandished weaponry merely to cull out rejects in their search for meaningful relationships. Cave-beings only used clubs to paste the babes who had obvious deficiencies in the breast and stern department, for which we should express our gratitude. This process, called "natural selection," assisted in the onward march of evolution and finally gave us some women with queen-sized chest-biscuits.

For the rest, cosmetic surgery became popular. Fossil records are clear on this point. Soon, methods associated with knocker enhancement began to increase in popularity. This took place in the late Plastecine Period, from which the name "plastic-seen" surgery is derived. We would be hard-pressed today to envision the agonizing conditions a flat-chested gal was forced to endure back then in her desire to get big boobies. The procedure entailed using huge rocks to sock what little chest-meat was available until those things swelled up like an elephant's used condom. But the sweeties who survived the operation were rewarded with lots of attention from the guys, though most of these quasi-male specimens were, sadly, the ugliest examples you can imagine. Courting habits in those days were far from the sophisticated rituals of today. Researchers have recently determined that a group of young men became incredibly aroused when exposed to images of scantily-clad honeys and developed the most despicable, unclean sexual thoughts. Of course, the results were the same when they were exposed to steel wool or a tuning fork.

Back in the old days, a cave-guy indicated his interest in a woman by hiding on a ledge, jumping on her, and humping her butt off. It was gross, but it was direct and prevented the misinterpretation of intentions. The "pounce routine," as this methodology came to be called, had its drawbacks, though, especially for slower cave-grunts with big bellies who were also near-sighted. After they recorded a number of failed attempts resulting in considerable shaft damage, many of the less-desirable suitors gave up and resorted to whistling. As time went on, pouncing became increasingly dangerous, due mostly to an early feminist movement. Some of the babes gathered together and formed defensive groups aimed at protecting the most precious aspect of their personalities. This is the stage in history that saw the origin of nut-kicking, ass-punting and rod-twisting, a system that is still in use today, I am unhappy to report, although my bruises are healing nicely. Consequently, early man began to invite early girl up to his cave to see his pelt collection.

Evidence has recently been uncovered out behind the Two-Moose Tavern in Drizzledong, Idaho, that lends indisputable credence to my conclusions. For one thing, male cave-dwellers had definite deficiencies in the realm of home furnishings and cave décor. This lack of domestic sense has not changed in the intervening centuries. In my work I maintain that early beings from the Testikleeze Period sat around in a cave a lot and consumed some of the more tender parts of various dinosaur species while watching a guy paint pictures on the wall. I've visited some of these locations. In one cave I inspected, there was a huge male member drawn on the wall (I've noticed that phallic graffiti invariably leans toward large images). At any rate, this activity was eventually broken up into quarters and a half-time was later added, during which the gathering got laid.

Naturally, evolution took time out for a breather every few centuries. Sometimes during a span of several thousand years nothing continued to happen. This was primarily in the Jurassic Period and other, well-known Assic Periods. Forgive me if I digress for a moment, but I have always been attracted by the sight of women in abbreviated loin wrappings and chest-centered lollipops of the cantaloupe variety, similar to those sported by early Babedom. I had a secretary in New York who qualified in every category. She had the longest legs and the shortest hemlines of anybody I've ever seen. If Joanne stuck her lower lip out, it hiked her skirt up and you were treated to a foot-long swatch of her peachy rear, some of it covered in satin (but thankfully not all). Besides that, her prow melons were of the "Holy Shit!" variety. I never knew whether to take in the show from the front or the back.

But to return to the subject, it's at this point in my tome that I touch on the Neanderthal Period. As you are already aware, Neanderthal Man was the son of Stephanie Neander and Jerry Thal, and he represented a significant step forward in the process of human development. Some of the more revealing rocks from this era show that early cave-persons produced an alcohol-based stimulant and evolved the practice of frequently allowing a loud, ripe one to escape from the anatomical area that had at one time been covered with tail-feathers. The practice continues to this day in a viciously intense form, as you would know if anyone would. Flatulence is an interesting subject, but I don't have time for it. You might want to pursue some research in this area, so here is some background information to get you started. The average person expels a gas bomb fourteen times a day. Our survey has taken everyone into account excluding you, because it would skew the results way the hell out of line. During these smelly stunts, we have established that the mechanic billows out the back of his coveralls, the politician rushes to the other side of the aisle, and the glamorous movie star poots her shots through shiny underthings and blames the maid or her Irish wolfhound ("Naughty dog!"). Animals cannot be excluded, though, so the mutt is not above suspicion.

The fact remains that animals are partly responsible for the gaseous haze that threatens to poison our cherished atmosphere. Earl falls into this category. He seems to rejoice in the noise and associated serenity obtained from anal fireworks. At any gathering, it's painfully obvious to by-standers that the Earlster is the one responsible for intestinal-centered volcanic activity. He takes no one into consideration when he lays down a ten-pointer covered with ashes. This habit is dreadfully repellent, so it's no wonder he hasn't been laid in decades. In his case, it's been so long, the guy has plaque on his hose.

You can do the math on the pratt-package issue. There are almost ninety billion expulsions of dangerous, ultra-toxic butt disturbances daily. This biologically-generated mixture of hydrogen sulfide and methane is perpetrated *ad infinitum* (add one infinity) on our surroundings. It's a real gas. But where does it wind up? We look at the guy next to us and shake our heads. There is undoubtedly a layer of flatulent by-products floating in the upper atmosphere and eating away at the ozone. This fact is clear to anyone who has experienced Earl's sphincter shrapnel. The noise alone makes a dog's ears shoot skyward within a radius of ten blocks.

You may want to dramatize the event on film in the form of a documentary, though no one has netted a picture of a well-defined rectal comet yet, so it won't be easy to capture that elusive little trouser-culprit on cellophane. Spectrographic photography doesn't provide enough definition or optic impact to hold the attention of the lay viewer, and the experts are still working on computer-generated animation that will lend realism to the event. You might consider feeding popcorn, beer and pizza to a bubba from your town who is sitting in a vat of maple syrup, but this is only the suggestion of a person who is well-versed in laboratory techniques. The fact remains that you could obtain, as the scientific literature calls it, some "really nice bubbles." It should be noted, however, that one researcher plunged to his death from a ten-story balcony in his attempt to capture a particularly volatile bum spark with a gaucho hat, so take precautions. If this kind of work is unappealing, maybe you can take a look at two snowflakes I'm sending you by UPS. They're identical and I'd like you to tell me how the hell that's possible.

But to pursue my main theme, later on the Greeks (the first Geeks) invented two or three numbers so they could work out mathematical formulas to build the pyramids, which were originally supposed to be spherical. It was the basis for that famous Algebra theorem, proposed by

Calvin Algebra, that led to the invention of more numbers and now we have lots of them. The Greeks went on to develop a whole line of mathematical products that included the noose and the hypotenuse, in order to manufacture right triangles for export to other countries. Among these items were the parabola, the florb, the fringle, the square (or slightly rounded) root, and the phone number.

A sad commentary on the emergence of that abortive activity known as civilized behavior is the loathed erectile-dysfunction commercial. Early anthropology studies confirm that from the beginning males tried to obtain bigger and more stalwart love levers. It was all they had to attract the better honeys, so they resorted to some exotic recipes. Packing the faulty member in ice seems to be dumb now, but some idiots would do it today if they thought it would help. Don't use this method, Grover. I got very sick when I tried it. Current marketing makes my ass ache, especially the warning that if you experience an erection lasting more than six weeks you should call your doctor. I'm already on record here, but who are these butt-warts trying to kid? Medics don't talk on the phone! Did you ever get your doctor on the phone? They don't give a beaver's back bumper about your puny little stiffy. They're busy trying to think of some reason why the old lady in their examining room is covered in a three-inch-thick rash that's oozing some black gunk. Stick your Johnson in a scotch and water, for crissakes! The doc can give you an appointment a week from Thursday. And if you're really sick or injured and unable to move, they'll make you come to the doctor's office right away and sit in the waiting room for a day. Then they look at you as if you're an overflowing spittoon and take a sample of your blood and your urine. You think they do anything with that stuff? Don't be silly. They throw it in the bushes. Wouldn't you?

Why do guys swallow this rod-inflating crap in the first place? Despite what the commercials depict, if you've been married to some fat old broad for fifty years, she won't be after your Johnson any time in the foreseeable future and you should be grateful for that favor. But here's something interesting. I mean to somebody normal. Say a guy takes shaft-swelling medication and finds himself in the six-week erectional condition. This dizz-butt will readily admit it's not because of a muscle spasm brought on by the admiration of his wife's monstrous heinie. Wake up. He's trying to get into his neighbor's pants, and nine times out of ten we're talking about a female. At least he'll be honest about it because his boner is getting heavy and he needs somebody to give it a shot of drop-down.

These guys at least admit their "shortcomings." But when one of our respected professional athletes sucks down waves of steroid cocktails from a five-gallon industrial blender and goes from a wimp of one hundred and forty pounds to looking like the Rock of Gibraltar or a float in the Macy Thanksgiving Parade, he'll swear on his multi-million-dollar contract that it's due to weight training and weekly attendance at church, not jelly beans laced with organic dynamite. That is, until his urine test reveals the presence of horseshoes. Then he says, "Oh yeah, I remember now." Didn't we suspect anything? By this I mean you. Didn't we see what was happening? Barry Bonds was hitting over seventy home runs a year at an age when you and I started asking people to cut our meat for us.

We're unburdened by tradition or cultural curiosity. We take it all in stride. Who gives a chocolate-covered hoot about what's happening in the world—where's the remote? The masses, bless their little hearts, are happy in their cluelessness. The only time we feel really lousy is when we ingest huge quantities of alcohol and wake up naked in an unfamiliar city. People don't want much, just the chance to aim their protruding bellies at the yellow arches three or four times a week and tack on another six pounds. Life is good. Let's just try to look cool. Let's spend millions on what we think are the latest fashions. But to paraphrase an old Spanish proverb, "You can paint your ass gold, but it's still an ass."

In one of the later chapters of my document I mention modern art. I'm an art lover. When I have a little spare time, there's nothing I enjoy more than looking through the stuff I have at home and trying to decide if it's art. I love the old masters, guys like Buford Rembrandt and Howard da Vinci, who painted stuff like "Peasant Woman with Saxophone" or "Silly-Looking Old Coot Seated On The Can." I don't know a lot about art of any kind, but when the age of modern art was perpetrated on us, people with no talent came out of the woodwork in droves. A so-called artist paints a bull's ass on the top of a flagpole and people revere the guy. They wet their pants over this stuff.

None of these hollow-skulls ever says, "I don't understand this painting." They have the brains of a cashew. They praise everything, and the frame too, noting how it perfectly reflects the artist's well-known love of knotty pine. I read about a guy in New York who owned a Picasso for over thirty years and then found out from an art expert that it was hanging upside down. Nobody is an artist if I can do the same thing he does, like throw paint on a canvas. I've thrown up a lot of stuff that looks just as good.

By the way, I've taken up painting and I'm sending you my latest work by Express Mail. It's a landscape called *Still Life with Woodpecker* and I think I used the right lighting and choice of colors to capture the true dimensions of a plywood male member. You'll probably want to hang it (or someone close) in a prominent place.

Yours (and a lot of other people's),

Ludlow

38

Hey Grover,

I've collected correspondence that somehow wound up on my desk over the years. Since you are an accomplished observer of the social scene, in addition to possessing an admirable talent for putting your socks on without using your hands, I thought you would be interested in hearing the viewpoints of the writers. Here are some excerpts from portions of various partial segments located within fractional parts of snippets and fragments:

Dear Sir,

I am writing to tell you that I think you are the world's biggest horse's ass. The only person who is a bigger everyday horse's ass than you are is **you** on weekends. You are such a supreme horse's ass that you give normal horse's asses a bad name, and I should know because my brother-in-law is a real horse's ass. You're one of those horse's asses, along with the other horse's asses on the city council, who are always spending our cash on bullshit projects that aren't worth a venereal-diseased foreskin. Where do you come up with these crappy ideas, you horse's ass? Our town does not need to spend three hundred grand for a float in the Flatulence-Sufferers Parade, for crissakes! And forgive me if I seem picky, but I fail to see how you can justify flying in the Mormon Tabernacle Choir for the event to perform "Who Let the Dogs Out?" And pray tell, whose idea was it to pass out free condoms at the Senior Center? I didn't get one. You piss away city tax revenues faster than I can urinate at a beer-bust. Why don't I just put all my money in one pile and set fire to it? You horse's ass! Kind regards.
—Jerry Mander

Dear Sir,

My company, "Wee Dewitt 4 Yuh," provides services to busy clients who need our expertise because there are a lot of people out there who are burdened with time-consuming jobs and just don't have an opportunity to take care of routine chores. Let me give you some examples of what we offer. If you're lying in bed and your can itches, it's often hard to reach the right spot. We come to your home and do it for you. Our trained staff has received numerous letters of commendation expressing satisfaction with the kind of butt-raking in which we excel. Another of our most popular services involves a late-night dilemma where your fat-ass wife is horny and you just can't get up any enthusiasm (or lumber). A quick call to our 24-hour number brings a non-discriminating male (or something approximating that category) to take care of the revolting deed and save you the queasy feeling that such situations often initiate. With the lights off, our employees, who have the discrimination of weasels with a deep-seated rooster-perversion, will tackle anything. You'd be surprised how many people need our expertise and so would we.   —Shodda Droppertoo

Dear Sir,

I have been rejected by dating services in more than twenty states. The reason I'm writing to you about this is that nobody else wants to hear about it. You'd think people would be more sensitive. I am five-feet-two, weight 400 pounds and have, thankfully, no problems other than the boils.
—Finn Gerztuck

Dear Sir,

I think your company has the best toilet seat out there. I've used a lot of them and I can say without contradiction that your crapper lid beats them all. I tell everybody I meet about your exciting product. Many people slap me. I was telling a woman on the bus about it yesterday and she agreed. Then she jabbed me with a pair of knitting needles and went back to her book. The driver threw me off at the next stop, which was ten blocks from where I was going and I had to walk the rest of the way with one of your toilet seats under my arm. When my arms get tired I hang it around my neck. On many occasions I've used your toilet seat covers too, mainly as a hat at masquerade parties, but often for dusting while I'm waiting to be seated in a restaurant. I'm thinking of moving to Rangoon. Can I get your toilet seats there? If not, perhaps you can ship some to me. I use about six a month. Do you have any flavors besides plastic?
—Len DeHand

Dear Sir,

Do you know any good pebble vendors in your area? I just moved to town and don't know my way around yet. I am a trampoline demonstrator and gravel is essential for my work. I use a lot of gravel in the course of my demonstrations and I need somebody reliable who can make deliveries on short notice, sometimes to out-of-the-way places like cathedrals and bowling alleys. Thanks in advance.   —Shooda Seener

Dear Sir,

Here's a real opportunity for your publishing house. I have just written a book for children about a male prostitute who owns a mule with prostate problems and has to urinate a lot. It's great fun, especially for little tykes who have prostate problems of their own.   —Juan Sumdoe

Dear Sir,

I love your music and want to know where I can buy your CD's (Certificates of Deposit). I think you're the world's greatest harmonica player who churns butter at the same time. If you tell me where your fan club meets, I'll put on clean underwear and attend with my hearing-ear dog. How do you manage that super trick of accompanying yourself on the trombone? Do you have a photo you can send me? My cousin took off with the last one, and I called the police and they caught him and sedated him with a dart, but he had already been to the bathroom and used your picture for a disgusting act.   —Slipper Toomy

Dear Sir,

I'm the president of the Manureville, Tennessee, Chamber of Commerce and I'm looking for a venue to hold our next convention and exhibition. I understand that your town has a sports hall that can seat more than two dozen people, and that would be just right for us. We make a lot of money at these conventions by selling momentos from Manureville. They're kind of a brownish color and we box them in thick cardboard so the smell isn't overpowering if you're lucky. They travel well under refrigeration. Say Hi to Jimmy if you see him.   —Drew P. Drores

Dear Sir,

Do you know where I can buy Band-Aids by the truckload? I was recently in an industrial accident and need to put over eight hundred Band-Aids on my buttocks every day. It takes a lot of time. You'd be well-advised to benefit from my experience and not wear metal shower clogs that can come into contact with a high-tension power source near your hay-baler.   —Caesar Bunns

Dear Sir,

This is a note to tell you how much respect we have for you out here in Madagascar and how our club admires the way you handled the indictment and conviction. None of us believed for a minute that you did those things to that poor animal. We have bestowed honorary membership on you in the Madagascar Grunting and Grappling Club, an organization devoted to coed mud-wrestling and crotch-gouging sponsored by the Merkel Pest Control Company of greater Madagascar (serving the island for over seven months). We want you to be our honorary Treasurer.   Please send us some money —X. Tenzy Vass

Dear Sir,

I live here in your lovely city, in the same way that a lot of people do not, and I wonder if you would review the book I have just completed. My work of non-fiction is the story of a family that brought an example of virtuous behavior to the multitudes and favorably influenced the formation of our great nation. Ridley Barf, of the Kansas City Barfs, was a member of Congress at the turn of the century in 1848, the same year that the telephone wasn't invented. The Barf clan was known at that time as a bunch of loutish, caustic, and peevish undesirables. These rotten, no-good crooks took every opportunity to bilk their fellow man, cheating the poor out of their meager possessions and refusing to shut the screen door when they went outside. They drove simple farmers off their land and turned the properties into racetracks, ski resorts and hopscotch arenas. They evicted elderly widows with big asses from their homes and forced their daughters into lives of roller-derby participation. No horrible act was too base for them. A lousier group of greedy and criminal louts would be hard to find, except for office-holders in New Jersey. The males also had short members. But Ridley changed all that. Growing up in this despicable and contemptible family, he fought against the tide that would normally have produced a hardened cheat and turned out to be something different—a real prick. Ridley spent a lifetime manuring the ground he trod. Members of the extended Barf family are Ridley Barf, his wife Clovis Barf, their son Jed

288

Barf, their daughter (the lovely knocked-up) Daisy Barf, Grandma Belle Barf, Grandpa Clarence Barf, and Lowell Barf, the dog.

In the opening chapter, Clovis and Daisy are relaxing on the porch, shelling peas with a small artillery piece, while Clarence Barf is throwing a tire iron for Lowell to fetch. Ridley Barf is lying on the porch swing, which is on the floor where it fell when he got into it. The postman and part-time auto salesman, Carl Ott, brings the mail up to the porch and Lowell bites him in the butt, dropping the tire iron to do so. Screaming in pain, Ott leaves hastily with Lowell still attached to his caboose. Jed comes out on the porch, scratching his crotch, drinking an RC and munching on a pig's knuckle. The pig is putting up a dreadful fight. Ridley says, "I can't sleep with all that noise!" Clovis purrs, "The firemen can't put out the flames in the living room any quieter, dear." What do you think so far, doesn't it?
—Dummster Sfool

Dear Sir,

I'm looking for a good place to change a tire. Can you help me? In addition, I need an arena to stage whistling events. Your town sounds just right according to the description I read on the Internet under the heading "Slums in Decay," although the photos make me a little nauseous, mainly the ones with you in it.   —O. Beese Bottum

Dear Sir,

I can't tell you how delighted we are to hear that they are going to add the head of Michael Crowner, who used to be the sheriff of Lemon County, to Mount Rushmore. Former Sheriff Crowner from out there in Lemon County was sentenced last April to more than five years in prison for corruption and we feel that his head belongs in South Dakota. Please let us know where we should send it.   — A. Key Stones

Okay, Grover, you may now return to your *Gilligan's Island* reruns.

Ludlow

39

Hey Grover,

My latest film is the first in a five-part trilogy featuring portraits of famous individuals who have helped to make our country the great dysfunctional home of intelligence-deprived dolts that we love. The biographies of these uncommonly brave and selfless American turnips are taken from my latest book, "Brave and Selfless American Turnips." I hope you share my excitement. My work is supported by extensive research involving three people who were home when I called and a guy sitting next to me on the bus. I compiled these stories while serving a short sentence in Laguna Beach for jaywalking in a jewelry store that happened to be closed at the time. The film is set to come out just after the publication of my latest novel, "Sex Adventures with Ducks." I think I sent you a printer's proof. The one with tips on plow sharpening, soiled panty disposal and how to arrange buckets in the bathroom. As you read this, try not to ask yourself, "What is this crap?" but rather try to keep the puke down to a fine spray.

The first scene shows a production complex with dozens of huge buildings and a slit trench for employee bowel and bladder practices. The manufacturing facilities are among the gargantuan holdings of Vernon Plucker, the hero of our story and a name you instantly recognize, a business titan who has risen from humble origins in a service station restroom to build a monumental industrial empire envied by everyone except for one lowlife nut-case in Syracuse. Vernon became one of the wealthiest and most influential men in the history of our country, the name of which escapes me at the moment, and one of the initiators of the space program. He always maintained that Washington and Lincoln were his inspiration,

George Washington, as you learned on one of the rare occasions that you showed up at school, demonstrated his manly determination by throwing a cherry tree across the Mississipi, or something like that. And as we all know, Abraham Lincoln was famous for reciting the Gettysburg Address wherever he went. Fortunately, Vernon thought these two guys were losers.

In his case, he was actually inspired by Basil Washington and Kyle Lincoln, members of the "Wild Willie" Cub Scout Troop of Peoria, Illinois. Besides, Abe Lincoln had an embarrassingly puny poker, which is probably why he never smiles in his pictures. In other words, his crankiness may have been related to his crank. Penile size has a direct impact on feelings of well-being among men, and women like it too, as you would have learned if you fell into either of these two categories.

Some historians consider Lincoln's wife Mary the person behind her hubby's ballistic-induced demise because of what she called his amateurish use of the presidential pudd. Compelling eye-witness testimony of the time points to a person of her description at the theater flashing her biggies at Johnny Booth during the trained dog act that preceded the theater piece (and just before Booth plugged Abe in his seat). A police artist's sketch shows an open-shirted female rich in boobiness hanging over the railing and shaking her dairy vessels at John Wilkes (and a bunch of other guys). Contemporary photos of Mary unclothed and exiting the bathroom testify to the pleasing size of her bangers. Although the images are faded and a little grainy, experts point to the tattoo of an anchor above one nipple, with the words "Post No Bills," as clear proof that the bountiful balloons were those of Mrs. Lincoln (or maybe her mother).

It is important to note that Mary's actions at the theater went unnoticed by most people due to an urination mishap on the part of one of the canines in the mutt act, a terrier named Willard. And for a Civil War buff like you, I'm not telling you anything you don't already know when I point out that the Civil War was soon followed by the Franco-Prussian War, in which Francisco Franco lost the battle of Hastings, together with part of one nut.

But to resume the outline of my film, the scene changes to Vernon's sumptuous office. It is expensively decorated, with precious works of art by Pablo Pick-Asso on the walls, a Salvation Army rug on the floor and a chamber pot (full) in the corner. Vernon is an extinguished-looking, cross-eyed gentleman in his forties, with silver-gray hair and a gnarled, but adequate lever. A visitor comes into the office and is offered a chair. He chooses a piece of period furniture and leaves with it. At this point, a representative from the pentagon is ushered into Vernon's presence by his secretary, Esther Weeniepopper, a Momma with a delightfully grand bagful of bounteous knocker-steak and a gal we would all like to get our hands and our thumpers on (when our hands are not on our thumpers). Esther's role is played by Minnie Mumm, a name that is in indirect proportion to the square footage of theater screen she blocks out with her crowd-pleasing dairy accessories.

The military person is General Diskus Tingbawlz, kind of a grungy wimp. He is the loon who came up with the idea of having badgers serve on our perimeter defenses and man our missile silos. General Tingbawlz asks Vernon to convert one of his immense factories to the production of a combination space shuttle and high-tech school bus that can pull a toilet-trailer. The shuttle is to perform a pioneer mission in uncharted space to search for alien civilizations, in addition to taking travelers to the airport.

The general offers Vernon a lucrative contract from the government that involves several gazillion dollars and includes participation in a drawing for various undergarments once worn by Fatty Arbuckle's cousin. Floyd Arbuckle was a notorious cross-dresser who shocked the Hollywood crowd when he donned crosses pinched from local churches. General Tingbawlz's proposition comes at a propitious time in Vernon's life. He has tired of an unfulfilling materialistic existence, realizing that money can only buy him a fabulously luxurious lifestyle, allow him to collect native Mississipi art and be seated first at any New Jersey diner. One of the companies within his vast holdings already supplies Easter Bunny coasters to the federal prison system.

Vernon undergoes an epiphany during the conversation with the general. The word "epiphany" comes from the Greek and consists of two parts. The first part, "epiphan," means "he is taking a leak," while the second part, "y," means "on my sandals." I am grateful to that unequaled Greek scholar, Bojangles Pooper, for the authentic translation of a difficult linguistic fragment that ultimately cost him his life. Anyway, the hell with it. Vernon is drawn to the project by the appeal of space technology (and also by Dr. Grinella Sputch, a bimbo physicist with a bulging prow). Using his unmatched business skills and superior scientific knowledge, Vernon launches the creation of a monumental space ship, the USS Vapor-Belch.

Vernon's scientists work day and night and are eventually successful in separating him from Dr. Sputch. This requires a crowbar and a length of stout rope. In their spare time the engineers goose each other a lot, but also develop a break-through in rocket-fuel technology, when they combine nitro-chlorified sheep-dip and piddle protein taken from two elected federal officials (who are incidentally among the few not indicted on that particular day). The major portion of the film celebrates a pioneering mission in space that up to now has been kept from the public, mainly because it's just barely more interesting than a beaver's backside. Much of the action takes place on the farthest planet in our solar system, Pennsylpushia, although the rocket had been aimed at Idaho Falls. Anyway, the high-tech space trolley lands on a crowd of locals, incinerating most of the population and terminating a bocci-ball tournament in which live cats are used instead of balls, having been taped into the shape of spheroids prior to the contest. During the actual space mission on which my documentary is based, the real Vapor-Belch landed on the Moon, where local residents mooned the landing.

Various sub-plots in the film revolve around gripping love-stories, with graphic shots of Vernon doing most of the gripping. I concentrated on a detailed exposé of interstellar animal husbandry, nude grocery shopping, plywood breast implants, and a candid look at the world of toilet-seat abuse. In addition, I managed to weave comments on the complex social mores of our times into the narrative, especially those involving parallel parking. The film asks again those age-old questions, "How can a professional team lose a football during the game?" and "Why do teenagers insist on poking their erections into light sockets?" Let's pause for a moment and reflect on those themes.

The actors I chose to represent the USS Vapor-Belch crew consist primarily of hot chickies in revealing uniforms (not always incorporating underwear) who are outfitted by nature with some of the most noteworthy frontally-located bumpers I could find. The cast includes many recognizable Hollywood names. You'll be familiar with Tootsie Muck, Baddely Stakkt, Rival Tweet, Willbur Pisswissel, Jocko Fern, Fluster Smeek, Darren Mange, Izzy Stump and Earl. I've written Earl into the script because he forms a prime juxtaposition to higher life forms. No known bacterial strain could be located to approximate him. Because of his iffy charm he is forced to sit out much of the square-dancing that takes place at the weekly crew mixers. Even when Earl has total control over his dentures, he is not easily mistaken for Brad Pitt.

I'd like to get your expert opinion on a delicate subject, Grover. Do you think there's something wrong with Earl's rectum? As I have sometimes hinted, he is given to unfortunate anal incidents characterized by a resounding "thud." These ear-splitting pantaloon-pulverizers are normally coupled with copious smoke emanations. I have seen an entire room full of people galvanized by his sphincter-sparks who then look on in horror as he incinerates the drapes.

In many cultures rectal behavior of this sort is considered a sign of virility, but in Earl's case it's merely an example of anal treachery. I considered having you step in when he was unable, because of technical difficulties, to play the intestinal equivalent of "Pop goes the Weasel" in the film, because you are capable of at least letting the steam escape one subtle puff at a time. Earl's approach is, on the other hand, nothing short of impudent. He squirts off gaseous formations that stop inches short of scorching his pucker-string. These free-wheeling anal antics frequently lead to accidents in his shorts, the result of diarrhea-led pressure build-up and a paucity of ass control. The film crew got up a petition to have a zipper surgically installed in his sphincter. They expected to see liquefied brain parts dribble out of his nostrils at times of high butt activity.

But this all fits nicely into the story. At a later point in the action, Earl plays a crew member who is sacrificed to save the mission, subjected to a horrible, gut-wrenching and sickening death, torn slowly apart by monster alien squirrels.

A lot of the story reflects virtues you and I learned as youngsters, and I weave the most prominent of these (breast-mauling and butt-handling) into the narrative. We grew up knowing what values were important in life, Grover—or whatever your name is. At least you did, and those shrewd instincts are what made you so successful as a species, despite the lack of marketable skills. Strangely enough, you did a lot of stuff backwards, though. I recall that you once broke a neighbor's baseball by throwing a plate glass window through it. And when we went swimming I often watched in amazement as you emerged from the water by diving onto the beach.

Anyway, back to the documentary. The Vapor-Belch takes off from Cape Carnival, catapulted into space by a Civil War cannon at the incredible speed of 35 miles per hour. This high-velocity discharge coincides with the one experienced by most of the crew members (in their undies) and was required to overcome gravity and a kid behind a nearby shed screwing around with a magnet. Everyone is strapped into a reclining seat for lift-off. Playing the role of the heroic captain, Saul Sheerote, I chose to strap myself face-down in a seat already occupied by a nifty redhead named Svetlana Svetzalott, who appeared in one of my previous documentaries on how to steam-clean bathroom tiles while wearing see-through togs.

Frequent exposure of the heavily-nippled portion of Svetlana's physique is one of the artful devices I used to maintain viewing interest in an otherwise horseshit plot. The first stage of the rocket separates and is returned to Carnegie Hall in time for the evening performance. The second stage, consisting of a turnip sack filled with cannon balls and partially-dried sewage, is released next, but unfortunately lands in Duluth, where it crushes a dumpster behind a bowling alley, kills four teenagers and a fairly charming local figure named Scudball, but picks up a spare on alley number ten. The artillery piece deploys parachutes to bring it safely back to earth and it is once again installed in the square in your town, where pigeons resume defiling it and also much of the citizenry, although the results of this latter activity are not obvious even upon close inspection.

After years in outer space, the Vapor-Belch finally returns to Earth, crash-landing on an outhouse in Jersey City and spewing bowel-extract over a large portion of the county, improving many areas. Vernon's ground-breaking mission is completed, which I re-created with stunning camera work, although I am at a loss to explain the presence in several shots of a large dog named Lowell. During the mission, new planets were visited and distant civilizations were contacted. The crew discovered alien forms that possessed positive traits such as hospitality, good will, compassion, a rare enthusiasm for tap-dancing, and the desire to order pizza right after they got laid. Vernon and his space travelers were able to communicate with these extraterrestrial beings through the use of complex sign language and crotch-clutching, demonstrating the amazing similarity between all life forms in the universe. It also shows how virtually everyone is drawn to practices similar to those you have routinely inflicted on unsuspecting members of society throughout your miserable, stiffy-oriented existence, even though most of your despicable habits were condemned years ago by virtually every state in the Union, with the exception of Mississippi, where they are essential for raising farm animals.

The final scene shows Vernon at a gala White House affair in his honor, where the President acknowledges the heroic devotion of those connected with the historic mission. He ends his remarks with the inspiring words, "Ask not what your country can do for you. Ask if you can find a way to avoid gatherings like these." He then takes questions from the audience. I was there on that historic day when Earl suggested that we adopt a National Squirrel and call it Fenton. A senator-skinning was also on the agenda.

Vernon was asked to say a few words and obliged with half a dozen well-chosen remarks from a furnace manual. Our hero tweaked the First Lady's ample butt as he was praised for his accomplishments and was then presented with an honorary federal goosing device and a ceremonial spittoon. I was going to send you one, but UPS wanted me to empty if first. Vernon also received a a coveted set of jockey shorts that boasted a picture of a former governor of South Carolina in the defecation area.

For your information, Grover, Madge said she wanted to shed some weight, so she took up horseback riding. It was immediately successful. The horse lost eighty pounds in the first three days. I hope you're not upset to learn that Earl has to go to the hospital for waterfowl surgery. A duck flew up his butt and now it has a quack in it.

Ludlow

40

Hey Grover,

Can you imagine? My latest film has been rejected by a bunch of wusses. The Hollywood players who reviewed my work labeled it "on the level of rat shit," except for one brave dissenting voice that proclaimed, "It doesn't reach the level of rat shit." Not many people would stand up for their convictions like that. But as you would expect, this setback doesn't set me back. You know that I have been able, over the last couple of years, to use reams of perfectly good paper, so I am in a perfect position to simply dust off my notes and produce some other high-quality _____ that will be electrifyingly successful. My new project, in the form of a 450-page pamphlet, examines the various movements throughout history that have resulted in the onward march of social progress, arriving at that enviable level of culture at which we find ourselves today, a world in which hot-dog eating contests are reported in detail. This book is not dedicated to those who did nothing to help me from a financial standpoint, and you know who you are.

In this work I follow the trials and tribulations of our species in their struggle to overcome poverty, bad teeth and unhealthy sexual practices to reach a social level that most people would say without equivocation is completely irrelevant. I produced this monumental tome to point out the necessity of classifying the inhabitants of the world in general, and our peerless country in particular, into several main categories, and this is evident in the unfolding drama.

I use examples that I have encountered over the years to represent two main groups—those who invent conspiracy theories for every event and those from a higher level who crap in the bushes—dividing them further into the following sub-groups: (1) booger-brains with the collective intelligence of mayonnaise, (2) turkeys who incite tranquilizer consumption in everyone around them, (3) bladder-violators missing key brain components, (4) bottom-feeders with some fractional cerebral functionality, and (5) flubs possessing the common sense that God gave gravel. I am continually impressed by the unique and wondrous conditions that have allowed intelligent life to occur on earth but keep it out of my neighborhood. You may not have noticed anything special around your place.

In my work I quote many experts, including those revered Greek philosophers, Soccer Tease and Play Dough. They spent their lives trying to make sense of their environment, despite the limitations of their time and their poor fashion choices. I am burdened, as they were, with the search for answers to profound universal questions. For example, how can one lowly individual know what our Creator intends? I'm still trying to figure out what Yogi Berra is talking about. I know you have issues too, but I can't help you get that stuff out of your underwear by fax. While I have ever pursued the activities of the common man—travel, leisure, upscale architecture, gourmet cuisine and horizontal female companionship, I have managed to devote my creative time to matters of unbounded importance, at the same time lugging pants full of heavy equipment around.

I'm sending you this outline, but I urge you to go easy with the praise. I can take only so much limitless adulation. You were undoubtedly riveted by my previous description of cave-dweller history. Building on those insights, I can tell you that later on, though man's progress was frequently hampered by paths that diverged from the appropriate evolutionary forces, his ultimate composition took on influences that pointed our species toward the way we live today. Up until that time, humans much like you and me (perhaps not necessarily you) led the life of the "noble savage," as Jean-Jacques Rousseau proclaimed, unspoiled by the demanding and stultifying rules of society and imposed latrine maintenance.

These innocent creatures, our ancestors, went about their business in comparative freedom, foraging, hunting and looking for nice butt. They kept their noses clean, except for outings involving the investigation of trash receptacles, evacuating where the mood (and their bowels) moved them, and treating themselves to a nice piece of tail as the spirit and the can of a hot babe dictated. These fine specimens, our forefathers, who were mangy, but nevertheless virtuous in their own way (as you are not in your way), had their peaceful existence altered by one of the first great events in a long line of experiences—the development of organized religion. This step forward in the evolution of barbarism cannot be underestimated.

We have many examples. Historians praise the achievements of ancient societies such as the Aztecs or the Mayas. They created advanced civilizations and built marvelous cities in which nobody had to wait long for a bus, while at the same time bullshitting their people in the name of some crackpot divinity.

Religions throughout history have thought up ceremonies to ensure the obedience of their followers. The Aztecs tore the heart out of a human being every day in order that their gods would make the sun rise. It was for a good cause, obviously. My thesis, however, is that practices like this are risky—at least for one of the participants. Thank goodness the Spanish brought their religious fervor to the New World in time to wipe out over fifteen million of the indigenous population in the name of the sweet Jesus.

We must remember that the impulse to religion originated in a period when nobody had the faintest idea what the hell was going on. They were grasping at straws to understand the tiniest aspect of their lives. Earl is still at it. All over the primitive world people felt that their existence was regulated by deities. They worshiped Sun gods, Moon gods, Water gods, Bowel gods and gods who provided guys with a nice Momma on a Saturday night. Religions encouraged virtuous behavior (you wisely ignored this suggestion) and that has led to a planet that now enjoys the utmost in non-violence, as you have noticed.

If we look around, we are able to recognize our greatest blessing, namely that virtually every religion is ready to kill my trembling carcass to ensure that I follow the correct precepts. The faithful know what God wants us to do, including what we eat, how we worship, and what to do with our thingies. The religious, bless their little hearts, have always demonstrated divine virtue as they killed the unbelievers or burned their temples. Well, excuse me, but it happens to be my mission to point out the true path to salvation, and it leads through a turnstile outside my home. A tear-out order form is at the end of this book.

I think I learned the most about religion when I met Esther Krapotnik, a young lady with an admirable lack of virtue. Our relationship must have been ordained by the true religion, because I praised the heavens for the experience. In addition to possessing absurdly swollen booby-mutton, Esther suffered from a malady in the presence of males that resulted in a frenzied inattention to clothing. She was a volunteer when I was in the hospital, and she asked if I wanted to donate an organ. I told her I didn't want to wait until I was dead so she got in bed with me. We fortunately had some privacy, because the guy in the bed next to me had just kicked the bucket. He seemed to be doing well under the circumstances, and this reminded me that we should not laugh at funerals unless we just can't help ourselves, such as when the corpse's fly is open. But what a struggle I had with Esther! She showed me that old railroad-car trick that later became known as high-speed coupling. They later had to vacuum the bed and then burn it.

Although I digress, I must point out that history has been vague on many subjects. A little-known fact is that the bow was invented many years before the arrow, since fossil evidence clearly points to archery targets with rock damage. But the strangest distortion of all is the myth that Alexander Graham Bell first said to his assistant, "Watson, come here. I want you." What he actually said was, "Watson, what the hell are you doing on the line? I was trying to call Mitzi."

Something is always happening to Earl, as you'd expect. The latest problem involved a gas leak that allowed propane to seep into the city water supply, and the lethal accumulation of flammable vapors transformed some toilets into explosive devices. The situation quickly loses its humor if you find yourself camped on the apparatus at the time of detonation. Sadly, Earl was located on just that spot at the wrong time, propelled skyward with considerable force. Unfortunately, he managed to pull through and was taken to the local pre-burial medical establishment, where it was determined that he experiences regular discomfort from porcelain in his feces.

Your closest relative, though writing from some distance,

Ludlow

41

Hey Grover,

The commentators at golf tournaments make my ass ache. They want you to think they're experts, so they give you detailed crap on every shot. "He didn't keep the putter blade square to the outthouse and the ball hopped off the hosel and spun out at the last moment." Give me a break. What happened is that the guy didn't hit a perfect putt. What a big surprise! I love the interviews too. They ask eight-part questions that last for twenty minutes and the golfer doesn't have the faintest idea what they mean, so his answers have no bearing on the issue. The dork is usually devoid of cranial life anyway. Here's a transcript of a recent telecast to prove my point.

Nintz: That ball is way left. Peter Costplus, take us through the tee shot.
Costplus: Let's look at this swing with the aid of the Revolta Swing-Vision Pecker-Level Camera. First, you can see how Bludgin Hammerswipe takes the club back in one piece instead of leaving part of it on the tee. He makes a full turn with one shoulder and the club is parallel to the ground at the top of his backswing, all the way around under his chin and almost stuck in his anus. The club-head is pointing directly away from the target. Now he starts his downswing because he doesn't know what the hell else to do at this point. He could go to the clubhouse and take a dump, but he manages to relieve the pressure with a smell-heavy trouser-buster. Keeping in mind that severe pronation at the impact area often produces extensive diarrhea, his hips get out of the way so he doesn't club himself in the sack and he pushes off his back leg, sliding his front foot into a pile of dog-dung, wiping the club-face across the ball to create the left-to-right shot that has become so familiar to the owners of severely damaged homes adjacent to the fairway.
Nintz: But why did the ball finish two fairways over to the left behind an exposed unisex urinal after it creamed a bystander who was taking a leak and a large dog—whose name, we understand, is Lowell?
Costplus: He came over the top.
Nintz: Oh. Where's the ball now, Peter?

Costplus: It finished up on a sprinkler head. So he'll have to play the ball as it lies, but he's entitled to drop the sprinkler head with no penalty.

Nintz: I guess these guys could benefit from your instruction, right Peter?

Costplus: Bludgin really needs my help, Jim. A couple of millimeters pointing wrong at the top of the swing can throw the flight of the ball off one or two inches and his Johnson will flop out—the way yours does when you go into your serpent-killing routine on the course. Ha-ha.

Nintz: Very funny. But how do you explain Doug Sanders, John Daly, Lee Trevino and Jim Furyk? They have some of the most screwed-up swings in the game. Sanders had a forward press and a follow-through. Daly sticks the club in the crack of his butt on his backswing. Trevino's arc was so flat he could hit the ball standing behind a phone pole, and Furyk's swing has so many loops it looks like medieval calligraphy tracing a new-car warranty in the air. Why are they successful?

Costplus: They didn't come over the top.

Nintz: Oh. Nick Faulto, I see Wissel Dicksie's ball finished up behind the green. He's leaving the pin in. When you were chipping, where did you want the flag?

Faulto: I wanted it attached to the flagstick.

Nintz____   I mean did you prefer to have the flagstick in or out?

Faulto: I wanted it jammed in my caddy's rectum for handing me the wrong club.

Nintz: Ian Bagel-Fink, it's great to see Walter Pidgeon's son, Clay, out here after trying to get through the Q-School for twenty-eight years. He's probably the best putter on the tour. A fantastic reader of the greens, with a marvelous putting stroke.

Faulto: Good call, Jim. He missed that putt on the low side and it finished up a good fifty feet from the hole.

Bagel-Fink: As you can see, he hit the ball right through the break of some eleven feet and it finished in his playing partner's bag. I detected a slight shoulder movement and heard a wicked pants-greaser as he lifted the putter over his head and hit straight down on the ball. I thought he was fixing a ball mark. But his stroke imparted a counter-clockwise, sideways spin and made the ball hop in the air about six feet. I also have a problem with his choice of putter. It looks like a pipe wrench welded to a leaf blower. And I hate to see a flat stick with square grooves.

Nintz: Let's check in with David Farty on number three. How much does Rufus Turdledong have left for his next shot to the par seven, David?

Farty: He has ninety yards for his twenty-second shot, Jim, and the ball is below his feet.

Nintz: It's a side-hill lie?

Farty: No, he's standing on the damn thing. There goes his shot. It's up in the air and it landed right next to the pin. Too bad the pin is in a shed down by the creek. The groundskeepers put it there after the previous group finished.

Nintz: Now it's time for "The Rules of the Game" with Minnie Driver's brother, Skrue. This segment is brought to you by Wonder Bread, for you golfers who have a slice.

Driver: Here's a good tip for the folks at home. When the wind is blowing hard, you're allowed to mark your ball with a concrete block. Remember, if you want to play this game, you must bloody nuts.

Nintz: Insightful as always, Skrue. Now let's go down to Roger Maltwhiskey.

Maltwhiskey: Thanks Jim. I'm here with Svelte Bladder, executive vice-president of the tournament's sponsor, Bare Buttocks Sportswear. Mr. Bladder, you must be very happy with the turnout this week.

Bladder: Frankly, I don't give a hairy horse's ass. I have a hot-tailed Momma stowed in my hotel room and every minute I spend with you clowns cuts into my reaming work. My wife is also a gorgeous blond supermodel and when I get home I'm going to bang her until she screams for mercy. Can you top that?

Maltwhiskey: I don't know. Let me have your address and I'll give it a shot.

Bladder: I'm out of here.

Maltwhiskey: Before you go, I understand your company has some financial problems and will go belly-up right after the tournament. It seems you misstated your profits by five billion dollars and manufactured a hundred thousand women's swimsuits with a large hole in the pubic area. Do you want to comment on that?

Bladder: No.

Maltwhiskey: Back to you, Jim.

Nintz: Let's go out to the seventh hole and our own Upchuck N. Rolfing.

Rolfing: Thanks Jim. I'm standing here in the bunker with Slappum Atschuh. He hit a perfectly miserable shot that was only slightly better than the previous twelve catastrophes he uncorked on this hole. In fact, it's the most brutal exhibition of rodent-maiming I have ever witnessed. In addition, he's got a buried lie.

Nintz: How did that happen, Upchuck?

Rolfing: I spoke with one of the groundskeepers and he told me he shoveled dirt over it because he couldn't bear to see any more havoc wreaked on the property. How do you plan to play this shot, Slappum?

Slappum: What the hell are you doing? Get out of this bunker or I'll take your head off with my wedge.

Rolfing: Good luck. So far, you haven't hit anything you've aimed at.

Nintz: Peter Costplus, how should Atschuh play this bunker shot?

Costplus: Jim, this calls for a 365-degree sand wedge and several hours of prayer. He'll have to play the ball, wherever he thinks it is, back in his stance about eight feet and break his wrists quickly....

Rolfing: He already broke both wrists batting the ball out of the quarry, Peter.

Costplus: .... he should keep his rear end out of the way and pick the club or the rake up quickly to ensure the proper backspin. On the downswing, he'll want to hit behind the ball three-quarters of an inch to compensate for the uphill angle of the weasel sitting on his foot. Oh no!

Nintz: What happened, Peter!? Did he nail the weasel?

Costplus: No, thank god, the animal is okay. But he smacked Rolfing right in the scrotum. It was the best swing he's made all day.

Nintz: Where did the ball end up?

Costplus: Under some blonde's skirt. She was sitting in a portable crapper with the door open so she wouldn't miss the action. We're going to help him clean and place it.

Nintz: The ball?

Costplus: No, the blonde.

Nintz: What about Rolfing?

Costplus: Piss on Rolfing. Let him find his own blonde.

Nintz: Now for the "Shot of the Day" brought to you by Ralph Suckledinger's Barbequed Chicken Innards. Chomp down on some of Ralph's gizzards and you never eat anything else. Just ask the family of the late Henry Chewmaster. Our Shot of the Day took place on the fourth hole, where Digby Duffer blew his brains out after carding a twenty-seven, two strokes higher than his score on the previous hole. And now, Peter Roosterhouse is going to bring us a few words from our first-round leader, Stabb Attum.

Roosterhouse: Thank you, Jim. I'm here with Morty Fyde, whose score of thirty-nine over par is leading after the first round. Morty, you've never made a cut before in six hundred and eighty-three attempts after receiving five hundred sponsor's exemptions, bribing several dozen PGA officials and crying like a baby until they let you into the rest of the tournaments. You must be awfully proud of your performance today, coming back at the last hole after seventeen consecutive quadruple bogies. What prompted you to use a three wood out of the greenside bunker?

Fyde: I have a cousin who is undergoing extensive penile surgery back in Alabama. It's got a wicked bend in it, so I want to wish him length.

Roosterhouse: The wind was blowing straight up today. Did it give you any trouble?

Fyde: I picked these clubs up at a church bazaar in Anus Dribble, Montana. I didn't even have to re-grip them. They were already wrapped with electrician's tape and the Honduran flag, except for the thirteen-iron.

Roosterhouse: Did you know that you'll be paired with the starter for tomorrow's round?

Fyde: The pins were pretty accessible today. Too bad they weren't anywhere near the holes. My mother told me to keep my chin in my pants and my Willie up. Or maybe it was the other way around.

Roosterhouse: Who was your role model when you started playing golf, Morty?

Fyde: I like a three-piece ball because it comes in three pieces. You can hit them all and then choose the one that winds up closest to the clubhouse.

Nintz: Tayga Mulligan is on the tee at the second hole, Nick. He's coming off a hole where he putted out for a forty, so he seems a little upset. The crowd got on him when he kicked that nice old lady in the ass after she called him a "shit-puss." Did you see what happened, Peter Roosterhouse?

Roosterhouse: I was right behind him, Jim. Mulligan's caddy kicked her in the ass too. I booted the old broad one in her fat keister myself.

Ninz: The final group of the day is coming up the last fairway, Nick. This is the threesome of Hammy Neggs, Rocco Vayjuss, and Dustin Fernitscher. Listen to the crowd reaction.

Faulto: Yes, it's pretty quiet, Jim. The four people who came to watch this tournament left a couple of hours ago. This group was originally a six-some, but I understand they lost Hakkin Punschitt, Cumming Throoh and Shank Tabadwunn to wild dogs and a farmer with a shotgun out there near the dogleg and the cat's rectum.

Ninz: It just goes to show how difficult the U.S. Hackers Union and Gopher-Mining Confederation has set the course up.

Faulto: On the other hand, they reduced the number of holes from eighteen to ten, so it's a fair test of skill.

Ninz: We'll be back right after this message from Ping. The company has recently merged with the Pong Corporation to manufacture bobsleds.

By the way, Grover, I called Madge to wish her a happy birthday. Her seventieth birthday isn't far away. Only fifteen years ago. She told me that Earl is now with the FBI. They captured him in Albany. I guess he took off after one of their famous pugilistic encounters and got into a bit of trouble involving a bank, a Sunday School class and an open gravesite full of chickens. It all started during a visit by the Rev. Harold Smidgen and his wife Harriet. The good pastor was offering a simple prayer when Earl leaned sideways to get a better view of Harriet's topside, which was hanging out a little and is not half bad. As usually occurs when he finds himself tipped onto one cheek, Earl's automatic exhaust system kicked in and he launched one of his resounding ordnance-class fanny-flares, followed by a series of glass-breaking poots that were impossible to disguise even with lead shielding. Seems he pulled an ass muscle this time, along with some rectal ligaments. The pious couple departed with scorched olfactory nerves and a renewed respect for many of the Commandments.

The best friend you have at this address,

Ludlow

42

Hey Grover,

Our town recently launched a local television station, KRUD, and they asked me to come up with a program for the children. I racked my brain, which was kind of risky because I was in the pool hall at the time, but I came up with a great idea. The show I'm putting on for the little putzes is modeled after "Bill Nye the Science Guy." My version is called "Chet McFeeny the Techno-Weenie." Science and technology never had such an exciting forum. I play the part of Chet, of course, providing the youngsters with explanations of physical, mathematical and chemical phenomena of all sorts. The show can't miss. Here's the transcript of the first telecast. You'll probably learn a pot-full of scientific stuff yourself, at least from a different point of view.

Hi Gang! Here's your Uncle Chet with a barrel of critical scientific information from the world of technology. How are you all doing? I feel good, and my curve ball has some real pop in it today. So huddle up close to the TV and tell your Mom and Dad to piss off, because this program is for Kids! I know you're dying to find out all abut those neutrons, protons and croutons, so we're going to talk about lots of technical phenomena that have been puzzling you. I mean besides genital fixation or that rash on your little cans. So listen up or I'll come to your house and kick some ass.

Let's start with a subject that has probably been bothering you for some time—Newton's Three Laws of Motion. Isaac Newton was kind of a short-shafted nerd who tried to be a comic as well as a scientist. He wrote his massive work on Natural Philosophy entirely in Latin. What kind of a jerk would pull a stunt like that? Nobody could read the damn thing. And he originally concluded that there were four laws of motion, but then he realized that the fourth one was a case of the "shuddering shakes" he contracted during a night slogging down some cold ones with a bunch of his buddies. So he went back to three laws, a reduction of over, say, 60 percent. Now, I'm sure all you youngsters out there have the same head-banging experience when you get into Daddy's liquor cabinet. And if you haven't, I suggest you give it a shot right away. Nothing lightens the load like getting a load on.

Anyway, Newton's First Law of Motion goes like this: "A body at rest tends to remain at rest until you boot it one in the can." You can perform this experiment at home with your younger siblings and you'll see that it works without fail. Sneak up and drop-kick one of them and stand back. Good for Newtonian motion and laughs too. And if they give you any trouble, tell them you're working on a project for Uncle Chet and boot them another one in the tail.

Moving on, Newty's Second Law states: "A body in motion tends to proceed in a straight line unless it is acted upon by an outside vector quantity and assumes a new direction that is dependent on the vector force and its angle." A 12-gauge shotgun loaded with bird pellets is excellent for this purpose. It'll change somebody's direction for you in a hurry. You may want to experiment with this using a kid brother or uncle, but aim for the scrotum. A head shot is known to do real damage. I know it did to me.

Where were we? Oh yeah, Newton's Third Law postulates: "For every action there is a reaction that is equal in force and opposite in direction." Let me give you an example. If Johnny puts his thingie in Emily's little opening and pushes hard, Emily will push back with equal force and giggle at the same time. But if I get Miss Abernathy from Accounting in the sack and I push, she falls out of bed. I know, I've tried it. It just shows you that Newton didn't know what the hell he was talking about half the time. If your parents walk in while you're buck-assed naked and pursuing this project, tell them you're involved in some kind of cross-pollination ritual.

Sticking with Newton, we're now going to examine what he knew about gravity, which wasn't much. You probably heard the story about an apple hitting Isaac on the head and leading to his theory of gravitational forces. This story is bullshit. You can trust me. The

Newster did not get pasted with an item from the produce aisle. If you fart around under a tree in the middle of the afternoon when you should be helping your folks bail bowel products out of the barn, what is likely to hit you in the guard? It ain't no apple, believe me. It has been proved through extensive research conducted at the sports pub down the street that parents who are trying to get their kids off their big lazy butts are known for their fierce projectile-launching enthusiasm, so you can bet your ass that the stuff raining down on Isaac's head was an extremely close relative of the dung family. It's amazing how some people screw up the facts.

At any rate, this propitious accident led to two vital discoveries in the history of science. First, gravity made its long-awaited appearance, and, second, it was determined that a tankard of ale is a poor choice for getting manure off your noggin. But we are fortunate today that Newton could still apply his stupendous brain-power under those conditions. Though his skull was covered with viscous defecatory matter, he was able to see the relationship between trees and the sucking power of the Earth. Thus, gravity was born, and we still use it today, although not always in the way Isaac envisioned. He wanted this major source of energy to be applied only for good or occasional practical jokes, but as we have seen throughout our barbaric history, mostly in your homes, mankind has managed to usurp the benevolent characteristics of gravity and use it to make Christmas trees tip over, toilets back up, and asses sag. But nobody gives a damn about that (except Miss Abernathy, who has a real problem there).

Let's quit diddling around with this gravity crap and turn our attention to the sensational mathematical innovation that proceeded from Newton's incomparable cerebellum. No, I don't mean how to clean your ears while taking a dump. I'm talking about Calculus, the miraculous derivation process that allows us to compute the areas and volumes of irregular-shaped figures, many of which you see in shopping malls all over the country. I have to tell you, though, I don't understand why anybody would want to tackle this junk in the first place. I've tried to avoid irregular-shaped figures all my life and with the exception of Miss Abernathy I have been relatively successful. But if you want to buck the trend and you're just shitting your pants to compute the sums of derivative quantities, you go right ahead. You make my ass ache.

Let's change the subject and pursue the world of chemistry, kids. Do you have your "Chet McFeeny Hair-Trigger Chemistry Set" ready? Then what the hell are you waiting for? Get your pasty little asses in gear! I'll give you five minutes to set it up, during which we can bring you a message from one of our sponsors, The Brown Lump Septic Tank Corporation. Kids, does your house have the lingering odor of human waste? Does poop figure in your household decorative style? Are you uncomfortable on the crapper because you have to hold your nostrils shut with both hands? Well, get on Daddy's ass and tell him to look into the septic tank at your place. The Brown Lump Corporation can install a new dung-box in your front yard in just five days, and you'll thrill to the fragrance of newly-treated rectal discharge once again. You'll have to get rid of the dirt from the excavation, though. Dig another hole and put it in there. For just a couple of bucks more, Brown Lump will convert your old dung receptacle into a swimming pool or indoor Jacuzzi just off the living room, completing the sewage process that will make your home and your discharge-treatment area a community showcase. Call the number on our screen and the first four hundred callers will receive a free septic tank check-up without obligation—except for lunch.

Okay, you little demons, back to the show. Have you got "Uncle Chet's Chemistry Set" ready? Some of you pint-sized warts need to shake your cans a little. We don't have all day here, for crissakes. Today's project is a roadside explosive device that can knock the balls off a cat, regardless of size—maybe two of them (cats I mean). Do you have any cats around your place? If so, get a few of them and keep them handy. If you don't have cats, any pet will do, or write down my directions so you can destabilize the molecules in any cats you run across in the future. The more the better. Shattered cats are welcome in the best circles, and even lame ones are viewed with pleasure where I come from, with second place going to pissy little yapping dogs that have bows around their necks, the furry bastards.

Here's how our experiment works. Take one of those little sticks of dynamite from the Raw-Materials Container that comes with your "Hair-Trigger Chemistry Set" (with the skull and crossbones on it) and ram it in the rectum of the nearest cat. This is best accomplished by standing on the cat's head with one foot and prying tabby's cute little anus open with the ass-stretching tool you'll find in the Chemistry Set's Wine-Making Section. Make sure the dynamite is all the way in and fits snugly in the feline's nether orifice. Only the fuse should be protruding.

Now carefully tamp some Krazy Glue around the stick so it doesn't come loose. The animal may become uncooperative at some point, so you need to whack it in its little gourd a few times with Uncle Chet's "Cat-Hammer," the twelve-pound ball-peen instrument right next to the "Fungo-Bat Cat-Anesthesia Device." Now light the fuse and let the cat loose. You're in for tons of fun, kids! The result of the explosion will look like the neighborhood where my brother lives. The tough part is that you'll have to clean the place up a little before Mommy gets home and beats on your ass. I want you to collect all the cat shards and put them in Uncle Chet's Porcelain Cat-Shard Receptacle. Then you just add the contents of the bottle marked H2SO4. **Don't get any of this shit on you!!!!** Sulfuric Acid will eat your skin off right down to your skeleton—and the floorboards too! Which may improve the looks on some of you friggin' mules.

Let's proceed to the next event. We're talking about real physics here—the rate of acceleration of a falling body. Keep a cat handy for this one too. I'll let you in on a secret. The physics text books say that every falling body accelerates at the same rate. They try to make you believe that if you drop a dime and a musk-ox from a tall building, both objects will strike the ground at the same time. Now, even senseless ninnies like you know that this is a crock. It's not logical. So we're going to perform a test to show those dunderheads they don't know their ass from the blister on a buffalo's nuts. Take a cat and tape its legs to its belly. Now go up on the roof of a building that has more than ten floors and take a bowling ball with you. I'll wait for you. All set? Good. Now drop the cat and the bowling ball at the same time and see which object splats on the sidewalk first. If you're not sure, repeat the experiment. Get another cat and this time tape the bowling ball to the cat.

That brings us to the fire-walking segment. You'll need to crank up the barbeque for this one, so you may want to throw a couple of hot dogs on the grill at the same time. The object here is to see if a cat can hoof it across a bed of glowing charcoal without losing its composure. Get the charcoal really red-hot and spread it out in a pit you dig in the back yard. Quit bitching, for crissakes! Grab a shovel and start digging! Now take the cat, immerse it in wood alcohol and then toss it in the pit. Some of your Daddy's scotch will work if you can't locate the alcohol, but don't drink any. Seal the bottle when you're done and FedEx it to the address you see on the screen. But keep your eye on the cat. If you never saw an animal whiz over hot coals with its fur on fire and screaming like hell just before it becomes a pile of cinders, you'll love this. Cats are a real howl sometimes.

It's time now for our mathematics puzzle of the week, gang! And it was tough for me to choose one that would challenge and entertain you, as if I give a rabbit pellet. I didn't know whether to pick something from the field of trigger-knob-itry or a quadriplegic equation. I decided to use two word problems sent in by Gotek Ashower of Custer's Grave, North Dakota. The problems go like this:

1.   Harold drives his car into a crowd of people who have gathered to watch the redneck rights parade in Selma, Alabama. His initial speed is seventy miles per hour, but each person he runs over reduces the car's velocity by three mph. How many quasi-people does Harold have to crush in order to bring the car to a halt on top of a hillbilly? (Answer at end of chapter.)

2.   Harold has seven gumballs. He refuses to give you any. How many gumballs does he have remaining. (Answer at end of chapter.)

Uncle Chet's guest today is Tori Adorr. Tori is eight years old and she's in the third grade at the Al Capone Middle School and Casino in El Pequeño Pene, California.   What have you brought for us, Tori?

Tori: I brought the ham sandwich you ordered. And take your hand off my rear.

Chet: Sorry. I mean what scientific breakthrough will you demonstrate?

Tori: This is a polymerized ionization model of a pro-benzene-ring molecule that I attached to four ferrous-oxide atoms to form a photo-synthetic proton fluid cell with an argon nucleus. And your hand is on my rear again.

Chet: Totally inadvertent.   What is your invention good for, dear?

Tori: It can be used for cleaning bird-crap from intercontinental ballistics missiles and it makes a nice after-dinner drink. Your hand! Off!

Chet: You're so sensitive, dear. And what are the raw materials for your invention?

Tori: I start with orange peels and football cleats, but it also works with discarded underpants and a baggie filled with mouse remains. You can put your hand back on my rear now.

Chet: That was terrific, Tori. So is your rear. I'll make sure you get a prize right after the show.

Wasn't she great, boys and girls? Aw, quit bitching. Well, that's all for today. Tune in again for our next show, when we will perform an experiment that entails stripping the electrons from a cesium atom and using them to make a device that can flush toilets by remote-control. You'll soon enjoy the sound of flowing fecal matter in your home without getting out of bed. And also in your neighbor's house (because the range of our apparatus is five hundred yards). What a great surprise for the whole family and those slowpokes in the neighborhood when you flood the bowl from the confines of your own room.

We're also going to do some serious atom-smashing, so get your gear together. All you need is a medium-size cyclotron, an acetylene torch, fifteen cents in change and a catcher's mitt. If we have enough time, maybe we can squeeze in instructions for destroying a city council meeting with tactical weapons. But don't forget, not all technology is good. Some is the opposite (bad). And keep in mind that there is a limited market for songs about welding Tupperware shut. I want to remind you kids out there in scientific land that you should keep learning and improving your technical skills. Use whatever means you consider appropriate to further your education, including frequent casual sex. And remember—cats are made to be taken apart.

Until next time, this is your old Uncle Chet saying, "This is your old Uncle Chet." Now you can go back to playing with yourselves—I mean with each other.

Well, Grover, I have often spoken of Earl's butt criminality, in addition to an odor that interferes with radio transmission, but I recently uncovered evidence showing that sphincter fizzlers occur equally as often among the upper classes. Now we know why the Prince of Wales is always surrounded by men with bagpipes.

Yours for better poultry plucking,

Kat Shoor-Schmidt

Answers to word problems:
1. All of them if he's lucky.
2. None. You knock him on his ass and take the gumballs.

43

Hey Grover,

Alas, Earl has been throwing up squirrel parts again. It started after he went to that restaurant with the buffet where you can eat all you want. He was there for five days. Before that, he was severely hurt at the city center when he fell off a high ladder while putting up a sign that reads, "**This Is An Injury-Free Workplace**." Earl says he feels fine and the flatulence is unimpeded, so I don't really see anything different, but Madge claims he doesn't look good. I don't know what she uses to compare him with. She always feeds him some beans before he goes to sleep. They provide escape velocity to help him get out of bed in the morning.

He was okay last week when he and I teamed up to win the Two-Man Windshield Scrape Competition down at the Senior Center. This is a contest to see who can remove the most bird droppings from the windshield of a 1949 Plymouth in the allotted time. Our town goes all out to promote activities like this and that's another reason why they piss me off. They had bleachers set up in the parking lot and everybody turned out for the event, which gives you an idea of the miserable lives these people lead.

At halftime the Senior Center Cheerleaders came out and put on a show, if you can call it that. Ten wrinkled old broads in walkers doing unsynchronized "bumping-into-each-other" is not my idea of entertainment, but a couple of them always forget to don underwear, so it's not without its charm.

I let Earl do most of the work for our squad, even though he moves at the speed of soybean growth. It doesn't matter, though, because none of the other competitors know what the hell they're doing. During the final minutes of the contest I had to carry some of the load, because my large-bellied partner was the victim of a severe bladder mishap, soaking his fashion-heavy Bermuda togs (and several onlookers) in the process. This happens to people who have a very high bladder-to-brain ratio and Earl is at the top of that list.

You can count on Earl to enliven any gathering and endanger innocent people with some sort of random discharge. But I came through in the clutch, able to pick off a large clump of excreted bowel extract from a distance of eight feet with my slingshot. That sealed the victory. Several contestants told me later they were on the verge of lodging a protest at my use of a "Mary Magdalene Model" weapon, but the rock caromed off the car and pasted Earl between the eyes, so they figured it was adequate compensation. He regained consciousness after ten minutes or so, as if anybody could tell.

Stepford Sludge and his partner, Matt Azoah (they call him "Spur Matt"), almost came in second. They were convinced that they could beat us, but reality is often inclined to disrupt our plans. They really seemed to have their poop together and would have nosed us out in the finals, but the Stepper stretched way over to snag a really thick piece of woodpecker-dung and when he grunted, he filled his shorts. Immediate disqualification. Plus his team had to haul away all the defecatory matter from the contest site. They put it in Earl's car.

Spur is a retired bus driver from Pasadena who was forced to take an early buyout when he was thirty-two because of his driving record, which some people alluded to as "iffy." In his first year, he was involved in seventy-eight serious accidents, many of which resulted in fatalities. The only reason they kept him on is that it's hard to get rid of an employee in California who relies on a seeing-eye dog. Everything would have been okay with Spur's bus work, but the dog they gave him was a Chihuahua and the little bastard couldn't see out the window. The transit authority subsequently gave all their other employees "driving-eye" dogs. After his collision-heavy career behind the wheel, Spur turned to a life of heinous crime and became a mortgage lender.

The old Stepper was philosophical about the loss, although I'm sure he was disappointed. At the awards ceremony he pushed the microphone halfway up one nostril and said, "I'm sorry we let our fans down, but we're going to work hard and come back next year to take the trophy." One of the old ladies in the audience called out, "That's what you said last year, you dickhead!" I guess she dropped a bundle betting the wrong way. Another gal whacked Stepford right in the ass with her cane. She said later that she was aiming for Earl, but was glad she at least hit somebody.

Some people threw rocks and bottles at the losers, but the wings on those old misfits wouldn't qualify them for a baseball tryout in Munchkin Land, so most of the stuff landed on the folks just in front of them. As you've suspected all along, the Senior Center is a den of geriatric violence. A fight breaks out every five minutes in that place. It doesn't take much to set them off. A day without a brawl is a day in another town.

Following the contest, we were seated at the interview table for the trophy presentation and Lou Spung, the Tournament Director, stood up and said a few words about sportsmanship that were totally inaudible. He couldn't be heard over the screaming, swearing and fighting that was taking place in the audience. Two aisles were filled with people rolling around and punching the bajeezus out of each other, and folding chairs were flying all over the place. Lou sat down and said, "Screw it!" just as the noise abated.

Stepford extended his hand to us in congratulation and Earl chose that moment to stand up and adjust his crotch. The Stepster inadvertently gave him a karate chop to the nuts, kind of like a poke in the eye, but farther south. Earl's well-known lightning reflexes kicked in. He messed his pants and fell down. That guy spends more time on the floor than wall-to-wall carpeting. You really can't blame the Sludger, though. He originally came from a country with no plumbing, so he's not current with Bird-Shit Trophy protocol.

A couple of the wheelchair-mounted attendees took the occasion to roll over Earl while he was lying there trying to figure out which direction was vertical. I grabbed a vacant rolly-stool and made a few passes myself. He had prosthetic marks all over his ass. That's in addition to the footprints Madge normally leaves on him. A terrible bout of fisticuffs took place in the back of the room involving four people in walkers. To show you the extent of their short-ranging intellects, the women were trying to get autographs because they thought Earl was a celebrity. One old biddy told me he looked like that actor who's always lying on an autopsy table in one of the crime shows. In my opinion, that's where he belongs. It's a crime show wherever he shows up.

I managed to keep out of the battles that raged around us and limited myself to watching these dingbats paste each other in the mouth and kick whatever shins they could reach. I also took advantage of the opportunity to pull down a few knickers, so I can report that Stepford wears boxers with little hearts on them. The whole affair had "long day" written all over it. But I got a lot of good photos and I know you'll enjoy them. They'll add a lot to your album. You can leaf through it while you're waiting for Partridge Family reruns to come on.

When things threatened to get out of hand, I pulled out a bullhorn and hollered, "Let's get naked!" That usually points the action in the right direction and it did the trick this time too. I learned this approach in my business career and found it went a long way toward increasing morale. Uppya Whatziss lost her dentures when she fell on her ass in the attempt to kick Casey Kwittz in the groin. Stiffy Plopper tried to prevent Enda Rownd from stomping on Elroy Berpp, who had fallen down on Betty Kant and wound up with one of her enormous bazoomers in his jaws—lucky bastard. Enda turned around and head-butted poor Stiffy, sending him flying across Foxie Buddox's lap. Foxie immediately grabbed his hammer, which was hanging out. That precipitated a rather swinish sex act, because Foxie has Parkinson's disease pretty bad and Stiffy's Johnson got a real workout. I think you get the picture, especially since I recall that it happened to you a couple of times.

In recognition of our record-setting performance, Earl and I each received a certificate suitable for framing. He lost his in the washroom. We also got a five-dollar gift card, redeemable in the cavernous Relationship-Devices Section at Jorgensen's Discount Mini-Mall and Livery Stable.

I strongly urge you to plan a trip out here soon, preferably for Christmas. Hopefully, you didn't take issue with some of the words I've used to describe you in the past. I never thought you would actually look them up. Just try to forget them and let the healing begin. To make up for it, I can take you by the Center and introduce you to Foxie. December is crammed with holiday activities that a guy with your interests can't afford to miss. Last year we got together and beat Earl senseless with a Yule log. We'll have the

Skeet-Shooting tournament, with real skeets that have been fattened just for the occasion. Miss Grossbutt's first-grade class is going to present a water ballet on the lake, and that's always a crowd pleaser, because the little tykes thrash around and lose their swimsuits all the time and wind up doing it in the nude. Now, you might think at first that this is a sensational event and a feast for the eyes, but that would be a mistake. The keisters on the kids aren't bad, but the truth of the matter is that Miss Grossbutt gets in the agua with them and she's just slightly more diminutive than one of our local mountains (before the rains cause it to slide down to the shore).

This gal has busted nearly every weigh-station truck scale in the southern part of the state without generating a believable result. Nobody knows the exact avoirdupois-number her gravity-challenging ass registers, but it ain't below four to five hundred, I can tell you that. A couple of the kids secretly slipped a bumper sticker on her can that read, "Up Yours, Captain Ahab." She'll never spot it. The crowd moves up ten rows in the stands when this Mamma hits the surf and then they head for the refreshment stands, where the holiday buffet is laid out.

Every year there's a different gourmet-food theme to delight the masses. This year it's going to be "Especialidades Puerto-Ricañas" (Tokyo Noodle Delights). Last year, which you managed in a bout of extreme cowardice to miss, the main repast consisted of "Specialità tipici italiani" (Munchies from Madagascar).

The Lake Association is holding a speedboat contest again for senior citizens and you still have time to enter. I know what you're thinking. It could be perilous for older folks to crank up those supercharged little craft on the water, especially since they're powered by 1,500 horses and driven by 60-IQ horse's asses. But to reduce the high number of drownings that have plagued this event for the past ten years, the race is going to take place on the beach, so flying sand will be the only danger. They block out an expanse of beach down at the ocean for contestants to practice before the big event, which means you can get in some pre-contest sand runs. You're free to arrange to have your boat shipped out here or pull it cross-country behind your Hummer. I'd let you use mine, but it's in the shop.

Two weeks ago, I opened the throttle to cut in front of a boat I was trying to swamp, but I didn't quite make the turn and ran it up onto the terrace of one of our lakeside restaurants and bent the propeller. I also bent maybe twenty diners when I landed in the middle of a birthday celebration and knocked a few of the celebrants around. Teeth, hair and eyeballs all over the place, as usual. Man, some people are really excitable, especially the women whose clothes were shredded before I could shut off the motor. I did get a chance to squeeze some well-packed chest-flesh, though. My propeller could be straightened fairly easily, but I can't say the same for the diners. I'm afraid a few of them are condemned to a life of Origami-ness. The trial is scheduled on the April docket.

My attorney, Hugh Sedditt, assures me that I have nothing to worry about if you come out here and appear in my place to say you were the one driving the craft when it left the water and precipitated what I would call minor lakeside carnage. I showed him a photo from our high school yearbook, and he says juries are reluctant to convict anyone exhibiting what looks like the absence of thought overload. How about it? If you don't want to help, I'll just show up and try to look like you.

In other news, my attempt to sell glow-in-the-dark combat gear to the army did not go well, but I'm not giving up. They laughed at Robert Fulton when he invented the steam iron too, mainly because his pants fell down during the initial presentation. But also because it was difficult to lift the appliance with a log-fire raging in it and people tended to leave it burning when they went on vacation.

I wonder if you would be willing to take part in the Genital Enhancement Program that I'm managing at our community college laboratories. The project is designed to determine the level of resistance to contact with power lines and involves some inconsequential instrumentation and a direct current feed. You'll get a handsome coffee mug for participating, along with an electronic banana-peeler. Don't stand too close to it. We can do the experiments by phone if you don't make it out here. Let me know. I'll send you the apparatus and instructions for attaching it to a number of your prime organs. I'll also include a whistle for the event that you begin to feel some discomfort or if the sounds of high-tension crackling and burnt flesh become disquieting. It will encourage you to know that we used Earl as a subject. He resisted at first, but I beat the hell out of him. There is no research to support that method, but it just felt right.

Your ever-loving

Ludlow

44

Hey Grover,

I was asked again this year to present the town's first annual Good Citizen Awards, a ceremony that recognizes the accomplishments of the most respected and successful people in our community. The Civic Center was packed for the occasion, mainly with people who couldn't get into the cattle auction down the street. The high school band perpetrated a malicious medley of unrelated notes and I opened the program with a few well-chosen words, mocking the city council and the bleeding hearts who get all blubbery when they see their pets run over in fast-moving traffic. I proceeded to call the recipients to the stage to receive their prizes—a certificate suitable for framing, two free passes to the petting zoo in Bugwarts, Arkansas, and a gift card for half a pound of select lunchmeat from Rusty's Trading Post and Sheep Dip Station.

Marlon Futch was the first honoree. Marlon's grandfather, whose name was actually Zbiegnew Schmuckbuster, started a business in the nineteenth century in what is now a swamp in Eastern Slovakia, manufacturing musical instruments such as the Alto-Swinette, the Bass Horse-o-Phone, the Double-B-Flat Leaf Blower, and the 45-Caliber Bassoon. I should also mention the Puntable Percussion Package, which is basically a leather-covered chicken that requires a second person to hold the snap from center. At the appropriate moment in the score, the performer boots it through goalposts on which a network of harp strings has been draped. All of these finely-tuned devices are required in the production of the seventeen operas written by Dmitri Dungsniffer, a famous Lithuanian composer of the fifteenth century who was hanged by the scrotum in the town square, thereby absolving the populace of an accusation of crappy taste.

Marlon's father came to the U.S. in the early twentieth century, leaving his wife and nine children to starve to death, and continued the rich family tradition of creating horseshit products. He changed his name to Futch, based on the exclamations he heard from those who met him for the first

323

time, and soon ran the business into the ground. In a fit of depression, but excellent judgment, he killed himself by leaping into the path of a small child on roller skates who was carrying a machete. Marlon, who had made the voyage with his father stowed away in the ship's crapper, making it difficult to distinguish him from the surrounding digestive by-products, used the family fortune ($4.25) to open a hot dog stand on the corner of "Road Work Ahead" and "Do Not Enter." His plan was simple, like Earl. But unlike Earl, it worked for a while. Unfortunately, the venture eventually became notorious for poisoning half the population, and a dissatisfied customer shot Marlon in the ass, which resulted in a life of disability payments on which Futch and his whole futching family subsisted. When I gave Marlon his award, he hugged it to his chest and said, "You don't know how much this means to me." I shoved him into the band's trombone section.

Clinton Snark was then called to the podium, although we had to wait a while for him to finish taking a leak. Clinton is a manufacturing mogul with a lucrative business employing two people, both on welfare. Besides selling his streamlined coffins (featuring chrome racing stripes and a sun roof) to mortuaries around the country, he also rents out burial products for people who want to get used to them before the big day. The Snark "Snap-Lock Sarcophagus" Company fills a consumer niche with keen marketing savvy. Now people can keep a coffin in the house prior to the funereal festivities, purchased on an easy monthly-payment plan, to help them sneak up gradually on the big day. "Having a casket around the house helps you relate in advance to the final event," Clinton explained to me. At least I think that's what he said. I wasn't paying much attention to the guy because I was focused on a Momma in the front row in a short skirt who was lacking in complete crotch coverage.

Gerald Muff was named an honoree for his significant contribution to the economic growth of the city. Using his well-tuned antenna for profitable business activities and a mind deprived of brain fluid, he identified an opportunity that was just waiting for exploitation and opened a trampoline store. Gerald is a harmless twit, but his wife is a short woman with an abysmally fat ass and the brains of a canary. The distance between her cerebellum and whatever molecules operate her mental compartment come in second to the total of Walter Peyton's record for rushing yards. I wouldn't touch her with your Willie (I wouldn't touch your Willie either, for that matter). I wouldn't even touch her with Earl's Willie, but that's because I can't figure out what his Willie is good for. Madge has pondered this question for years.

We next celebrated the owner of the high-end dog-training academy run by Holdsworth Fern called "Hounds R Us." Although I hate dogs with a passion, I have to admit that Holdsworth really knows his business. After a few weeks in his care, a mutt can dance on his hind legs, turn somersaults, fetch sticks, bring his master's slippers, wash up after dinner, and shake hands with any of his four paws (although manipulating those in the rear can sometimes lead to a urinary event). The dogs who show exceptional ability at retrieving the morning news are often given a paper route of their own.

I suspect that Holdsworth's wife, Sharon de Bedd, is the real reason he made the final cut. In contrast to Gerald Muff's Frau, this babe is a rod-stiffener of the first order, with an astounding feel for lethal booby positioning. Drawing on my years of experience as a semi-professional jug-checker, I am led to give her a score of several million on the "Yowzuh" Meter.

We decided to recognize the achievements of Miss Dubbel Tayke, the head mistress of the private girls academy down by the sewer department. Miss Tayke has molded the lives and manners of young ladies for several generations, teaching them liberal arts, etiquette, aristocratic bearing and how to sit erect on the toilet. Miss Tayke, as her alums call her (except for a couple who insist on referring to her as "Old Princess Tight-Ass"), gravitated naturally to the field of education. In other words, she was devoid of any real talent. She claims that her father always doted on her. I looked up "dote" in the dictionary and found that it means "to take a healthy dump."

A new venture that has become wildly profitable in our area was started by Ben and Hannah Dover, a husband and wife team who saw an opportunity to serve a sector that had never before been approached. We tend to think that you can find a greeting card for any occasion, but until Ben and Hannah came along there were no cards for people you despise. Well, this couple has a card for every desirable insult. Here's an example of their clever greetings:

> Just a note to let
> you know I think you're
> a genuine prick !
> Happy Holidays !
> And may the shit fairy
> visit you nightly.

I can honestly say that I've dropped a bundle at their store already and I haven't come close to sending out all the cards I want. Well, as Archimedes used to say, it's the principle of the thing.

The panel considered giving Millicent Nikkertwyst an award. She is one of the premier society hostesses in our part of the state, known for her frequent candlelight suppers and evenings of entertainment, even though her cuisine challenges the digestive workings of the most resilient anatomy. Millicent loves to show off her plates with intricate French borders (some near Belgium). She didn't make the cut.

Several other bums were nominated for recognition by the council, but failed to be selected. There was Wes Bazkitt, who raises parrots that recite the Lord's Prayer several times a day, inserting unwholesome obscenities of the commonest kind and lending a pronounced vulgar tone to an otherwise devotional message. Wes is notorious for spreading crap like buckshot and has never been known to utter a single sentence containing fewer than seven outright lies.

Lee Kinrod, who runs an outhouse-tipping firm, was almost chosen for an award, but was told at the last minute that he wouldn't be chosen after he got up in the middle of the interview and relieved himself behind the drapes.

We were able, however, to include Rafer Arside in the ceremony. He's the proprietor of a successful fertilizer business, having worked out a method for getting cattle to poop directly into fifty-pound bags. Rafer has an impressive pedigree. He has an uncle who is an eye doctor in Alaska. Sort of an optical Aleutian.

I think I'm the only brother who writes to you.
(You never mention anybody else),

Ludlow

45

Hey Grover,

Well, I still haven't heard back from the Metropolitan Opera about staging my operatic masterpiece, but that should come through any day now. In the meantime, I'm writing an unauthorized autobiography, and I'm currently revising it to include myself. I figure people can gain a lot of inspiration from my experience and profit from the opportunity to admire my many accomplishments. Even though I have sometimes overstepped the bounds of common decency, most of my prior punishable offenses can no longer be prosecuted thanks to the statute of limitations and that's good news for you, as well.

I should caution you that some of the facts in my book have been modified slightly to give a more accurate picture of the true heroic proportions of my life. I originally thought I'd ask you to write a chapter, but then I had a better idea: **NO!** Following is an overview of an edited version of a pre-draft of the general notes from my first rough outline. I sent it to a publisher and they may want to make a board game out of it.

First of all, I intend to downplay our physical resemblance. It wasn't easy to ignore when we were together, of course. People would cringe when I walked by, but when they saw you come along, the tendency to gag was geometrically reinforced. We've been through a lot together, and most of it was your fault. Some of it can be traced back to basic sibling rivalry. Although it never became a significant issue, I recently came across a sonogram that was taken a month before we were born where you had me in a headlock. I soon developed the maturity to move beyond that, but even today intimacy is a problem for me. I feel uncomfortable in situations where I wind up hugging close friends. I think it's because of the nudity.

In my book, our family will be described as intelligent, well-educated and financially independent, so you may not recognize us. I wonder if I should describe father with a pipe (3/4" I.D.) and wearing a smoking jacket (preferably ignited), working on Wall Street and amassing the fortune which he so generously placed at our disposal. I know I should work some sort of disposal into the narrative. I think I'll set our childhood in New York, because it makes me sound much more sophisticated. I can still see us on the way to school, you with your fly open and me basking in the shade of your charming but felonious nature. And you were so playful. I'll probably leave out the part where you felt it was necessary to whack me with a tree limb or a dead cat all the time. Ever the playful sibling. And it was almost impossible to keep you from rooting around in the garbage wherever we went. I never told you that I was often irritated by the things you brought home from rubbish cans in the neighborhood, mainly because you never let me wear any of them.

The image of those little red chairs at the front of the classroom will always remain with me. I sat on similar ones in college. As we grew, I recall that I was constantly busy in my capacity as your role model. It was good to have you as one of my brothers, though, as we confronted the practical world together. You were always at my side, so I learned to deal with that handicap quite early. I still laugh at your cute habit of promising to push me on the swings and then kicking me in the ass every time I swung back. You kept telling me you were trying out for the Radio City Rockettes, and I had no reason to doubt your veracity, although I knew you were shitting me.

I plan to reveal something in my memoirs that I never shared with you, mainly because you wouldn't give a rat's ass,, but from the beginning I was endowed with an oversized hammer. That particular characteristic helped me to overcome a paucity of social skills and made my later life significantly easier wherever I went. As Descartes so often phrased it, "I hump, therefore I am." It's a rule worth remembering. Many are those who are unaware of the benefit of an over-sized trouser hound as an ice-breaker. I only know it accelerated my acceptance into society and led to friendly relations with Mommas of all nationalities, often after church services or during funerals. It also enabled me to become a charter member of the Hooter Pullers Club of Hong Kong, as well as the International Association of Ass Masters.

Wealthy matrons and rich housewives throughout the world devoted their time to coach me in the proper way to mingle with the upper classes.

With their help I found out which fingers to put in my mouth when I whistled for a waiter, and I have them to thank for the ability to wipe my can with the proper drapes. They instructed me in things like keeping my fly zipped at the dinner table. How often I've heard the phrase, "Dinner's ready, so pull up your pants and get in here!" A bit of information I wish you had picked up on along the way.

My military heroics will surely be of interest to my readers, although my social activities were curtailed when the army asked me to join them as a consultant, those bastards. I especially relished my assignments to Fort Leonard Wood in Missouri (for basic training and relieving myself in the snow) and then to Fort Sill, Oklahoma, those two god-forsaken pieces of crap that caused God to vomit when it was time to choose between them for the worst spot on earth. I just know they send proctologists to both places for their final exams. If they can stomach those two regions of hell, they can deal with any anus-oriented situation.

It was a relief when I was assigned to Fort Huachuca, Arizona, right down on the Mexican border, where the whole desert blows through every day. The place was an old cavalry fort and looked just like a set for a John Wayne movie. Smelled like horseshit, and I'm not kidding. So did John Wayne, by the way. It was about fifteen miles (as the crow staggers) straight south of Tombstone, called "the town too tough to die." The natives obviously hadn't been paying much attention, because that bloody dump bit the dust a long time ago.

Being in the artillery was interesting. I was in an outfit that calculated target coordinates for the firing batteries, and we kidded around a lot, giving them numbers most of the time to zero in on outhouses in the town beyond the firing range. Probably the happiest day of my life was when I entered the army—because I knew they would never get me to do it again. I'll probably gloss over my teaching career, but I was able to inspire many young people to be the best they could be after graduation and to stay well away from the edge of the highway when they were sweeping the road. My story would be incomplete without acknowledging my many romantic encounters. I witnessed numerous perversions, things that were strange, sick, twisted, godless and evil, but you remember high school as well as I do. This type of behavior is what separates us from the weasels, which is how the weasels want it.

Then, engaged in various assignments on the international business stage (and sometimes beyond our borders), I was simultaneously drawn to the shadow world of espionage and jockstrap theft, recruited by some of the legends in the business. This is where my true talents emerged. They recognized my capacity for amoral dealings of the most disgusting sort. Picture one of our high school shop classes. I was able to satisfy the requirements with no training, because of my ability to mimic your perverse behavior. You don't know the full extent of your influence on me, but it's well-documented in the files of law enforcement agencies on five continents, including New Jersey. It's been my pleasure to follow your example when dealing with the underworld and the underwear. I feel I may have failed to thank you properly, though, and if that's the case, the hell with it. During my years working with various secret agencies, I often recounted some of your exploits to the more jaded and war-hardened veterans among my colleagues, then watched them recoil in horror and vomit. I never told you, but I was so proud.

I plan to feature you prominently in my tome, although you are only peripherally related to me (the DNA sample came back marked "possibly mammal"). Despite the lack of real evidence, I have always considered you part of the family, and one of the things I just can't resist describing is your impressive exploits on the golf course. It was easy to follow you around a course. The trail of divots and uprooted trees didn't require an Indian scout to locate you. Members of the grounds crew chose many times to follow you, taking advantage of the trenches you opened that allowed them to lay new sprinkler lines. I know that after one particularly excavational round, the management of one course decided to shut it down and just plant corn.

I think they're gaining on us.

Pass it On

46

Hey Grover,

Since you asked, I want you to know that I am fully engaged in meaningful activities as a concerned citizen, just as you are, although from your recliner. We went to a city council meeting the other night, because it's an opportunity to witness politics in action and mental vacuity at its apex. The inhabitants of our town are special examples. Many fugitives from the Midwest have settled here, maybe some you know—disgraced scoutmasters, defrocked priests, child murderers, adulterers, arsonists, perverts, and bank tellers who have suddenly come into a lot of money. And we welcome them all, because we know they'll improve the community. Those who bring their petitions before the city council are among the highest intellects in the city. And that's the problem.

The session was called to order by Mayor Reelie O'Beese, and in doing so she whacked Nick O'Teene, who is a heavy smoker, on the fingers with her gavel. She had to reach across four people to do it and he bitched all night. Hall Hizzashes sang the national anthem. At least that's what he was supposed to do with it. Those who know him joined in loudly to drown out his voice, which on a good day resembles the cry of an elk with a hernia caught on an electrified fence.

The first speaker was Cashew Laytor, who gave a short speech for a long time. It was something incoherent involving the Armenian heritage, the Holy Grail, the male identity crisis, and the myth of the Easter Bunny. Listening to him talk is like waiting at the crossing for a freight train to pass and then have it stop and back up. Cashew barely makes it out of the slug category. He's a slow talker, one of those mouth breathers. As a boy, he fell down a mine shaft and couldn't be located for years. It was determined much later that he had been raised by moles and he returned to society after many years with poor eyesight but an uncanny ability to plow vast farm fields without the benefit of machinery. Cashew cornered me at one of Madge's dinner parties last year and guided me into a state of semi-consciousness with an account of his so-called life: "I originally wanted to go to the Mike Tyson Institute of Technology in West Virginia. But for reasons having to do with failure to turn in a final paper for the course on toenail growth, I was transferred under heavy guard to Saint Myron's College, a conservative arts school in Crotch Rock, Maine, that applies a layer of education to students who can benefit from low admission requirements. I still remember the Gothic style of the outhouses and the happy cries emanating from them. The chapel organ sounded like a terminally ill dinosaur with heartburn about to move its bowels. Nobody ever used the library for academic purposes, so we used to party there a lot. We could get naked without fear of being interrupted. The librarians were thrilled if one of us took a book off the shelf and flipped through the pages after we got dressed again.

"I later applied for work as a window dresser at Macy's because I thought it meant I could dress in the window and I was without a fixed residence at the time. With my job application I submitted three references. Two were written by homeless guys who had just been released from an institution for the brain-imploded and I wrote the other one. All three praised me highly. On the basis of these three recommendations they kicked the crap out of me during the interview and tossed me out on the street. It was the defining moment of my life and set me on the road to what I am today—a dismal failure whom parents can use to frighten their children."

We had all heard this bull-sediment from Cashew before, but frequent repetition of the story has not diminished the appeal it holds for him. An old aunt left him some money, so he bought a bar in the country. He changed the name of the joint from *The Hog Trough* to *Maxims's* and put in new knotty-pine interiors to produce what is commonly referred to as a crapper motif, complete with snot, constructed to look like the pooper at the bus station in Albuquerque. The joint is usually peopled with heavy drinkers, mostly hookers and fat guys with pitted skin, open flies and bloodshot noses and wearing caps that feature agricultural themes. It's a good place to go to get away from the lower classes. I don't know if anybody with a thimble-full of brains would be seen there twice. I usually hit it on Friday nights.

Cashew reminds me of a dolt I worked for once. This guy would sign anything you put in front of him. I tried it. I had his signature on extradition papers, a check for fifty thousand dollars, a search warrant for his home, and a death certificate on which his name figured prominently. He met a tragic fate when one of his kids ran over him in his garage. It seems he was sleeping there after his wife kicked him out of the house. You probably think I'm kidding. Somebody finally pushed Cashew out of the way and I got up and said a few words concerning the Polish origin of the polka as a martial art and followed it with a short reflection on spanking your secretary. I admit that neither activity has been the object of clinical trials, but that in my case it has offered definite therapeutic value as a stress-reliever.

Hilda Flupp was next to address the august gathering. Kind of a ditz, but she has an adequate foredeck and a fairly attractive, though substantial, rudder section. She made a stirring plea for recognition of The Grapefruit County Ass Institute, The Hangover and Short-Wand Clinic, and a request for funds to support The Friends of Diseased Donkeys. She claims handicapped muskrats are getting too much attention. Hilda likes to sing Wagnerian arias while seated on the toilet. I know this to be true because I observed her doing it once, and it wasn't easy, because her bathroom windows are very high.

When she finally got done whining, I was recognized by the council and rebutted Hilda's position, stating that she should also be "re-butted" by a cosmetic surgeon. She countered with derogatory remarks about my relatives, which happened to be true but irritated me anyway, and in your defense I pointed out that you couldn't help it. I told Hilda that she was unattractive and that I would rather sleep next to a dead black woman. Or on top of one. Again. The Sergeant at Arms kicked her in the ass. Cashew tried and missed.

Hilda reminds me vaguely of a young lady I fell in lust with back in Italy, but then many women remind me of her simply because of the gender issue. I met Magdalena Grabbaweeni during a perversion tour of Rome (she was the guide). Maggie had all the qualifications of a desirable woman. For one thing, she was female and that often counted in her favor. In addition, there were intervals when she was sober, she bathed regularly, the police were no longer looking for her, and she spoke in complete sentences, although they were laced with profanity. She was also willing to engage in carnal activity without the use of electrical appliances or spaghetti, although the sight of exposed wiring made her tremble and frequently empty her bladder.

Next to speak before the council was Goheddin Assmee, a guy who looks a little like a ball of snot. He presented a film documentary about menopause in teenagers and its negative impact on sphincter tightness and dental fillings. Very informative. Goheddin is well-known in the community for celebrating the anniversary of the Eskimo independence from Spain. Also for being an idiot. He dresses in a thick parka and furs every First of August and participates in his own parade, driving sled dogs down the main thoroughfare until he passes out from the heat (the dogs do too) and the emergency squad reluctantly picks him out of the gutter—after they've carted the dogs away. If it weren't for the opportunity to kick him in the ass, I think they'd leave him there. As it is, they don't take him away until some of the locals have had a few good boots at him.

According to the respected historical reference work, "Bullshit through the Centuries," the King of Spain at the time of the Great Eskimo Uprising was Alfonso "El Feo" (Jim the Ugly). This is the same book that lists the children of the Norse gods Wotan and Frida as Quentin and Toots. I had run into Goheddin once before when I was standing on a crowded bus and this guy with a surfboard approached me. It was Goheddin and he was naked. He said, "I get off when the bus hits a pothole."

Ray Kyabawls came before the council with a suggestion that one of the main streets be diverted to pass through the drive-through lane at the bank he runs. This guy is a crook, a blot on humanity and a chiseler, not necessarily in that sequence. He knows as much about running a bank as a cocker spaniel knows about internal combustion. Ray is one of those eternally jolly con-man types whose smile would delight the entire orthodontic faculty at the New Jersey School of Dentistry. The council, to a man, acted as though they didn't hear him. They then took fifteen minutes out to present some entertainment by a local musician. It's their intention to support artists who are attempting to develop their fledgling careers and I guess that's what this blot on the arts was aimed at, but somehow "Malagueña" doesn't sound that great played on the bagpipes.

Hans Awff asked for permission to address the council and they told him to hurry. I can understand why. The medical community will probably never include him in one of their clinical studies, because he doesn't have much time left. He has high blood pressure, a clogged heart, soaring cholesterol, diabetes, Parkinson's Ass Syndrome, the shitty shakes, strep nuts, and he's ninety-six. He said, "I just want to mention something that could be helpful to everyone. My family has recently benefited from group therapy after years of friction, open antagonism and rancor of the worst kind. We went into group sessions together, all thirty-seven of us. The meetings were filled with open warfare, hate and barbaric personal attacks. We fought and shouted and described how much we loathed one other, and on several occasions the gathering erupted in fisticuffs that required hospitalization. My cousin Mert hit me with a chair. It brought us together." Everybody in the room told him to shut up and sit down.

Tayka Dowt was scheduled to speak next and we turned to see her pass through the double doors. Tayka is an aspiring actress, like so many gorgeous but thought-challenged pieces of tail around here. We have wannabe movie stars up the wazzoo living in the area, those pleasant, nose-powder-oriented bunches of shallow neurotics with the intellectual motoring speed of water buffalo. Anyway, if you wanted to set a record for understatement, you would describe Tayka as loaded with sex appeal. She entered the room wearing clothing that would be revealing on a toothpick, cut low enough to show off her magnificent prow swag, covering only one-tenth of her nippledom, and short enough to barely hide her urinating facilities. Male interest swelled, confined to the pants.

Tayka approached the podium and took out her notes, which were thicker than a governor's indictment. She smiled sweetly and began, "There are four main pleasures in life: the love of knowledge, the love of good food, the love of music and the one you thought of first. In our community we have two opposing factions. We're divided over the role of polar bears in society and how much potato salad is required for a really satisfying sex act, and I would like to see us eliminate our differences. Let us remember that the cornerstone of every reasonable philosophy has always been nudity, and more important, nudity that can be shared with friends." She cried and the room cried with her. Weeping is contagious in some circles, like vomiting. She sat down to thunderous applause, mainly from me.

Horace Sezzass was at the meeting to petition the council for a zoning change. He runs an empire that includes a publishing house, and his company puts out erotic novels that have vivid physical scenes, but also contain educational passages concerning botany, architecture and carpet cleaning. He also sells pre-dug latrines to the army. The council told him they would take his request under advisement and get back to him as soon as they had determined just what the hell that means. Horace has not had an easy life. During the Gary, Indiana military campaign he served as a prisoner of war and a hostage. In his spare time he sits for hours and weaves throw rugs. Then he throws them away.

I hadn't expected to see Stepford Sludge at the meeting, but there he was holding a sign that read, "The City Council Members Are Pricks!" When admonished for this seemingly churlish act, he advised the room that he was only holding the sign for a friend who was in the washroom. There were forty-nine further petitioners and then I was asked to pronounce the benediction. I first gave thanks that the mayor's swimsuit didn't fall off at the lake the preceding weekend, sparing those present from a view of her world-record cellulite saddlebags. After the sordid mess was adjourned, I took a picture of the entire group while they held up a sign that said "Cheese."

Well, Grover, I would like to see a sign from God, like somebody taking me seriously for instance. I don't know what you wanted to be when you grew up, maybe because I didn't care, but I dreamed of becoming a member of a government organization, similar to the House Subcommittee on Shin Guards and Bicycle Chains. I'm willing to concede that picking Bruno Hauptmann as my role model may not have been the best choice. I'm considering a surgical procedure called "laproscopic tool-tightening." It may have something to do with advanced age, but my poker keeps flopping out of my pants at inappropriate moments and although it doesn't bother me, for some reason it seems to embarrass bystanders. I don't think it's anybody's business. An old couple behind us in the ticket line at the movies expressed their displeasure a little too loudly for my taste on one occasion, and one rather uptight biddy at the library fainted when I approached the desk to check out a smutty novel. I believe everybody should react the way the pastor of our church did. He reached down to shake my hand and spotted my wand hanging forth in all its rigid glory. He was a real trouper. He said, "I hope your wiener gets better."

Too much time watching *Gilligan's Island* reruns can ruin your eyes. And your stomach,

Ludlow

47

Hey Grover,

I thought nobody could find me, but some of the companies I used to work for have started to forward mail to me. I wonder if you would mind answering these letters. I have a lot of other stuff to do, and I know this is a project that can benefit from your caring nature. You can get started on this bunch before the truck pulls in to your place with the rest of them.

Dear Sir. I wrote to you before about my brother-in-law with the teeth problem. He died, so you shouldn't worry about that crap anymore. I want to let you know that I've managed to trim down from 400 pounds to a stunning 382. The boils have cleared up a lot and only cover about 80% of my body now, but they're still concentrated around the genitals. I continue to soil my pants a few times every day, but I entered the New York Marathon and came in second to last in twenty-two days and nine minutes, so I'm still excited about that accomplishment. It's not that easy running all that distance with your pants full, as I understand you've experienced on many occasions. The guy crawling behind me was legally blind and had a wooden leg and he was last seen on a garbage barge heading out of the harbor according to his family, who accused me of elbowing him off the Williamsburg Bridge. But he started it, the bastard. Not everyone is blessed with athletic prowess, including you, I hear.   —Finn Gerz Tuck

Dear Sir. If you ever come to our little town here in New Mexico, we'd like to have you stop at the Serpentville Indian Museum. We boast the largest exhibit of Indian artifacts in the country, mostly rocks that were used by the Indians back in the nineteenth century. At least we think that's who used them. If they didn't, they missed a fine opportunity, because there's a shit-pot full of rocks just lying around here waiting to be used. There are round ones and jagged ones and some that defy description except for the fact that they're definitely from the stone family. Many well-known tribes are represented in our museum. Among lots of others, there were the Sooxes, the Semaphores, the Hop-Ons, and the Pawnees, who ran a hockshop for the other tribes. Take the 22 out of Deadbutt and you can't miss our plywood storefront on the left.   —Hiram Bluttz

Dear Sir. There are many people living in your neighborhood, but who doesn't? This is a chance to get in on the ground floor and reap boundless wealth by investing in a dozen or so of my inventions. I have perfected a folding toilet seat that a person can easily carry around and slip over the seats in public washrooms in order to protect against fungus and other ass infections. The Pentagon is currently studying my submission of a mega-ton bomb that offers guaranteed precision and unqualified accuracy. The delivery system is a camouflaged donkey cart that positions the device at the exact target coordinates and once the bomb is in place, a trained technician hits it with a hammer. I'm also working on an electronic flatulence-catcher, but those things are hard to bag. Besides these ground-breaking ground-breakers, one of my best ideas is in the final creative stages. It's a mass-circumcision device that I plan to sell to hospitals near synagogues. Trial runs are proceeding as I write, and a gentleman named Earl from out your way is helping us. I can provide testimonials from members of the medical community who wish to remain anonymous and who are in the witness-protection program until next weekend when the bus leaves. Send a check to me, but make it out to my cousin, Show.   —Hattie Nuff

Dear Sir. I am fifty-seven and have been in an abusive relationship for two years. I really like it. Everyone in my family was abused at one time or another, often by total strangers, so it's something we've enjoyed all our lives. I still have two cauliflower ears from a previous marriage. Now my boyfriend is moving to another state and says he has found lots of women there who are willing to be abused, so he's looking for something new and feels it will provide him with some advancement in his chosen field. This means I have to start all over again. Do you know where I can find a church that specializes in abusing women my age? I like it when somebody kicks me in the ass.   —Mae B. Nudds

Dear Sir. Do you suffer from low self-esteem but high erectional activity? Do babes reject you because of your undesirable physical condition and bad breath? Are you tempted to grab female butt in a darkened movie theater or rub against women in a crowd? A successful career may be awaiting you in the field of Serial Rape. This activity is currently suffering from a shortage of qualified attackers, and the School of Assault and Molestation is ready to train those who demonstrate the proper aptitude. We specialize in the instruction of depraved seduction methods and the use of profane and smutty language while committing the outrage. You can learn how to use proven immoral behavior to ravage and violate members of the opposite sex on your way to becoming a respected member of the rapist community. Deflowering underage girls is our specialty. Return the attached form, and one of our caring assistants will contact you with more information. Don't waste an opportunity to perpetrate a criminal act on the person of your choice. —Goosum Awl, President

Dear Sir. I represent the Trowel Manufacturers Association of China and we would like you to be the principal speaker at our annual convention, to be held this year in your fine city. You would go on right after the tombstone-throwing contest. Some of our staff have heard you fling the bullshit before and claim they were spellbound for days after the event. One guy got the shits. There will be a collection taken up to pay you for your words of inspiration. Please let us know if you can make it the day after tomorrow. I'd appreciate it if you would work some trowel praise into your address. —Hoo Yoo Kiddun

Dear Sir. My company makes plastic washers and lunchmeat. We are one of the largest plastic washer and lunchmeat processors in Dry River, Idaho, and are looking for guidance to help us penetrate the North Dakota market. In the past, we sent flyers to the entire population of that admirable state with the catchy heading, "What do you bastards have against our lunchmeat?" That increased our washer sales, but lunchmeat tanked. What do you think of the idea of including a dozen washers in each package of lunchmeat? Do you think the residents of North Dakota would react favorably to a powerful marketing campaign like this? Or maybe we should just shut the damn place down and open a cathouse. I'm relying on your expertise in this matter, although a lot of people say you're a shit-ass. —Doug A. Deepwunn

Dear Sir. Every year about this time, the Missouri River Barge and Surfboard Symphony Orchestra asks you to open your hearts, your wallets and your bathrooms to benefit this vital community organization. Our board of directors has decided to conduct a Dog-and-Weasel Washing Service, as well as a High-Diving Contest, on the Dungstrummer Street Bridge between the hours of midnight and six in the morning on February 20th for the purpose of raising the money to get our instruments out of hock. The weather report for the big day is not too good, with two feet of driving snow, sleet, and arctic temperatures predicted, but we like to think we can count on the good citizens of your condominium complex to come through for us (like you didn't last year, you tightwad bunch of jerks). Thanks in advance. —Needja Coynes.

Loretta, don't send the letter out with the phrase in parentheses still in it.

Dear Sir. You don't know me, but we met during a seminar for Sexual Deviates last November. You were serving as a terminally hopeless example. I have just been unjustly convicted of stealing urinals from public washrooms (while in use) and was sentenced to twelve years in an institution for incorrigible urinal thieves, although I'm confident I can get two weeks off for good behavior. But I swear I didn't do it. I just took some underwear. Anyway, I wonder if you could water my plants while I'm gone. The key is under a flower pot on the front porch, and the plants are nicely arranged in white porcelain containers throughout the house and probably look a little like urinals in the right light.   —Luvdem Pissers

Dear Sir.   I was rejected by your production company when I auditioned for the part of Snow White in your new musical, "Rapist Assassins of Bombay." The impression I got is that your people were unwilling to consider a black person for the role, and a senior citizen at that, so this is a clear case of discrimination. The dance that I was asked to perform was exceedingly intricate, but with the aid of a walker I was able to do it satisfactorily, although I had to slow the tempo a little and dance sitting down. The songs are easy if you had just given me the chance to put my teeth in. I didn't like the way the big guys pitched my butt out on the sidewalk, so you creeps are going to hear from my lawyer. One more thing. Do you have any other parts I could try out for?   —Blyne Syddud

Dear Sir. I don't know how to thank you for the wonderful response and heartwarming sympathy expressed by your firm when my husband was

dying of lung-rot and ass-rickets at the time you fired him, after forty-eight years of loyal service with your company. It's perfectly understandable that you chose not to provide severance payment or a pension of any kind on the occasion of his dismissal. I'm sure you have other weighty issues to deal with. I want you to know that I will forever cherish the certificate you sent that featured a space to insert his name, even though he never got a chance to see it, considering the fact that it arrived fifteen months after the funeral. I'm currently trying to stay busy, writing this note during a break in my adult education class dealing with the assembly of major explosive devices.
—Pullda Pinn

Dear Sir. I am the president of Ayness Barber College here in beautiful Ayness, Kentucky and I am writing to inform you that we would like to award you an honorary degree at our graduation ceremonies, to be held on the last day in June. That is, if the four people in our graduating class pass the finals. We seem to get all the dumb-asses from up north in your state. A lot of the big schools give honorary doctorates to famous political figures, celebrities from the entertainment world and people engaged in the garbage arts, so we want to start a trend here at our humble institution of higher learning. You would receive an honorary "Bachelor of Light Trim" degree and a pencil drawing of electric butt shears. We hope you will just take the diploma and won't be moved to make a speech, because your habit of bullshitting the troops is well-known even in these parts. The featured speaker has not been determined yet, but we are beginning to contact those who are on the fourth page of our preferred speaker list. It seems that a lot of people are too busy this time of year and can't take the damn time out from their tight schedules to come and say a few words of encouragement to our students. Yeah, right. —Noughtu Offen

Dear Sir. There are only two people in the world who know my terrible secret and you are the fifth. It's been haunting me for decades and I have to tell someone. Since I don't know you, I feel you will be able to keep my secret. Years ago, while traveling on a paddle-wheeler on the Passaic River in New Jersey, I was involved in a card game with professional gamblers who plied the river and made their living by cheating at one-card stud. Despite my better judgement, which is attested to by my recent release from the Home for Wayward Bank Presidents and Convicted Public Officials, I sat in on a game and lost an excellent pair of Fruit-Of-The-Loom shorts, along with my father's watch, which I had to remove from his wrist as the coffin was closed.

Anyway, I accused one of the players of unfair card practices when I caught him dealing from a pocket sewn into his jockstrap, and he pulled a gun on me. Thanks to my agility and incredible swiftness, I was able to leap through a window to safety, but not before grabbing the money, while performing a chorus of "Let Go My Shorts" to distract the affronted person. What I never revealed until now is that I completely forgot to tip the cabin steward on the boat and I may have sung the aforementioned number in the wrong key. It's not completely my fault. My musical ability was honed by listening to duct tapes of a guy named Grover from the Midwest, and it is said that when he performed in Key West it was the only time he knew what key he was singing in.   —X. Krooshy Ayting

Dear Sir.   It is no easy task to write these lines. Life is full of unexpected drama and even the noblest of human beings among us is subject on occasion to a capricious destiny. It is with this thought in mind that I am prompted to contact your firm, Christian Bible Publishers of Ohio. I head a talent agency that currently represents Colin Soars, a person we expect to become the next super-celebrity of our time. A world tour is planned beginning next month and we would like to offer your company the opportunity to sponsor this exciting event. Colin has a rare talent and, as you can see from the accompanying photograph, his sex organ is a marvelous departure from the usual anatomical construction. The numerous cysts, gouges and gnarled veins, along with the deep scars and delightful tattoos, put his spanker in a class by itself. We expect audiences everywhere to be thrilled at the sight of his appendage, and we have sent copies of the photo to all the major talk shows, event arenas, and the Vatican.

Colin began his career in the exposure field in a small way. He started by goosing old ladies in supermarkets and department stores, working up to squeezing buns in churches and cathedrals, pulling panties down at political rallies, and finally unsheathing his dong in subway cars and cross-town buses. In other words, things went well. Our plan is to have your corporate logo imprinted boldly across the back of Colin's shorts and prominently displayed on a large screen in the background as his article of interest is unfurled. We expect an enthusiastic response wherever Colin appears, so you can see how beneficial it could be for Bible sales, as well as related items. Awaiting your quick reply.   —Marlon Froop, for "Scabs R Us."

Dear Sir.   We are sending this letter to every corporate office and household in the U.S. in order to increase name recognition. We are the Acme Ransom Company of South Northington, West Virginia. Are you planning to kidnap someone in the near future? If that's the case, our company can be of great assistance, because we assume the messy details associated with lodging the victim and collecting the ransom money. We know how to cut through red tape and elude federal agents in order to achieve perfect completion of the desired felony. For a reasonable fee, our trained professionals hide the captured individual in a secure location, monitor law enforcement activity and negotiate the appropriate payment. We take the uncertainty and stress out of the post-snatch period and eliminate the worry associated with obtaining the cash and making the getaway. Our staff provides room and board for the kidnapped person in a place completely inaccessible to search parties. If the mark is female and reasonably hot, we also make sure she is adequately abused and molested, assuring satisfaction in every instance.

In the event that the injured party's family fails to pay the ransom, we are prepared to charge only half our normal fee to eliminate the unwanted person, providing for his or her disappearance in one of our many shallow gravesites throughout the Southwest. Ask about our "Two-for-One" promotion. You can perpetrate one abduction and get the second one at half-price, a tremendous bargain, considering the time and effort that we put into making your crime a success. References available on request.
—Hugh Needuss, CEO

Dear Sir.   I am writing to you under confidential cover and would like to know if you are interested in assassinating well-known politicians for us. This is a growing career area. All of the hit-men in our employ are currently busy on assignment, and we have heard that you would do practically anything for money, including removing your clothing in crowded venues and eating soup with a straw. We have a long list of elected officials who qualify for immediate removal from our midst, and we are prepared to pay high rates for satisfactory work. There is virtually no danger associated with our missions, since the public has come to welcome the service we provide without reservation. Likewise, little training or expertise in the use of firearms is necessary. You can dispatch the target with a rock if you so choose. Mail us the completed form and we will contact you within seven business days.

—Drillum Goode, Director of Removals

I'm expecting you to do your usual first-class job on this correspondence, Grover. You outdid yourself in the phrasing you used on the eviction notices I sent to the Mafia families across the country. Don't worry, it was okay for you to sign them.

Your pen-pal (hopefully never having to write from the pen),

Ludlow

EPILOGUE

Don't worry, Grover. I'll be writing again soon.

To order this book
please visit:

www.ludlowsmutt.com

or:

http://www.createspace.com/3497478

Ludlow Smutt